The Ends of History

D1013617

The Ends of History

Victorians and
"The Woman Question"
Christina Crosby

New York and London

First published 1991
by Routledge
a division of Routledge, Chapman and Hall, Inc.
29 West 35th Street, New York, NY 10001

Simultaneously published in Great Britain
by Routledge
11 New Fetter Lane, London EC4P 4EE

Typeset in 10/12 Times by
Butler & Tanner Ltd, Frome and London
Printed in Great Britain by
Butler & Tanner Ltd

British Library Cataloguing in Publication Data
Crosby, Christina
  The ends of history: Victorians and "the woman question"
  1. Great Britain. 1837
  I. Title
  941.081

Library of Congress Cataloging in Publication Data
Crosby, Christina
    The ends of history: Victorians and "the woman question" /
  Christina Crosby.
      p.   cm.
  1. English fiction – 19th century – History and criticism.
  2. Feminism and literature – Great Britain – History – 19th century.
  3. Women and literature – Great Britain – History – 19th century.
  4. Social problems in literature. 5. Women in literature.
  I. Title
  PR878.F45C76   1991
  820.9′008′082 – dc20   90–8166

ISBN 0–415–00935–9
ISBN 0–415–00936–7 pbk

For
Jane Miller Crosby
and
Kenneth Ward Crosby

Contents

Acknowledgments

The conventions of the scholarly study are strict, and dictate that any book must have an aura of completion and internal sufficiency. Framed by an introduction and a conclusion, a book offers little evidence of the processes by which it is produced: the inexplicable false starts, corrected only with the help of others; the fortunate encounters, which in retrospect are so indispensable; the revisions which are revised again on the strength of another reading. Only the acknowledgments explicitly open up the text and gesture towards the innumerable relations which are its condition of possibility – which is why I always read them first when I pick up a book.

The fortunes of this project, from its initial prospectus to its completion as a book, have everything to do with the critical intelligence and unsparing generosity of Joan Scott, who has taught me about the politics of institutions and about gender and the politics of history. Denise Riley, in her contributions to the weekly seminar of the Pembroke Center for Teaching and Research on Women at Brown University, and in her conversations with me, helped me formulate my thesis at a crucial moment in the writing of this book. My feminist reading group, Mary Ann Doane, Coppélia Kahn, Karen Newman, Ellen Rooney, and Naomi Schor, kept me on track, criticized when necessary, praised when appropriate, and educated me with their own work. Our regular meetings made all the difference.

Back even before this book is Roger Henkle, who introduced me to the attractive extremes of Victorian novels and encouraged me in my early efforts to think about the social and political dimensions of literature, and who has since offered helpful comments on parts of this study. A more recent connection with Nancy Armstrong, who also read several chapters in progress, and whose own work is inspiring, has confirmed my sense of the importance of *reading*

Victorian Britain. Thanks of another sort are due to my students at Wesleyan University, who have taken so passionately to the theoretical-political issues of this project, who every year encourage me about the future production of knowledge.

I have a special regard for Janice Price, my editor at Routledge, who has supported this project over the years it has taken to reach the end of *The Ends of History*, whose faith in it has meant a great deal to me at difficult moments.

For proofreading and indexing I thank Anne Sunshine and Nicole Cunningham.

Without institutional support I never could have written this book. Thanks to the National Endowment for the Humanities, I had a fellowship which I took to the Pembroke Center, where a year of reading and writing and participation in the research seminar established the basic design of the project. The time was invaluable, as was a semester at the Center for the Humanities at Wesleyan which was followed by a sabbatical leave. The Department of English and the Women's Studies Program have made Wesleyan a most congenial place to teach and think; thanks are due to many colleagues.

I am most fortunate in my family, all of whom have encouraged me in my work. Thanks to Jeff Crosby and Beth McMillen Crosby, and to Kirsten and Colin. Above all, thanks to my parents, Jane and Ken, whose lives and work I admire so much, who talk with me about my teaching and my research and enthusiastically read what I write, and to whom I gratefully dedicate this book.

Now I am tempted to resort to an *aposiopesis*, the figure of speech by which one indicates an inability to go on, to say what is needful. To acknowledge all that Elizabeth Weed has contributed to this project is indeed impossible, for I hardly know myself what ideas of hers I have made my own, or what shape the chapters were in before her vigilant readings. For all that she contributed to this book, and for so much more. . . .

Introduction

Nineteenth-century British thought is indelibly marked by two inter-related features, a passion for "history" and faith in historical expla-nation of all sorts, and a fascination with "women," the ceaseless posing of "the woman question." The logic of the relation of "his-tory" and "women" is the subject of this book: I argue that in the nineteenth century "history" is produced as man's truth, the truth of a necessarily historical Humanity, which in turn requires that "women" be outside history, above, below, or beyond properly historical and political life. Constructing history as the necessary condition of human life, as so many nineteenth-century texts do, ensures that "man" can emerge as an abstraction, can know himself in history, find his origin there and project his end – but only if there is something other than history, something intrinsically unhistorical. "Women" are the unhistorical other of history.

All the texts I consider, from Hegel's *Philosophy of History* to Wilkie Collins's melodrama, *The Frozen Deep*, from Patrick Fair-bairn's *The Typology of Scripture Viewed in Connection with the Whole Series of the Divine Dispensations* to Mayhew's survey of "labour and the poor," from *Daniel Deronda* to *Villette*, are engaged in some way with this conception of history. Indeed, all participate in a widespread discourse about history. Whether novels or journalism, philosophy or history or theology, these texts actively produce history as an object of knowledge and as a way of knowing. History becomes in the nineteenth century a specific method of investigation, a discipline with its own rules of evidence and methods; a narrative mode, characteristic of nineteenth-century novels; a principle of social investigation, guiding the work of social reformers; an object of philosophical speculation, developed in systematic philosophies of history. Indeed, in the nineteenth century history becomes both an epistemological and an ontological principle, the determining condition of all life and therefore of all knowledge.[1] At this foundational level, the ends of history, its limits and its goals, are both positive and negative, a tension which makes the concept almost infinitely productive.[2] As negativity, history is the end of the theological, the disappearance of God and the loss of the guarantee of immortality: human life is ineradicably marked by finitude, by death. Moreover, as a finite being, "man" – in this sense a particular modern concept – is disqualified from immediate self-presence; he cannot know himself simply through reflection because he is inscribed in a history that precedes and exceeds him, which, in fact, determines his mode of being. Yet this history in all its rigors is also profoundly positive, for history is the evidence of the collective life of humanity, and the positive end of history, its purpose, is to reveal man to himself, show where humanity has been and where it is tending. History is, thus, first a displacement and then a reconfirmation, at a more profound, more abstract level, of man himself.

Producing "history" as the truth of man has very important social and political effects, for this project necessarily entails constituting various categories which relate to history in quite different ways. "Women" is such a category, a collectivity that is positioned outside of history proper, identified rather with the immediacy and intimacy of social life. "Savages" and all "primitive" men are another; either they stand at the threshold of history, or, like the Jews of Orientalism, are the outmoded remnants of an historical "moment" now past. "The poor," too, are like "savages," barbaric but capable of development. In these ways, "man," that generic, universal category typifying everything human, is in fact constituted through violently hierarchical differences.[3] "Women" must be radically other to history and to men; "primitive" men must be barely human, potentially but not actually historical.

Women live most intimately with the white men of the English bourgeoisie (those properly manly men), thus the Victorian obsession with "women," with their nature, their functions, their aptitudes, their desires, with, above all, their difference from men. The nineteenth century is the time both of history and "the woman question," the time of Hegel and the angel in the house, of the progress of history and the fallen women. Men are constituted as historical subjects and find "man" in history by virtue of locating women elsewhere. The spectacular inflation of women's value is inextricably a part of the Victorian investment in history, and the tremendous effort to understand women, to manage them, to find out what they want – the ceaseless asking of the woman question – is the price of discovering the truth of man in the far reaches of history.

To read the relation of "women" and "history," then, is to consider "history" more as a concept than as an event or the record of events, and "women" more as a collectivity generated by discursive operations than as a phenomenal entity in itself. This is not to dissolve either women or history into "nothing but" language, but to approach both as the effects of a production of knowledge. Further, it is to consider how such a production is inseparable from politics, from the construction of specifically English and middle-class subjects and the achievement of middle-class hegemony. This achievement depends crucially on sexual politics and on a conception of knowledge that identifies knowledge with history, which makes history "itself" an epistemological foundation, the guarantee of truth.

Thomas Carlyle sets out the terms of this guarantee in his 1829 essay, "On History," in which he declares,

> The Past is the true fountain of knowledge. . . . [W]e do nothing but enact history, we say little but recite it: nay, rather, in that widest sense, our whole spiritual life is built thereon. For strictly considered, what is all Knowledge too but recorded Experience, and product of History, of which, therefore, Reasoning and Belief, no less than Action and Passion, are essential materials? [4]

History is indeed self-consciously embraced over the course of the century, from the early and great popularity of Sir Walter Scott's historical novels, to the introduction of "modern history" as a discipline in the universities and the founding of the scholarly *English Historical Review* in 1886. From mid-century on, various antiquarian, archaeological, and historical societies for the preservation of buildings, the collection and printing of manuscripts, and the exploration of ancient remains are organized, with local branches across the country;[5] the medieval revival is fueled by an enthusiasm for the feudal past and all things "gothic"; massive historical narratives such as Macaulay's *History of England* are published to popular acclaim. This fascination with history is itself much-observed and discussed, not least by Victorians themselves. To John Stuart Mill the concept of history, of the relation of the present to the past and to the imagined future, distinguishes his "age," for, he says, "[t]he idea of comparing one's own age with former ages, or with our notion of those which are yet to come, has occurred to philosophers; but it never before was itself the dominant idea of any age."[6]

The "dominant idea" of Victorian Britain is indeed profoundly historical. It is equally teleological, as the present necessarily issues from the past and will lead ineluctably to the future. The *telos* of history may be rendered in patently ideological terms, as when J. C. Bruce, in *The Roman Wall: A Historical, Topographical, and Descriptive Account of the Barrier of the Lower Isthmus*, compares Britain to ancient Rome:

> Another empire has sprung into being, of which Rome dreamt not.... Her empire is three-fold that of Rome in the hour of its prime. But power is not her brightest diadem. The holiness of the domestic circle irradiates her literature, and all the arts of peace flourish under her sway. Her people bless her. We may ... learn ... on the one hand to emulate the virtues that adorned [Rome's] prosperity, and on the other to shun the vices that were punished by her downfall. The sceptre which Rome relinquished, we have taken up. Great is our Honour – great our Responsibility.[7]

Here the Roman wall is as much a site of ideological investment as of archaeological remains; historical comparison sanctifies domesticity and imperialism. But the crassly obvious ideology of this "history" is not to be separated from the judicious statements made by the editors of the *English Historical Review* in the inaugural issue of their journal in which they write:

> We believe that history, in an even greater degree than its votaries have as yet generally recognised, is the central study among human studies, capable of illuminating and enriching all the rest. And this is one of the reasons why we desire, while pursuing it for its own sake in a calm and scientific spirit, to make this Review so far as possible a means of interesting thinking men in historical study, of accustoming them to its methods of inquiry, and of showing them how to appropriate its large results.[8]

Thinking men need to know how their thoughts, how they themselves are historical, how scientific enquiry can reveal what human life has been and what it might be. The results of historical study are so large precisely because history is everything. It is both something to know and the way of knowing, and ensures that men will know themselves if they will but learn how to think through history. "History" thus leads inexorably to the men who can think it, to educated Englishmen, to the most historically advanced men of the most historically advanced nation.

In this way, history, even when described as an "unseen power" and an "ever-acting force," is also home-like, the guarantee that the present – and the present order of society – is the necessary development of the past. Frederic Harrison, who so characterizes the irresistible power of "the Past" in his 1862 lecture "The Use of History," is equally certain of its consolations: "We see intelligible structure, consistent unity, and common laws in the earth on which we live, with the view, I presume, of feeling more at home in it, of becoming more attached to it, of living in it more happily." For history is nothing but the history of man ("[w]hilst Man is wanting, all the rest remains vague, and incomplete, and aimless"); and man is nothing but his history ("in all ... human questions whatever, history is the main resource of the inquirer").[9]

This logical circle ensures that man's subjection to the irresistible force of history will in the end confirm him as the subject of knowledge. The "unseen power" manifests itself in the world, is intelligible, and acknowledging its laws is the way to feel at home, no longer alien. Indeed, the intelligibility of history, the fact that this invisible force can be read in its effects, transforms it from the end of man, his dissolution in finitude, to the end towards which he aims. As Matthew Arnold writes, to survey the past is first to be oppressed by "that impatient irritation of mind which we feel in the presence of an immense, moving, confused spectacle, which, while it perpetually excites our curiosity, perpetually baffles our comprehension." In this view, history depresses and alienates, is a vision of heterogeneity and purposeless movement which seems indifferent to order. But Arnold finds in this same history man's salvation from aimless disorder: "The deliverance consists in man's comprehension of this present and past. It begins when our mind begins to enter into possession of the general ideas which are the law of this vast multitude of facts."[10] In this way history is not so much a displacement of the theological as a repetition of its logic, a secular guarantee of order and meaning, of the necessary relations of origins and ends, and, above all, of the man who enters into possession of himself through the possession of this history.

Indeed when the *Antiquary: A Magazine Devoted to the Study of the Past* published its first issue in 1880, its editor took as an epigraph these lines attributed to Schiller, " 'Time doth consecrate;/ And what is grey with age becomes religion,' " and went on to declare,

There is in the breast of our "nation of shopkeepers" a deep-
seated reverence for antiquity, a *religio loci*, which shows itself in
the popular devotion to ancient art, whether in architecture, in
painting, in design, or in furniture, and in the eager reception
accorded to fresh discoveries of relics or works of antiquarian
interest.[11]

This reverence for the past on which the *Antiquary* sought to capi-
talize is, in fact, a confirmation of the "nation of shopkeepers" which
strips that phrase of its critical force, which lifts up the commercial
middle class from the material to the spiritual. "History" is imbued
with religious properties, and what is more, this sacred past has led
ineluctably to the present, to 1880, to the domestic and imperial
triumphs of the English bourgeoisie. The very difference of past ages,
legible in the "relics" of history, reveals the deep continuity between
what has been and what is now, and affirms the "spiritual life," as
Carlyle says, of those who recognize their historical condition.

In his study, *The Victorian Mirror of History*, Dwight Culler
observes that thinking historically is a "habit of mind" of nineteenth-
century Englishmen, and "[t]heir historical consciousness [is] a mode
of self-consciousness, an awareness of the self by means of the
other."[12] Culler's book is a carefully detailed discovery of this habit
as it manifests itself in a wide variety of texts, but like so many who
have recognized history as the "dominant idea" of the nineteenth
century, he explicates the idea of history without ever questioning
the terms of the concept, its consequences or its costs.[13] "Self-consciousness" is no innocent achievement, and if middle-class Victorian
men become aware of themselves by means of "the other," then
"otherness" is only conceivable as the means to an end. The otherness
of history must be read as a problem, not an answer, a process in
which differences are produced only to reflect the truths of certain
men, a process which constructs an imaginary unity of Englishmen
then projected as the image of universal man, a process which entails
the radical exclusion of "women" from the historical, which makes
women "other" to history itself. To look at the mirror of Victorian
history without asking how it produces these images is necessarily
to reflect its "truths."

The chapters which follow are all essays in reading the work of
"otherness," the strange familiarity of "history" and the troubling
but necessary difference of "women." I begin with Eliot's *Daniel
Deronda* because, of the various texts, it is driven most powerfully

to produce "history" and to speak the truth of "man." Its famous double plot, with Gwendolen Harleth's story making up one half and Deronda and Mordecai's story the other, sets "women" in their necessary relation to a "history" which guarantees man's transcendence: here the Jews represent what Eliot calls the "ideal forces" of history, while women (most notably Gwendolen and Deronda's mother) are shown to be essentially unhistorical. The women characters are systematically excluded from the properly "world-historical" realm; "women" are imagined as the bearers of human affection, the medium of cultural transmission. As the representatives of historical man, the Jews are raised up, elevated at the expense of the women who are forced to assume a strictly limited, unhistoric position. For all her sympathy with Gwendolen and her unhappy life, Eliot must do violence both to Gwendolen and Deronda's mother to ensure the historical humanity of man.

Further, the Jews, who are evidently lifted up at women's expense, are actually no more exempt from the covert violence which produces historical totality, for the text effects a transformation of Judaism quite as fatal to Jewish principles as "history" is to the women in the novel. To make the Jews represent historical "man," Eliot must imagine Judaism as an idealism and conceptualize the Jews as the incarnation, the embodiment of history. She assimilates the Jews to a Greco-Christian philosophical tradition; more precisely, she transforms Judaism into a kind of Hegelianism, making Mordecai, her Jewish prophet, speak Hegelian concepts while referring to Jewish literature, the Talmud, the Midrash, the Kabbala, the Bible. Most importantly, she makes Mordecai a Zionist. If history is to be transcendental, Judaism must be Zionism and Israel must be a nation again, for in Eliot's Hegelian terms, unhistorical time becomes history only through the abstraction of a national life, the corporate existence of a nation-state.[14]

In *Daniel Deronda* the violence done to women in the name of history is more obvious than the forced assimilation of the Jews to an alien philosophy of incarnation and transcendence, for women must be radically excluded while the Jews are sublated, cancelled, *and* preserved in the totality of history. To read these processes, especially to read them in their interrelation, is to see both "history" and "humanity" as decidedly political concepts which confirm Anglo-European men at the expense of others, at the cost of producing historical differences only to eradicate them. This clearly is not a reading authorized by Eliot; it is at odds with what she "herself" says she is doing and does not accept her humanist thesis. None the less, it is a reading made possible by her very project of totality, for "history" is marked by what it must repress and refuse in constituting itself as universal, is disfigured by difference. And further, the reading is a necessary one, called for by the logic of the text's concepts and by their consequences, required by the politics of a certain production of knowledge.

This necessity (the necessity of politics), and this possibility (the possibility of reading), motivate the present study and bring together the diverse texts I consider, all of which have to do both with "history" and "women." In Chapter 2, a discussion of Thackeray's historical novel, *The History of Henry Esmond*, and Macaulay's historical narrative, the *History of England from the Accession of James II*, I take up the questions which are posed by these authors and their texts: what is proper to history? what is proper historical representation? Macaulay envisioned his narrative as a vital and authentic account of historical truth – the truth of the progress of England since the Glorious Revolution of 1688 – and hoped to rid history of the falseness of fiction, while *Esmond* insists on fiction – not as falsehood, but as the place of what disciplined history represses: questions of subjectivity, of identity, of the instability of representation. Indeed, in Thackeray's text history turns on the most intimate of questions – "what makes one little hand the dearest of all?" – a question posed but not answered by Colonel Esmond in writing his "memoirs." With his emphasis on the mystery of desire, the power of memory and its malleability, the work of remembrance and the uncertainty of representation, Thackeray makes Esmond into the historian of the feminized sphere of family life. A generation later, Freud will establish himself as an historian of subjectivity and interpreter of the family drama, always the same drama of triangulated desire, of an Oedipal past which makes its indelible, obscure mark on the present. But rather than finding an explanatory principle in Oedipus and the Oedipal trajectory of desire, as Freud will do, Thackeray offers more questions than he answers. For Esmond is Oedipus with a difference: he is the unwitting cause of his adoptive father's death, and he marries his "mother," but this is no transgression, no law is broken, there is no price to pay. *Esmond* is Oedipus with a happy ending, a text in which desire simply proliferates, a text without closure. In this it is a counter-text to history proper: history implodes in the figure of Colonel Esmond, his narrative is continually qualified by the corrosive play of irony, by

repetitions and reversals – a reminder of how uncertain reconstruction and representation may be.

"History" is in *Esmond* a contested concept, a problem addressed
directly by the narrator and indirectly by the fictionality of the text –
by the design of its plot and by an insistent irony which hopelessly
compromises Colonel Esmond's authority. But history is apparently
nowhere to be seen in a melodrama such as Wilkie Collins's play,
The Frozen Deep, and is hard to find in Dickens's melodramatic
Little Dorrit, texts I read in Chapter 3 along with Henry Mayhew's
survey of "labour and the poor." It is the very structure of melodrama, however, its staging of absence and presence, loss and recovery, which is a strong instance of the Victorian fix on "history,"
the confirmation of "man" which moves from loss to gain. In
melodrama, polarities are exaggerated and intensified to construct a
self-evident ethical order, and the maternal woman – who once was
present but is now absent – is at the center of the system. It is she
who is an originary site of total love and complete satisfaction that
must be found again. This is the logic of *Little Dorrit*, of "the
ravishing little family history" of the Clennam household. In this
history, the title character, so angelic as to be unearthly, is the
"vanishing point" of Arthur Clennam's life story, "the termination
of everything that was good or pleasant in it." Absent itself, such a
vanishing point orders all around it; invisible, it makes everything
else come into focus.

In melodrama, history becomes nostalgia, and the social is identified with the familial. This has important political effects, not the
least of which is to make power invisible. "History" is domesticated
and "society" is prepared for the tutelary interventions of the state.
Both are sentimentalized and moralized; the alienating and unconsoling fact of political struggle and the systematic exploitations of
capitalism disappear. Reading Mayhew's work on London laborers,
artisans, and the unemployed, which was published in the *Morning
Chronicle* newspaper a few years before Dickens began *Little Dorrit*,
helps to put these processes in sharp relief. For although Mayhew's
work is not free of the melodramatic fix, his letters to the *Chronicle*
represent the consequences of unregulated competition, depressed
wages, high mortality, the Poor Law, and the police. In Mayhew
history is "what hurts" (in Jameson's phrase), and what vanishes in
melodrama becomes more visible.

Throughout this book I am concerned with what must be overlooked to ensure the truth of "history," what must be excluded to

close the circle in which knowledge and history are one. Thus in Chapter 4 I turn to *Villette* to read in detail the ways in which Brontë's representation of the "inner life" is articulated with history, the ways in which the life of the spirit and of the mind are imagined in terms of history – in this case history as typology. Typology is a hermeneutics which finds in the events, people, and prophecies of the Old Testament "types and shadows" which are fulfilled in the New; it is a theory of history as a totality of perfect correspondence between past, present, and future in which every event emanates from and returns to God. Brontë appropriates the discourse of typology to tell the story of Lucy Snowe, the solitary and troubled protagonist who must learn to read and then to write the book of life, to interpret the events of her life and discover in them an order of intelligibility. Lucy must move from the material to the spiritual, must learn to interpret the "signs and tokens" which surround her if she is ever to know herself.

Villette thus engages the problems of representation and consciousness by way of typology. Indeed, the novel suggests that to understand representation as the adequation of phenomenon and concept is inseparable from a conceptualization of history as the revelation of meaning. What is striking, then, is the way in which the style of the text subverts this order of intelligibility. Promising semantic depth, this intensely figurative text instead develops bizarrely allegorical passages in which "correspondences" do not hold, in which a wild metonymy overwhelms any hope of resemblance or resolution. To overlook this metonymic ruin of representation, or to regard the stylistic excesses of *Villette* as the "expression" of Brontë's own history – as many readers have – is to reinscribe the circle in which representation is the belated expression of an absent real, in which knowledge is "but recorded Experience and product of History."

This circle configures history as a totality, a totality in which differences proliferate only to be transformed into "otherness," into that which is other to the same. Such a configuration ensures that history will in the end reflect man's truth, the truth of those men who are typically human, who fulfill past history and anticipate the future, the Englishmen of Britain's hegemonic class. In Victorian England, history is much more than the events of the past or the account of those events. History is a regime of truth to which knowledge in general is subject, which governs philosophy and philosophical novels (Chapter 1); historical novels and history "proper"

(Chapter 2); melodrama and social studies (Chapter 3); theology, aesthetics, and autobiographical fiction (Chapter 4). The texts I read all are subject to this regime, though very differently, and the diversity of the texts is perhaps the strongest evidence of the extent to which "history" functions as a concept of foundational significance.

While history is not the "dominant idea" of the late twentieth century as it was of the nineteenth (identity and subjectivity now prevail, in the West at least), the historical problematic has none the less long held sway – indeed, has been modified but not displaced by other concerns. In the concluding chapter I consider the high cost of this problematic, not only as it adds up in Victorian Britain, but also as a continuing theoretical and political concern. History is often said to be the foundation of politics and the source of knowledge, the ground which provides a particular standpoint, the Necessity which governs theory and sets inviolable limits to practice. How different is this "history" from Carlyle's "true fountain of knowledge," from Harrison's "unseen power" and "ever-acting force"? How can history and politics be thought together, without endowing the former with foundational status, without being driven by the logic of total history? Can feminist theory conceptualize a history which breaks the circle in which history returns man to himself by way of his others, by way of history "itself"; more importantly, perhaps, can feminism theorize history without replacing "man" with "woman," and without discovering in history the reality of all "women"? The necessity for feminism of theorizing history differently is pressing. The possibility is given by the impossibility of totality, an impossibility which the following readings are an effort to trace.

Chapter 1

George Eliot's apocalypse of history

When reading reviews of *Daniel Deronda*, George Eliot's last, big novel, one must be impressed with her pre-eminent position among British novelists in the 1870s. She is hailed as a "Prophetess of Humanity," her books are acclaimed as a "national blessing," and are said to be "more like Bibles than books of mere amusement."[1] Eliot is no longer a "Prophetess," perhaps, but she is canonized, celebrated as a great philosophical novelist who represents crucial issues of modern life: the relation of the individual to society, the necessity of knowing the limits of individual life and of submitting to the corporate, historical life of humanity as a whole. Read by her contemporaries as a guide to living rightly, Eliot still enjoys the prestige of the moralist, and is known as the great author of humanism.

Much of the voluminous criticism of her work has concentrated on analyzing the complex development of her characters as moral subjects and on studying the paradoxical relations of individual will and historical determinism developed in her books. Critics have explicated Eliot's repeated insistence on submission, her conviction that the individual must submit to the great impersonal forces of history which work on and through one, and her sometimes violent demonstrations of the impossibility of escaping from the determining influences of the past. Tito's horrible death at the hands of his adoptive father in *Romola* is an instance of this logic, as is the fall of Bulstrode in *Middlemarch*. But the book which insists most relentlessly on submission is *Daniel Deronda*. In this, Eliot's most strikingly "world-historical" novel, she develops in detail the workings of the "Invisible Power," as she calls the forces of history, and dramatizes the sometimes painful pressure this impersonal power exerts on individual lives. The overriding question, then, is how the individual will respond to this pressure, whether he or she will be knowledgeable enough to comprehend both the absolute limits of mortal human life and the glory of man's "corporate existence."

There is in *Daniel Deronda* a very explicit, even obsessive development of the problems of power, submission, and knowledge. But rather than accepting the terms of Eliot's humanism, I take *Daniel Deronda* to be a coercive text, a text which is not so much the apocalyptic revelation of the Invisible Power of world history as it is a dramatization of the workings of knowledge and power which produce the moral and historical subject as an effect.[2] Explicitly concerned with the discipline that is crucial to the great humanist project, *Daniel Deronda* is simultaneously Eliot's most strongly idealist book and her most disturbing text, disturbing precisely because the idealizing moves are also power plays, and the emphasis on the ideal is matched by an obsession with power which collapses the comforting opposition of the individual and society by suggesting that the humanist subject is in part an effect of a distinctly untranscendent exercise of power.[3]

Further, *Daniel Deronda* makes strikingly manifest the link between a certain concept of history and the production of the subject. This is especially evident in the famous division of the novel into two parts, an ideal, world-historical half (the Jewish half), and an experiential, psychological, domestic half (Gwendolen Harleth's half). The story of Gwendolen is in many ways a familiar one, that of a vain young woman's moral education. But the story of the prophetic Mordecai, his vision of the restoration of Israel as a modern state, and Deronda's enthusiastic embrace of Judaism has little precedence in British literature, and readers from Eliot's time to now have wondered what Gwendolen has to do with the Jews and vice versa. Why raise "the woman question" (for Gwendolen is exemplary of the woman as spectacle, enigma, problem) and "the Jewish question" (the question of the "superlative peculiarity" of the Jews, to use Eliot's phrase, the problem of their difference) in the same book?

An answer is suggested by the insistent duality of the text which is organized around a related series of paired oppositions: individual and collective, empirical and ideal, psychologic and philosophic, particular and world-historical. The text is structured by these distinctions, and in each case the second term, defined in contrast to the first, subsumes its opposite. Eliot's last novel produces differences only to overcome them, demonstrating repeatedly how the ideal triumphantly incorporates the diversity of "facts" into an all-embracing totality. Indeed, *Daniel Deronda* displays the necessary conceptual link between empiricism and idealism, the two poles of modern thought, demonstrating that neither can function without the other. This is the logic, then, which produces the duality of the novel's plot in which man's historical identity, his ideal humanity, is secured at woman's expense. These are the abstract categories – Man, Woman – which this richly detailed novel helps to consolidate.

That Gwendolen comes to stand for the unhistorical, untranscendent particularity of woman is not surprising, but it does seem strange that Eliot would choose the Jews to represent historical man, given that nineteenth-century anti-Semitism positions the Jews as alien, anachronistic, a foreign body inimical to collective health. In fact, it is precisely to combat such vulgar prejudice that Eliot idealizes the Jews, for she sees in anti-Semitism a pernicious ignorance of history. For Eliot, the Jews are no anachronism, but rather the embodiment of the "ideal forces" of history, and the survival of Judaism over millennia is the best evidence of the power of history to conserve as well as to destroy. However, as we will see, idealizing the Jews and punishing women are but two poles of the same problem, and both Jews and women are set up in *Daniel Deronda* only to confirm the everlasting unity of Man. Eliot works in this novel to account for two troubling threats to the unity of humanity, the difference of the Jews and the difference of women, finding in the first an ideal instance of history and in the second the absolute limit of world history. But in fact, the Jews fare little better than women in this scheme, since before they can become the representative historical subjects, the specificity and materiality of the Jews and Judaism must be radically disavowed.

While writing *Daniel Deronda* (the book was begun in 1873 and published in eight parts, beginning in 1876), Eliot offered in a letter a now famous definition of her work.

> My writing is simply a set of experiments in life – an endeavour to see what our thought and emotion may be capable of – what stores of motive, actual or hinted as possible, give promise of a better after which we may strive – what gains from past revelations and discipline we must strive to keep hold of as something more sure than shifting theory.

She goes on to say, "I become more and more timid, with less daring to adopt any formula which does not get itself clothed for me in some human figure and individual experience. . . ."[4] While Eliot speaks of her timidity, the effect of this definition is quite the contrary, for she is laying claim to the authority of the scientist and the veracity of the scientific experiment. The characteristically Victorian deference to science is evident in her definition of her writing as a scientific enterprise; further, the respect due to science should be due also to her novels, these "experiments" designed to investigate hypotheses about human life. Certainly Eliot anticipated the social sciences in the extensive research she undertook when preparing to write her later large books, and her accumulation of information is evident in the detail with which she is able to reproduce fifteenth-century Florence in *Romola* or the particulars of Jewish history and controversies about Jewish identity in *Daniel Deronda*. As George Henry Lewes wrote to her publisher, "You are surprised at her knowledge of the Jews? But only learned Rabbis are so profoundly versed in Jewish history and literature as she is. . . . What a stupendous genius it is!"[5] It is clear that her contemporaries were rather awe-struck with her learning, and there is something awesome in a "research program" that includes mastering Hebrew in order to write a novel.

Eliot's declared timidity is not to be dismissed as a false note, however, for in Eliot's conception of her work as experimental there is a double gesture of submitting to the facts and mastering the facts. Indeed, her mastery, and the truths she is able to discover, depend on her attentiveness to particular human figures and individual experience, and the results of her investigations depend on her restricting herself to the evidence. Lord Acton, in a letter written to a friend a few days after Eliot's death, offers a suggestive description of this process:

> George Eliot seemed to me capable not only of reading the diverse hearts of men, but of creeping into their skin, seeing the world through their eyes, feeling their latent background of conviction, discerning theory and habit, influences of thought and knowledge, of life and of descent, and having obtained this experience, recovering her independence, stripping off the borrowed shell, and exposing scientifically and indifferently the soul of a Vestal, a Crusader, an Anabaptist. . . .[6]

The objects of Eliot's investigations are stripped, exposed, discarded in a thoroughly objectifying operation, but not before Eliot has assumed their positions. Further, the second move, the reduction of the subjects of the experiments to objects, is for Acton the condition of the truth of the books, and Eliot's revelation of how men think "who live in the grasp of various systems" suggests the possibility of being free from such a grasp, the promise of pure knowledge.

As readers of Eliot rather than Eliot herself we are evidently to do as Acton does, submit to her superior knowledge and be thankful that she can, as he says, "give rational form to motives [one has] imperfectly analysed." This submission is the condition of a better life, one conducted in fuller knowledge of both limits and possibilities. But there is another kind of coercion here, one more problematic. For Eliot, all research always reveals the same thing, the truth of man's social and historical being, the promise that man may one day live in the full knowledge of his individual mortality and his corporate potential. That is, Eliot's "experiments" always have the same results. No matter what the evidence, in every novel the same philosophical–moral dilemmas are posed and the same revelations of man's paradoxically historical being are made. Thus the experiment in fifteenth-century Florentine life made in *Romola*, for instance, and the Jewish experiment of *Daniel Deronda* come to the same conclusions. Savonarola's Catholicism and republicanism are identical to Mordecai's Judaism and Zionism; identical, that is, in their latent meanings known only to Eliot – who then takes care that we readers can also analyse the truths inherent in any great religious system or political movement. So when Eliot strips off the borrowed shell of a particular human figure or individual experience, she also strips away the specificity of that figure, of that historical time. The massive accumulation of evidence is crucial for the creation of certain reality-effects, but finally every fact is only the means to an end, man himself – man reduced to an object of study yet full of almost unthinkable potential.[7]

Eliot, of course, was widely read in modern philosophy – she was perhaps the most masterfully informed of Victorian novelists – and her philosophical positions repeat and justify her "experimental" method. In *Daniel Deronda*, as elsewhere in her writing, Eliot is engaged with the problem of managing finitude, of making the limits of human being the condition of transcendence. When writing *Daniel Deronda*, Eliot thought often of death, of her own death and perhaps even more of Lewes's. In her letters she repeatedly mentions their bad health, and the unavoidable fact of their corporeal existence. Death, Eliot writes, is what I think of almost daily. For death seems to me now a close, real experience, like the approach of autumn or winter, and I am glad to find that advancing life brings this power of imagining the nearness of death....[8]

The rather unexpected turn in which Eliot is glad to be able to imagine death is of interest not so much as a biographical detail, but as a wonderfully clear instance of the particular sacrifices she believes are required if one is to realize the ideal, the higher, historical life of humanity which supersedes one's own. Recognizing that being human is a subjection to forces beyond one's control, knowing that human life depends on conditions that are barely comprehensible – this is the submission that is necessary if one is ever to grasp the workings of what Eliot calls in *Daniel Deronda* the "Invisible Power." But, of course, although this power is invisible, its effects are evident. Indeed, the only way Eliot can know this transcendent force is through the observable facts of human life.

Knowledge of the Invisible Power is thus available to a "powerful imagination," which Eliot defines in a late essay as

a creative energy constantly fed by susceptibility to the veriest minutiae of experience, which it reproduces and constructs in fresh wholes; ... a breadth of ideal association which informs every material object, every incidental fact with far-reaching memories, ... bringing into new light the less obvious relations of human existence.[9]

But this "veracious imagination" (as she calls it in another place) might be better known as the voracious imagination: it swallows up even the tiniest bit of experience, even the smallest fact, in a process which transforms everything into an embodiment of the ideal.[10] The facts of life, then, including the fact of death, become the evidence of a totality which transcends individual experience. While Eliot is by no means alone in the project of managing finitude – the period is famous for the disappearance of God and the consequences of that absence – she is one of the most "ardently theoretical" of novelists dedicated to the project of finding in history a deferred transcendence.[11]

Of her novels, her last one displays most clearly the triumph of the ideal and the costs of transcendence. *Daniel Deronda* is a lengthy demonstration of the effects of the impersonal invisible power of history and insists in no uncertain terms on the necessity of submission to this power as the condition for the salvation of human life. But in the recurrent insistence on submission, and especially in the different effects of power in the divided plot of the novel, *Daniel Deronda* displays power working in decidedly untranscendent ways.

The Jewish half of the novel represents the ideal union of individual and collective life in the character of Mordecai and his vision of the restoration of Israel as a nation in Palestine. This part is philosophical, didactic, prophetic. The Gwendolen half domesticates the novel by telling a familiar story of a proud young woman's moral education by way of courtship and marriage. It is distinctly unideal, showing English life as shallow, mercenary, and exploitative. Gwendolen, as the heroine of this half, is granted a sensitivity lacking in the rest of the English, a susceptibility that will allow her to comprehend, to a point, the insignificance of her individual life, the forces of world history, the higher knowledge that comes from submission to the invisible power. Whereas the Jewish half is dominated by philosophical discussions and prophetic visions, Gwendolen's half is much more dramatically developed, more psychological than philosophical. George Eliot, disturbed at "readers who cut the book into scraps, and talk of nothing in it but Gwendolen" defended the unity of the novel, writing in a letter, "I meant everything in the book to be related to everything else there."[12] However, this frequently cited declaration of her intent hasn't stopped critics from objecting to the incongruity of the parts, perhaps the most famous recent criticism coming from F. R. Leavis even as he induced Eliot into The Great Tradition.[13] He dismisses the Jewish sections of the novel as "fervid and wordy," and proposes to save the novel by keeping what's good – Gwendolen's story, which develops her as "a responsible moral agent ... amenable to moral judgement" – and throwing away the rest. But an earlier reviewer of the novel realized that turning *Daniel Deronda* into *Gwendolen Harleth* won't work, because everything in the novel *is* related to everything else, even if not quite in the ideal way Eliot imagines. Henry James recognized the centrality of Gwendolen in the novel, the way her "history," as he says, is "admirably typical," showing the painful discovery of one's insignificance: "The universe, forcing itself with a slow, inexorable pressure into a narrow, complacent, and yet after all extremely sensitive mind, and making it ache with the pain of the process – that is Gwendolen's story."[14] Such a realization surely is typical in Eliot's terms, since, as we have seen, for her all human life is subjected to history, and this is the condition of transcendence. In *Daniel Deronda*, Mordecai and the "corporate entity" of Judaism are evidence of the transcendence which comes of subjection, so Eliot could well claim that the Jewish part stands in a necessary relation to Gwendolen's story as an instance of what she calls "a larger life." But, as James so rightly observes,

> [Gwendolen] is punished for being narrow and she is not allowed a chance to expand. Her finding Deronda preengaged to go to the East and stir up the race-feeling of the Jews strikes one as a wonderfully happy invention. The irony of the situation, for poor Gwendolen, is almost grotesque, and it makes one wonder whether the whole heavy structure of the Jewish question in the story was not built up by the author for the express purpose of giving its proper force to this particular stroke.[15]

This is a crucial question, for if the "whole heavy structure" of the Jewish half presses on Gwendolen solely as a punishment which is not transformed into a redemption, then the relation of real to ideal, empirical to transcendental is seriously compromised. Surely juxtaposing Gwendolen's life with the "world-historical" dimensions of Deronda's Zionist calling is a particularly forceful stroke, and one that is applied quite mercilessly to Gwendolen. When Deronda reveals to her his mission " 'of restoring a political existence to my people, making them a nation again, giving them a national centre, such as the English have,' " she is massively overwhelmed. Earlier in this final interview between them, she has already experienced "a dreadful presentiment of mountainous travel for her mind before it could reach Deronda's," and now "the world seemed getting larger round poor Gwendolen, and she more solitary and helpless in the midst." "Reduced to a mere speck," she has reached "a terrible moment" in her life:

> Then it is as if the Invisible Power that has been the object of lip-worship and lip-resignation became visible, according to the imagery of the Hebrew poet, making the flames his chariot and riding on the wings of the wind, till the mountains smoke and the plains shudder under the rolling, fiery visitation.[16]

Gwendolen is rolled quite flat in these closing pages of the novel, and in the rhetorical overkill of this scene there is perhaps a displaced recognition of the exercise of power implicit in any idealizing operation. But to understand this scene of punishment more fully, and to appreciate the reference to "the Hebrew poet," we need first to consider how Eliot uses the Jews in *Daniel Deronda*.

She takes the Jews, a long oppressed and suffering people, and finds in them a representative of what she calls in an essay "the ideal forces in human history," for Jews have maintained their culture and religion in the face of vicious prejudice. The destruction of Israel's national center and the dispersal of the Jews has not obliterated Judaism; rather, in Eliot's view, this national tragedy has elevated those who are still ready to say, " 'I am a Jew,' " since "the pride which identifies us with a great historic body is a humanizing, elevating habit of mind, inspiring sacrifices of individual comfort, gain, or other selfish ambition, for the sake of that ideal whole."[17] Indeed, Eliot imagines the Jews as the most radically conservative of men, who assiduously conserve a culture despised by much of the world, a culture which she argues is in fact of originary significance. Mordecai, in one of his prophetic moments, declares that

> "Israel is the heart of mankind, if we mean by heart the core of affection which binds a race and its families in dutiful love, and the reverence for the human body which lifts the needs of our animal life into religion, and the tenderness which is merciful to the poor and weak and to the dumb creature that wears the yoke for us...."

(p. 590)

That is, at the heart of mankind is the law; the law which regulates kinship, which orders bodies, which distinguishes between man and animal.[18] This humanizing law has been transmitted through the centuries as the organizing principle of a collective life – Eliot's "ideal whole" – greater than any individual. Thus to say "I am a Jew" is significant not as a matter of personal identity, but as an acknowledgment of the law and of mankind's necessarily corporate existence. To "be" a Jew in *Daniel Deronda*, to claim that identity, is to submit to the law and the history incarnated in the corporate entity of Judaism, and to do so even at the sacrifice of personal gratification and advancement.

It is no surprise, then, that Daniel Deronda is a Jew, even though the secret of his birth isn't revealed until the seventh of eight books. From the beginning he is different from the English, disqualified by his apparently illegitimate birth from inheriting Sir Hugo's lands, and, feeling wronged by his illegitimacy, extraordinarily sensitive to the sufferings of others. Deprived of the proper relations of kinship, he longs to know the truth about his parents – "to Daniel the words

Father and Mother had the altar-fire in them" – because kinship brings with it duties greater than self-gratification, provides a connection to the past, places one in a regulated cultural order with a history (p. 526). Thus when Mordecai hails Deronda as the embodiment of his prophetic vision, the one who will be wholly devoted to the transmission of the law and restoration of Israel, Deronda willingly responds to his call, and although he points out to Mordecai, " 'What my birth was does not lie in my will,' " the confirmation of his Jewishness is but a formality of the plot (p. 560). In fact, when his mother finally summons him and makes the revelation, the scenes between them are far more significant in the violence done to her than as the disclosure of a determining fact. Deronda's Jewishness is determined long before this point by the logic of the novel, a logic comically and ironically demonstrated in a letter written to Deronda by a minor figure. Cynthia Chase, in an incisive essay on *Daniel Deronda*, has taken Hans Meyrick's letter as an indicator of how the text undoes certain classically realist assumptions, particularly the logical sequence of cause and effect.[19] In this letter, Deronda's friend Hans writes that he has been sketching Mordecai in Deronda's absence,

> getting credit with him as a learned young Gentile, who would have been a Jew if he could – and agreeing with him in the general principle, that whatever is best is for that reason Jewish. I never held it my *forte* to be a severe reasoner, but I can see that if whatever is best is A and B happens to be best, B must be A, however little you might have expected it beforehand.
>
> (p. 705)

This is, of course, a perfect description of the inevitability of Deronda's identity as a Jew, a cause transformed into an effect just as in Eliot's text all empirical facts are but effects of transcendent historical forces. That is, the fact of Deronda's birth, revealed to him by his mother, should be the cause of his Jewishness, but rather, this fact is produced by his effective Jewishness, his idealization.

That his meeting with his mother should be the occasion of a violence in the text rivaled only by the punishments meted out to Gwendolen suggests, first, that facts may be recalcitrant and sometimes difficult to transform successfully into evidence of the ideal, and second, that women pose problems for Eliot's idealizing, historicizing imagination. Eliot knows that the determining fact of Jewish identity is guaranteed by the mother, not the father, that the

evidence of Jewish birth is material and maternal. This is a real
problem for her, for while she will give Deronda a Jewish mother,
she cannot credit his Jewish identity, that evidence of the "ideal
forces" of history, to an accident of birth. Indeed, Deronda's mother
must appear only to disappear; she comes into the book suffering
horribly from a mortal disease and is soon forced out of the picture.
She is obviously a device to advance the plot, but is also instrumental
in a much more troubling way, for she is, as she herself says, "the
instrument" of her dead father's will. He had willed that she be a
good Jewish girl: as she says, " 'he only thought of fettering me into
obedience,' " and, later,

> "he never thought of his daughter except as an instrument. Because
> I had wants outside his purpose, I was to be put in a frame and
> tortured. If that is the right law for the world I will not say that I
> love it."
>
> (p. 726)

She refused to observe the law, she thwarted her father's will, but
now death is upon her and she is afraid. " 'I am forced to be withered,
to feel pain, to be dying slowly,' " she tells her son. " 'Do I love that?
Well, I have been forced to obey my dead father' " (p. 693). And
again,

> "I have after all been the instrument my father wanted. – 'I desire
> a grandson who shall have a true Jewish heart. Every Jew should
> rear his family as if he hoped that a Deliverer might spring from
> it.' " In uttering these last sentences the Princess ... spoke slowly
> ..., as if she were quoting unwillingly.
>
> (p. 726)

She is, we learn, in "an agony of pain" at times, and "a great horror"
comes over her. Thus terrified, thus punished, she reveals to Deronda
the secret of his birth and delivers to him what her father had
commanded her to deliver, a chest containing ancient and modern
Hebrew manuscripts. To be more precise, she doesn't deliver the
chest herself, but facilitates its transference from a friend of her
father's to that father's grandson. So the law is transmitted from
man to man, and the Princess who does not consent, who "was never
willingly subject to any man," disappears from the book (p. 730).

Eliot's severity to Deronda's mother has to do with her imagining
this character as unrepentant, coerced by a fear of death and retribution but closed to all knowledge of the ideal life. But why the

compulsion to punish her so? Mirah and Mordecai's father is a graceless enough character, but not tortured the way Eliot torments Deronda's mother. Why? An answer is suggested in an exchange between the Princess and her son. She addresses him abruptly and scornfully after he had pleaded with her to open her heart to her father: " 'You speak as men do – as if you felt yourself wise. What does it all mean?' " Deronda, of course, entreats her not to think him wise, personally, for he only strives to be truthful,

> "not ... keeping back facts which may – which should carry obligation within them. ... No wonder if such facts come to reveal themselves in spite of concealments. The effects prepared by generations are likely to triumph over a contrivance which would bend them all to the satisfaction of self."
>
> (p. 727)

Deronda understands "the effects of generations" as the forces of history which bear down equally on all people, men and women alike, but the Princess is right in arguing that the facts which carry obligation within them are produced to the advantage of men. Women are assigned the responsibility for social life, for ensuring that generation follows generation. They are obligated to reproduce life, not only to bear children but to rear them, to love them, to humanize them. In this obligation – the very one the Princess refuses in her rejection of maternity – women have a quite different relation to history than do men.

Given her explicit criticism of "the effects prepared by generations," and her rebellion against the forces of history, the Princess actually challenges the whole order of historical necessity Eliot slowly and carefully "proves" in the course of *Daniel Deronda*. Her eloquent presence, and the clear sympathy that the narrator also has for Gwendolen's longing for a more vital and meaningful life, are aspects of the novel which highlight the high cost for women of a history which is predicated on their exclusion and their relegation to the realm of reproduction. In quite explicit ways, then, Eliot recognizes the different relations men and women have to history, and directly addresses the effects of that difference. Yet this recognition is made only to assert more forcefully the "fact" of sexual difference. Women must submit – not to a conventional femininity of display nor to the dehumanizing exchanges of the marriage market, but to a higher necessity, that of reproducing social life.[20]

This necessary difference is especially clear in a question the narrator poses about Gwendolen:

> Could there be a slenderer, more insignificant thread in human history than this consciousness of a girl, busy with her small inferences of the way in which she could make her life pleasant? ... What in the midst of [the] mighty drama [of world history] are girls and their blind visions? They are the Yea or Nay of that good for which men are enduring and fighting. In these delicate vessels is borne through the ages the treasure of human affections.
>
> (p. 160)

Women are thus a medium of transmission, not "the great Transmitters" who, as Mordecai says, are the "philosophers and the great Masters who handed down the thought of our race" (p. 580). It is for men to discover man as an historical subject, to find themselves in history; women are disqualified from such a deferred consolation, for they are to be understood first and foremost as different from men. So the Princess in refusing her womanly place not only disrupts the continuity of social, affective life, but threatens history itself, for history, like all concepts, requires its other. This helps to explain why Mirah and Mordecai's father, while equally (or even more) culpable as a parent, is let off so lightly. As a man, his failure to safeguard the treasure of human affections is not nearly so troubling.

The Princess is punished for crimes of the heart, crimes which in Eliot's book are a capital offense for women. To use one of Eliot's favorite words, the "lot" of women is one of the crucial stakes guaranteeing the truth of humanity, which is to say the truth of man. As the great Victorian author of humanism, Eliot must ask the woman question, must try to calculate the particular value of women. How she assesses their worth is suggested in a letter of hers to Miss Davies on the issue of higher education for women. She writes,

> there lies just [a] kernel of truth in the vulgar alarm of men lest women should be "unsexed." We can no more afford to part with that exquisite type of gentleness, tenderness, possible maternity suffusing a woman's being with affectionateness, which makes what we mean by the feminine character, than we can afford to part with the human love, the mutual subjection of soul between a man and a woman – which is also a growth and revelation beginning before all history.[21]

Women, in this definition, quickly *become* love, and love is outside of history. The worst thing a woman can do is to "unsex" herself, to refuse femininity, maternity, affectionateness. The problem with the Princess is that she is too masculine, for all her beauty, for all her erotic charm.

But of course Eliot herself, pseudonym and all, is "too masculine," too. First, she is all too masculine in her championing of history and the historical subject at the expense of women. In this she confirms the Victorian fascination, even obsession, with the woman question, a question asked to consolidate the identity of men. But she is too masculine in another way, one that doesn't affirm the order of things. That is, Eliot's punishing of women who are not properly suffused with maternity, who are not self-sacrificing in their femininity, is a bit much – a bit too much – an exaggeration of the way men over- and under-value women. In fact, she can't get the woman question right because she herself is a woman, and for her the woman question doesn't hold the complex fascination that it does for some, for many men. She identifies with men, she sees women from the masculine point of view, but women can never be for her the wholly enigmatic other. They do, however, pose a problem that has to be solved if she is to make history work. Her solution is at once formulaic in its design (the woman's story: courtship, marriage, motherhood) and almost frightening in its violence. In *Daniel Deronda*, Eliot's women characters are either permitted a sort of secondary transcendence through history by virtue of their attachment to a properly transcendental man, or they are subjected to the worst sort of discipline in an effort to coerce them into a transcendence which is, in the end, impossible. Mirah, the perfect Jewess who is Mordecai's devoted sister and then devotedly attached to Deronda, is an instance of the first "solution" to the problem of women and transcendence, the Princess Halm-Eberstein of the second.

The punishment of Deronda's mother is nothing, however, compared to the long story of Gwendolen's torments. On the one hand, she is forced to submit to her husband Grandcourt who has married her precisely because he wants the pleasure of subduing her. Uniting two branches of nobility, commanding the lands and titles of both, Grandcourt embodies in his languid person a purely negative power of command. Once Gwendolen has married him for his wealth and social position, she is in his power. Under "the quiet massive pressure of his rule," as the narrator describes it, and subjected to his "continual presence and surveillance," Gwendolen "was undergoing a discipline for the refractory which was as little as possible like conversion ..." (pp. 656, 648, 656). Like the Princess, she is coerced but not converted.

But Eliot is determined, it seems, to save Gwendolen, to make her truly penitent, to make her see the truth of Deronda's declaration to her: "'The refuge you are needing from personal trouble is the higher, the religious life which holds an enthusiasm for something more than our own appetites and vanities'" (p. 508). To bring her to this "larger home," as Deronda calls it – the history in which, as Foucault says, man finds "what might be called his abode" – Eliot establishes Deronda as Gwendolen's "superior," and as the novel progresses we learn that "he was becoming a part of her conscience."[22] Indeed, she is aware of a "coercion he [exercises] over her thought" from the first, when he looks disapprovingly upon her gambling (p. 374). This coercion becomes more and more intense, she internalizes his words and his looks more and more, until, we are told, "she had learned to see all her acts through the impression they would make on Deronda. ... He seemed to her a terrible browed angel from whom she could not think of concealing any deed ..." (p. 737). The relation between these two reaches its first climax in the days after Grandcourt's death by drowning, a death for which Gwendolen feels herself guilty since she had wished her husband dead. She feels herself compelled to confess all to Deronda, every last nuance of every avaricious and murderous desire. He sits, she talks; he averts his eyes, she talks. It is, indeed, a talking cure, for all her desires have become torments: "'all the things I used to wish for – it is as if they had been made red-hot'" (p. 757). Part religious confession, part psychological therapy, part criminal trial (for Deronda pronounces on the degree of her legal culpability), these scenes between Deronda and Gwendolen are almost unbearable. But their last interview, the one in which Gwendolen is flattened by the "Invisible Power" is even worse, for at that point it is quite clear that, as James says, "[Gwendolen] is punished for being narrow and is not allowed a chance to expand." And, indeed, while Gwendolen is without a doubt sacrificed, she is not redeemed. Deronda may live happily ever after in the "larger home" of world history, but Gwendolen is doomed to a distinctly untranscendent life.[23]

The obsessive punishing of Gwendolen – her whole story really only sounds that one note – makes one think twice (at least) about the costs of transcendence, indeed, about the whole humanist project of consolidating man as an historical subject. The idea of Eliot's "experiments in life" comes to be distinctly ominous as we see how her subjects are objectified in order to be reconstituted in a properly ideal whole, how facts are produced only to be subsumed in the transcendent totality of history. Perhaps most importantly, the exercise of power in *Daniel Deronda* demonstrates that transcendence through history is an impossibility for women, and that articulating "man" as a being who finds himself in history (albeit after some searching) is predicated on the exclusion of women from history, her difference thus helping to ensure his identity. George Eliot's most determinedly transcendental and historical novel displays this logic, nowhere more clearly than in its bifurcated plot. For if the Jewish part is an apocalyptic revelation of man's true historical essence, Gwendolen's part is just as surely the sacrifice which enables it. Mordecai is the prophet of this revelation, which comes to pass when Deronda finally says, "'I am a Jew.'" At that moment, the truth of man is fully disclosed. When Deronda speaks these decisive words, Mordecai, who had been looking particularly deathly (he is dying of consumption) is brought back to life, and Deronda enjoys "one of those rare moments when our yearnings and our acts can be completely one, and the real we behold is our ideal good ..." (p. 817). The union of real and ideal makes Deronda history incarnate, but Gwendolen pays for this apotheosis. And pays. And pays.

*

But then so do the Jews, for George Eliot makes over Judaism so that it can do the world-historical work she requires. If women in this text are but instruments to further man's transcendence, so paradoxically are the Jews. They, too, are put in the service of Eliot's humanist project, and her idealization of Judaism ends up denying Jewish specificity. Judaism in *Daniel Deronda* becomes an idealism, an extension of a philosophical and theological tradition actually antipathetic to it.

Because Eliot evidently valorizes the Jews, this appropriation and quite thorough displacement is less obvious than her apparently high assessment of Jewish life. Her approval of the Jews and decision to make Mordecai the novel's best instance of "the higher, the religious life" is a challenge to widely-held prejudices against Jews and an explicit rejection of the idea that Jews are necessarily degenerate, an alien remnant of ancient times long since past their glory. Anti-Semitism is not everywhere and always the same, and nineteenth-century Europeans despised the Jews in distinctly modern terms, finding fault with them for not being properly historical. They were said to be unnatural, anachronistic, and obstinately devoted to a religion and a culture that had no place in the present: the time of Judaism was in the past, and living, observant Jews were an offence to civilization.

These ideas, part of what Edward Said has named "Orientalism," were widely current in Victorian Britain, part of even so apparently balanced and inclusive an essay as Matthew Arnold's *Culture and Anarchy*.[24] Published just four years before Eliot began writing *Daniel Deronda*, Arnold's discussion of England's ills turns on the distinction between Hebraic and Hellenic, and is an instructive contrast to Eliot's formulations in her novel. Both authors think that the condition of England in the second half of the century is distinctly troubling, tending to decline to the lowest common denominator, characterized by Arnold as the "ordinary self" and by Eliot as "the average man." Each is for raising the cultural standard, each is deeply critical of bourgeois taste and values, each turns to culture – for Arnold, "the best that has been thought and said," for Eliot "the spiritual products, the generous motives which sustain the charm and elevation of our social existence."[25] But their assessments of the values of the "Hebraic," the Jewish contribution to western culture, are significantly different.

Arnold's is a standard Orientalist position, however original his formulation may appear, for his final considered judgment is that Hebraism is and should be a thing of the past and that the future belongs rightly to Hellenism.[26] Arnold understands all of world history in terms of the relation between these two fundamental "forces" of human life, the Hellenic focus on intelligence and knowledge, the Hebraic on duty and morality. And he believes in a progressive history in which Hebraism – Judaic culture and the culture of primitive Christianity – is properly and necessarily superseded by Hellenic ideals. "Eighteen hundred years ago it was altogether the hour of Hebraism," Arnold writes, declaring that the Hebraic stress on action and morality was then "legitimately and truly the ascendent force in the world" (p. 474). It was, he says, a necessary corrective to the aestheticism of Greek culture which had no adequate way of addressing the facts of corruption and evil, focused as it was on "thinking clearly, seeing things in their essence and beauty." Arnold allows that this Greek "conception of human nature" was "premature" and that the world required the discipline of Hebraism. The ascendency of the forces of duty and morality had an absolute limit, however, reached in the Renaissance. At that crucial moment the world rediscovered the classical ideal, the humane rather than ascetic life. The progress of mankind depended on the overcoming of Hebraism at the proper moment, but the English, in their dogmatic Puritanism (an extension of Hebraic principles) have made the mistake of going against history, of reviving Hebraism after its time, of "checking the main stream of man's advance ... towards knowing himself and the world." The English have contravened the natural, historical order; they have

> made the secondary the principal at the wrong moment, and the principal they have treated as secondary. This contravention of the natural order has produced ... a certain confusion and false movement.... Everywhere we see the beginnings of confusion, and we want a clue to some sound order and authority.
>
> (p. 475)

The culture which is properly Hellenic, committed to "sweetness and light," beauty and knowledge, is for Arnold that authority, and Hebraism is relegated to the youth of the world which required its rigid and unreflective discipline.

For Arnold, then, the university education which left him "stuffed with Greek and Aristotle" is a civilizing influence since culture is the effort to "see things in their essence and beauty" – that is, culture is above all a Hellenic ideal. But Eliot is far less sanguine about a classical education which leaves educated Englishmen shamefully ignorant of all things Jewish. In a letter written after the publication of *Daniel Deronda* she refers scornfully to the English ignorance of Jews and Jewish history. "They hardly know that Christ was a Jew," she writes. "And I find men educated at Rugby supposing that Christ spoke Greek...."[27] For Eliot, as for Arnold, culture is that "by which man saves his soul alive," but she associates the classicism which long was the mark of English high culture not with salvation but with death – with the deadly influence of the pale and languid Grandcourt, most notably, but also with the killing stupidity of well-meaning (and classically educated) English characters like the Reverend Mr Gascoigne or Sir Hugo.

In a direct reversal of the common anti-Semitic relegation of the Jews to ancient history, which had as its corollary a contempt for the Jews who still adhered to a dead religion, Eliot makes Judaism vital not only in the past but in the present and the future. " 'The Jews,' " declares a minor character in the novel, " 'are a standstill people. They are the type of obstinate adherence to the superannuated.' " But Mordecai turns this adherence into a virtue, the evidence of Jewish respect for the law and the ground for future greatness. He proclaims,

> "In the multitudes of the ignorant on three continents who observe our rites and make the confession of the divine Unity, the soul of Judaism is not dead. Revive the organic centre: let the unity of Israel which has made the growth and form of its religion be an outward reality."

(p. 592)

Jews, even when ignorant and oppressed, have kept Judaism alive and maintain a vital connection to the past from which the future will grow organically. Observant Jews, then, embody a living history, while the English of the novel, however cultivated, however educated, are moribund. This Eliot emphasizes by setting Deronda and Grandcourt side by side. They make a "subject" for "those ... who liked contrasts of temperament. There was a calm intensity of life and richness of tone in [Deronda's] face," whereas of Grandcourt we know that "it was perhaps not possible for a breathing man wide awake to look less animated" (pp. 208, 145). And in the Theophrastus Such essays, she makes expressly clear her contempt for the putatively historical arguments of anti-Semitism, scorning those "personages who take up the attitude of philosophic thinkers and discriminating critics ... condemning the Jews on the ground that they are obstinate adherents of an outworn creed."[28]

Eliot objects strongly to received truths, especially when they distort what she understands to be the foundational truths of history. In "Leaves from a Note-book," she claims that "the grand elements of history require the illumination of special imaginative treatment" and "freedom from the vulgar coercion of conventional plot."[29] The unconventional double plot of her last novel, then, and the unexpected lifting up of the Jews as an ideal world-historical corporate entity are Eliot's efforts to provide a new illumination, to shed new light on man's historical condition, to reassess the "spiritual products" which comprise human culture. Hebraism, considered by Matthew Arnold to be a regressive, dogmatic, rigid, and finally unnatural force in modern life is in *Daniel Deronda* the most significant realization of the human spirit, and Israel a nation not only of the past but also of the future. In a move which discomfited numbers of her readers, Eliot reverses the hierarchy of Hellenic and Hebraic, Indo-European and Semitic, English and Jew.

Eliot wrote self-consciously against the general anti-Semitism of the English, and in doing so she took a calculated risk. "As to the Jewish element in 'Deronda,' I expected from first to last in writing it, that it would create much stronger resistance and even repulsion than it has actually met with," she wrote in a letter to Harriet Beecher Stowe. "[N]ot only towards the Jews, but towards all oriental peoples with whom we English come in contact, a spirit of arrogance and contemptuous dictatorialness is observable which has become a national disgrace to us."[30] Her wish is "to rouse the imagination of men and women to a vision of human claims in those races of their fellow-men who most differ from them in customs and beliefs." In both her last novel and in her final book of essays, Eliot presses the liberal claim that all men are fellows, united in their humanity although divided by cultural and racial differences. In fact, the logic of liberal humanism requires that differences be recognized in order to be overcome in a higher unity, difference being the manifest sign of deep historical rootedness, the specificity that makes all men the same, that makes all men subject to history. Eliot insists on difference because she finds in it the grounds of a common humanity. Thus she says through Theophrastus Such, "Let it be admitted that it is a calamity to the English ... to undergo a premature fusion with immigrants of alien blood," and although she recognizes that "the tendency of things is toward the quicker or slower fusion of races," she insists that there must be an effort "to moderate [this] course so as to hinder it from degrading the moral status of societies by too rapid effacement of those national traditions and customs which are the language of the national genius."[31] Her liberalism is therefore radically conservative, recognizing and preserving differences – national, racial, customary – so as to discover in the facts of diversity the root, the origin of a more profound likeness. Eliot's defense of "oriental peoples," then, and her unconventional development of "the Jewish element" in her final novel, has as its final result the discovery of sameness in difference, or as Eliot writes,

> The distinctive note of each bird species is ... exceptional, but the necessary ground of such distinction is a deeper likeness. The superlative peculiarity of the Jews admitted, our affinity with them is only the more apparent when the elements of their peculiarity are discerned.[32]

If Eliot's attention to the Jews is unconventional, her claim to the ground of a deeper likeness is the predictably necessary resolution of difference in universal humanity. Her political liberalism is the effect of an idealism which requires the reality of differences, of empirically verifiable diversity, of historical specificity, in order to reveal beneath, before, above this reality a principle of unity. In her choice of subject and plot in *Daniel Deronda*, Eliot asserts her freedom from vulgar convention, her commitment to a higher truth, but she is in fact compelled by the logic of humanism to enact a massive appropriation of the Jews, thereby ensuring that everything will always be the same. For the Jews in her novel are made over, are Hellenized and Christianized. Only then can they be claimed as *the* representative historical subjects, only then can the Jews be universal Man.

The humanism which Eliot prophecies is a secular, historicized extension of the dominant western tradition, and as such is founded on principles quite alien to Judaism, most importantly the concept of incarnation. This is, of course, a central Christian doctrine holding that in Christ the word is made flesh, that God and man are one, that subject and object attain a perfect union: God *is* man, the subject *is* the object. Further, incarnation and Greek idealism are philosophically compatible, sharing the premise that phenomena are an imperfect instance of ideal forms, that, ideally, the phenomenal world will realize the ideal. In the tradition of which Eliot is a part, being is imagined in onto-theological terms, as Derrida has observed:

> [I]n every proposition the binding, agglutinating, ligimentary position of the copula [*Bindwort*] *is* conciliates the subject and the predicate, laces one around the other, entwines one around the other, to form one sole being [Sein]. . . . Now this conciliation that supposes – already – a reconciliation, that produces in a way the ontological proposition in general is also the reconciliation of the infinite with itself, of God with himself, of man with man, of man with God as the unity of father-to-son.[33]

So when Daniel Deronda says " 'I am a Jew,' " the statement is, as we have seen, a revelation of historical essence, an ontological proposition in which subject and object, individual and collective, real and ideal, empirical and transcendental are joined. That her hero should be a Jew, and the Jews should be chosen as the incarnation of history is an irony that opens up the text, and in the gap between Eliot's idealizing, historicizing project and the recalcitrant difference of Judaism, one can see the degree to which Eliot's secular humanism is founded on deeply theological, deeply Christian, and idealizing premises.

In making history take the place of God, Eliot speaks as the prophetess of humanism, an oracle for modernity. Her declared truths are so powerful in part because they are a dramatic condensation of a philosophical discourse about history that was widely influential, developed most fully by Hegel and then by the "Young Hegelians." Eliot helped to disseminate the Hegelian philosophy of history, first as the English translator of Strauss and Feuerbach, then more widely in her novels. Mordecai speaks like an idealist philosopher well read in Jewish literature, and all of *Daniel Deronda* is designed to bear witness to the mysterious workings of the "Invisible Power." The key concepts of spirit and history are everywhere apparent in the novel, and are true to Hegel's philosophical system.

In Hegel's philosophy, history is the process of Spirit actualizing itself. In logical terms, Spirit is Absolute Reason; in phenomenological terms, it is Absolute Knowledge; in theological terms, it is God. Actualization is the philosophical equivalent of the theological concept of incarnation, so Hegel of course thinks that Christianity is superior to all other religions, including Judaism. Indeed, Christianity is for Hegel "the highest, and final, embodiment of religious truth," as one of his commentators has written.[34] The Christian incarnation is philosophically crucial, since at that moment God divides into Father, Son, and Holy Spirit, or Subject, Object, and Consciousness. God is realized in the world (embodied in Christ) and is knowable as Spirit in a simultaneous division and unity which Hegel takes as the ground of history. In *The Philosophy of History* he declares, "God is ... recognized as *Spirit*, only when known as the Triune. This new principle is the axis on which the history of the World turns. This is the *goal* and the *starting point* of History."[35] The Trinity, the Christian God that is three-in-one, is the starting point of History since God (Spirit) is then objectified, made manifest in the world (the process of this objectification being history). It is equally the end of History, the final overcoming of contradiction and division, the goal of achieved unity.

Judaism thus necessarily had for Hegel but a limited "world-historical importance," since the God of Judaism is not incarnate, is not realized in the world. His final judgment of the Jews is harsh: they are, he says, a primitive, exclusive, and superstitious people.[36] Most important, given what Eliot is to do with the Jews in *Daniel Deronda*, Hegel declares that the Jews are, philosophically speaking, a prehistoric people. They share this dismissive classification with all peoples who are not organized into a centralized state – India, for instance, although "rich in spiritual products of the greatest profundity, has no history."[37]

The state is of such philosophical importance because it is the political and social embodiment of Spirit. It is "the form which the complete realization of Spirit assumes in existence."[38] "All the value man has, all spiritual reality, he has only through the state," for it is the unity of individual and collective, of particular and universal. Without it there is no logic, no reason to human life, and therefore no history, only the repetitive passing of time. A state, however, is a collectivity organized by law, a "community of existence" in which "the subjective will of man subjects itself to the laws."[39] So organized, man is no longer simply finite, for the state is larger than any one subject. History is thus the overcoming of time, of finitude, as spirit realizes itself in the state, the objective manifestation of reason and law. To leave "the unhistorical night of time" for the illumination of Spirit requires a subjection to the state, a subjection which is salvation from the dissolution of the unhistorical, from unreflective primitive existence. The state, then, stands in the same relation to Spirit as Christ does to God, as the object to the subject: it is the objectification of Spirit, its self-realization, its phenomenal reality. Man can comprehend Spirit only through its historical realization, the material of human history itself, and Spirit has no existence except in men, events, and institutions.

This philosophy which can imagine being only as the realization of the subjective in the objective, the spiritual in the material, is onto-theological: incarnation by any other name is still incarnation – as is salvation. History as the realization of Spirit saves man from death, guarantees that absence exists only to be overcome, that nothing is ever lost. In history there is no simple negation, everything is always in a determinate relation to something else. As Hegel declares,

> ruin is at the same time emergence of a new life ... out of life arises death but out of death life. The spirit, devouring its worldly envelope, not only passes into another envelope, not only arises rejuvenated from the ashes of its embodiment, but it emerges from them exalted, transfigured, a purer spirit.... The present state of spirit contains all previous states within itself.[40]

Dialectics thus cancels and preserves every particular embodiment of Spirit, ensuring that death will always produce life, and life death, until the end when all contradictions are overcome.

Daniel Deronda, Eliot's most explicitly "world-historical" novel, works up these Hegelian concepts – the incarnation of Spirit in history, the dialectical *aufheben* of death – into the story of Gwendolen and of Mordecai and the Jews. Gwendolen, as we have seen, is cancelled but not preserved, not lifted up by history, for history – to be history – requires something else that is purely temporal and limited. Eliot is willing to sacrifice Gwendolen to guarantee the salvation of Deronda, of Mordecai, of the Jews as historical man. But in the Jewish half, too, the text is coercive, for to make the Jews properly historical, Eliot must make them anew, force them to embrace their salvation through the spirit of history, to assimilate to an idealist system actually inimical to Judaism.

To do this, Eliot consistently misreads the many Hebrew texts she studied in preparing to write her novel and makes them speak the truth of history, of humanity. Thus she makes the psalmist into her mouthpiece, declaring that the "Invisible Power" of history is just what "the Hebrew poet" writes of in the Bible. Drawing for her authority on the scripture, claiming the psalmist as the poet of world history, Eliot denies a whole textual and interpretive tradition which rejects incarnation while privileging interpretation, a tradition which is, as Derrida puts it, "grammatical" rather than "pneumatic," not spiritual, but based on writing, interpretation, citation, displacement, and deferral: the Messiah has not come, incarnation is idolatry, God is absent, exile and loss are the conditions of life. Eliot recognizes this Judaism only to overcome it, to transcend it, to spiritualize it in making it over into something else.

That something else is Zionism, for by turning all Judaism into Zionism, Eliot is able to imagine the Jews in terms of history, in terms of Spirit and a state. Her orthodox Jewish prophet may use Kabbalistic language, may cite the scriptures, the Midrash, and study the Talmud, but only to articulate a secular project: " 'The divine principle of our race is action, choice, resolved memory. Let us ... choose our full heritage, claim the brotherhood of our nation.... The Messianic time is the time when Israel shall will the planting of the national ensign' " (p. 598). In fact, the orthodoxy of nationalism is the only answer Eliot can imagine to "the Jewish question," for it ensures that the Jews are properly historical people, a nation that will be restored as a modern state, a people whose troubling differences are the very evidence of their historical authenticity, their collective identity. Mordecai's nationalism is his religion, and his strongest "spiritual need" is to meet the man who will be able to carry out his dream of restoring Israel, a need Eliot describes as "the passionate current of an ideal life straining to embody itself, made intense by resistance to imminent dissolution" (p. 532). The whole book strains in this way, creating Deronda as the Messiah to Mordecai's John the Baptist, giving flesh and blood to the vision the prophet sees in the wilderness of London. Further, Mordecai's consumption, his "imminent dissolution," makes him ever more immaterial, more spiritual, more "pneumatic" as his lungs grow weaker and weaker, so that his death can be demonstrably not an end at all, but a new beginning in Deronda, in the East, in Israel itself. " 'You will take up my life where it was broken ...,' " Mordecai says to Deronda. " 'I shall behold the lands and the people of the East, and I shall speak with a fuller vision' " (p. 600).[41]

But the salvation of the Jews is not deferred to the future when Israel shall be a "new Judea," "a power and an organ in the great body of the nations," nor is it limited to Mordecai's discovery of Deronda as his savior. To the contrary, Eliot devotes herself in *Daniel Deronda* to proving that the Jews have always been a coherent nation, a separate "race" – have, in fact, been history incarnate these many thousands of years. For Mordecai, the past is palpable, and to be "rational" is " 'to see more and more of the hidden bonds that bind and consecrate change as a dependent growth – yea, consecrate it with kinship: the past becomes my parent, and the future stretches towards me the appealing arms of children' " (p. 587). Bound by the past, observant of the laws which organize their cultural and spiritual – therefore national – life, the Jews are offered up as the prime instance of the reality of history, the best realization of the human spirit, evidence of the shaping power of history in the past and of the promise of the future. Whatever specificity there may be to Judaism is evoked only as evidence of the exemplary historicity of the Jews, and they become an instance of the very incarnation, the very structure of representation that Judaism forbids.

That Eliot should come up with this answer to "the Jewish question" in her last novel, that she should devote herself to transforming Judaism into just another variant of universal humanism makes sense when one considers that Jews and Judaism were a real difference right close to home. Indeed, European Jews themselves struggled with the problem of assimilation and difference, trying to account philosophically for the "superlative peculiarity" of the Jews. They felt, as Eliot did, the pressure to reconcile Jewish difference with a totalizing philosophical system. Nahman Krochmal was one such Jew, a philosopher who in 1851 wrote a *Guide to the Perplexed of the Time*, a remarkable transposition of Hegelian concepts into Jewish terms. This guide is a telling contrast with Eliot's assimilation of Judaism to idealism. Juxtaposing Hegelian and biblical language, Krochmal writes,

> God is the Absolute Spirit and there is none other beside Him. . . . Individual manifestations of spirit, which are attached to the hosts of heaven and earth, are all finite and transient; they possess true reality and absolute existence only to the extent that they have their being in the Lord, Blessed be He, the Absolute Spirit, the Infinite One.[42]

The Jewish insistence on one God, undivided and unrepresentable, here is what ensures Israel's survival: the Absolute Spirit "within" Israel "protects us and excludes us from the Judgment that falls upon all mortals." The Jews are not below the higher state of historical existence, as Hegel claims, but are rather beyond the contradictions, the negations of history since "there is no Absolute Spirit, infinite and truly existent in every respect, other than God alone; He is our portion and we are His."[43] Jewish monotheism lifts the Jews above particularity and guarantees their survival through the ages, for their indivisible God encompasses all time, their God is Spirit.

Krochmal's Hegelian Judaism is a *tour de force* which takes the very elements of Judaism said to disqualify it from the properly historical and makes them the guarantee of Israel's triumph over time. His *Guide* inserts Hegel into a Rabbinic tradition in an argument which mixes together Hegel, the Bible, the Talmud, and the Midrash. Unlike Mordecai's speeches, Krochmal's text is written from within the complex Jewish system of commentary and interpretation, written in Hebrew for a Jewish audience, referring explicitly to Maimonides's twelfth-century *Guide of the Perplexed*, a medieval response to the challenges of Aristotelian philosophy as Krochmal's is to Hegelianism. Eliot, although she read Hebrew, apparently never read this work, and if she had, one might wonder what she would have made of it. For Krochmal's "Hegelianism" is a direct challenge to Eliot's formulations. She accounts for the Jews by making them the embodiment of history, by claiming them as the most historical of people, while Krochmal, equally concerned to explain the continued existence of the Jews as a people apart, declares that they and their God transcend not only time, but history altogether. Krochmal's argument thus empties out the concept of history, and demonstrates the impasse inevitably reached when Hegel's absolute idealism is brought together with Judaism.[44]

While Krochmal rewrites Hegelian philosophy in Judaic terms – with questionable philosophic results – Eliot imagines an idealist Judaism which necessarily represses the difference of the Rabbinic tradition. She tries to find her point of leverage in Kabbalism, assuming that this mystical tradition will give her a way to lift up Judaism in its entirety to the higher reaches of history and humanism. She makes Mordecai familiar with the texts and concepts of the Kabbalah in order to demonstrate that Judaism, too, has an idealist tradition which understands the manifest world as but a sign of the spirit.[45] But Eliot must misconstrue Kabbalism to render it as an idealism since the Kabbalah is a matter of interpretation, not revelation, and conceives of God as without end, unknowable, beyond representation, without attributes. As Harold Bloom explains, in the Kabbalah, God is said to have created the world out of nothing, which is to say out of Himself, making creation not an emanation from God, but a process which takes place within God. The "nothing" of the Kabbalah bears no relation to Hegel's concept of determinate negation, for there is no contradiction of positive and negative, subject and object, interior and exterior – only difference, as it were, within God. There is, therefore, no distinction between presence and representation, and the complex commentaries on the Torah which are produced by the Kabbalists are not exegeses explaining the truth of God's word, but meditations on the combinations and permutations of the Name of God which is the text itself.[46]

In the Kabbalah, God is not incarnate. That is unthinkable since it entails a separation of spirit and matter. God may be approached – not comprehended totally, but approached – through the texts that are his Name. Text, writing, commentary produce the truths of God. Indeed, Judaism in general, whether Kabbalistic or not, is predicated on the importance of writing.[47] The text itself is privileged in Judaism since writing is all one has of God, and interpretation emphasizes not so much the idea represented, but what Joseph Dan calls "the total text,"

> not only the meaning of terms and words, but also their sound, the shape of the letters, the vocalization points and their shapes and sounds, the *te'amim* (the musical signs added to the Hebrew

words), the *tagin* (the small decorative additions to the letters), the frequency with which words and letters appear in a verse or a chapter ... and the countless ways, other than ideonic content and meaning by which the scriptures transmit a semiotic message.[48]

Unlike Christianity, which relies both theologically and practically on dogma, on the single truth revealed by an authoritative interpretation, Judaism is a religion of infinite commentary and an infinitely contestable text.

For all her prodigious research on the history of the Jews, for all her reading of Jewish literature, Eliot misconstrues Judaism in the most basic ways, a transformation especially marked in her discussion of Jewish law. In *Daniel Deronda* Mordecai declares that the Jewish respect for the laws which order social life make Israel "the heart of mankind," and in a poem called "The Death of Moses" Eliot laboriously dramatizes the originary moment of that law. "Mute" and "orphaned," the Jews grieve at Moses's death, but then, "The spirit's shaping light, mysterious speech, / Invisible Will wrought clear in sculptured sound / ... Thrilled on their listening sense: 'He has no tomb. / He dwells not with you dead but lives as Law.' "[49] Eliot hypostatizes law, making first Moses and then Israel as a whole embody the Law, just as Christianity creates the hypostatic union of human and divine in Christ. But by imagining Jewish law as fixed and substantial, Eliot denies the ways in which that law is produced. For in Judaism, as Richard Jacobson points out, "God is replaced by text. The impossibility of speaking *with* God is replaced by speaking *of* God. Practice becomes Law, engendering a skewed infinitude of legal discourse in the legal compendia of the Talmud and its progeny."[50]

A skewed infinitude of discourse is, of course, incomprehensible to Eliot. For her, writing is revelation, and this means that no matter how meticulous her research, how wide her reading, she will never understand the workings of the Rabbinic tradition, work that is also play – the play of citation, of unending interpretation. As one commentator has said, there is "something a bit joking" in the unexpected twists and turns of Midrash,[51] and as any reader of Eliot knows, she's not one for joking. She takes too seriously her call to prophecy. Her publisher may ask her if she has available "any lighter pieces written before the sense of what a great author should do for mankind came so strong upon you," but Eliot has no such writing to offer.[52] High seriousness is for Eliot not just a personal style, but the condition of her philosophical position. Hers may be, as Henry James declared, a "deep, strenuous, much-considering mind," but however profound and exhaustive her study of things Jewish, she only sees revealed in those texts and traditions a single serious truth, the truth of humanism.

Eliot thus imagines the Jews above all as the people of the law, the original instance of properly social, collective, national life. But her fixation on an originary law means that she cannot imagine the textuality of Judaism, the continual revisions, reinterpretations, relocations of Jewish thought. No more can Eliot understand that Judaism is an effect of God's absence from the world, an acknowledgment of the impossibility of presence and therefore of representation as revelation.   As Derrida argues in an essay on the Jewish poet Edmund Jabès, Jews are "the people of the book," and Judaism is untranscendent and therefore "unnatural." Because nature, to be "natural," must be contradicted by spirit, must be transcended, overcome in the end. The opposition of nature and spirit, of the flesh and the word is not Jewish, nor is immortality. Rather, in Judaism, "Death strolls between letters. To write, what is called writing, assumes an access to the mind through the courage to lose one's life, to die away from nature."[53] This is just what Eliot cannot think, for all her remarks about accepting death, and all her principled refusals of the consolations of personal immortality. She cannot "die away from nature," for nature, matter, flesh must be the embodiment of spirit, must realize spirit, in the last analysis must be overcome by spirit, lifted up in an incarnation which transforms death into life.

Eliot recognizes the difference of the Jews. She even acknowledges their difference as somehow special – "superlative" – a difference which is especially marked because the Jews both are and are not European or British, are both of the English nation and apart from it, have a crucial relation to Christianity yet are not Christian. The Jews are hard to place, and they are very close to home. Eliot's answer to the Jewish question is unconventional: she idolizes the Jews, makes them the embodiment of spirit, history, and law, makes their threatening difference into a representative instance of the embodiment of spirit in the world. Ironically, Eliot thus does to the Jews exactly what Judaism prohibits, making the Jews themselves a substantial realization of spirit. Because for the Jews, all incarnation is idolatry, a reification that places a concrete, particular, present object in the place of God – the unrepresentable. Idols are from this point of view fetishistic, as John Freccero has pointed out, "a desperate attempt to render presence."[54]

Eliot's treatment of the Jews is fetishistic in the structure of recognition and disavowal that marks her relation to Judaism. A fetish is a stopgap, a stand-in. It is put in place to meet the threat of absence and overcome difference. A fetish will cover over absence, make it disappear, and in this the fetish is an effective disavowal: nothing is missing, everything is the same. But a fetish also, by the very fact that it is an object invested with an inappropriate significance, calls attention to the fact that a cover-up is in progress, that something is missing, something is different. This recognition is equally a part of fetishism.[55] The double structure of the fetish accounts for the contradictory affect a fetish can produce: it is an object of both desire and fear, love and hate.

The Jews are such an object for Eliot, and the over-investment which characterizes fetishism is evident in her intensive development of "the whole heavy structure of the Jewish question" in *Daniel Deronda*. Eliot wrote her last novel with death on her mind and at every point the text is structured so as to transcend finitude, to deny that anything could be beyond comprehension, to ensure that differences are always a part of a larger totality. That totality is History itself, the Invisible Power which is realized in human activity, the spirit which is evident in world history. By embodying this spirit in the Jews, Eliot disavows the difference of Judaism, disavows the Jewish refusal of transcendence, but by choosing the Jews – in their particularity, textuality, and materiality – she also recognizes that difference. Eliot's make-over of the Jews is an intentional idealization, an Hegelian *aufheben* in which Judaism is lifted up to humanism. It is also a fetishization, a recognition and disavowal of difference, absence, death.

Moreover, Eliot's fetishizing of the Jews, her epic development of "the Jewish question" suggests the limits for her of "the woman question." She needs the Jews because she cannot fetishize women. She may make Gwendolen a spectacle, she may make her the object of Deronda's, the narrator's, the reader's gaze, but Gwendolen is never anything but a problem. From beginning to end Gwendolen points to the mortal limits of life. Eliot cannot quite manage what men so often do; she cannot find in women both a threat and a consolation, a fetishized object, a fantasy. But she knows that women have to be kept in their place if the transcendental project is to work, so she rigorously disciplines her women characters, making sure that they will be forever feminine. As Gwendolen is finally brought to realize, her highest calling is "to make others glad that [she] had been born" (p. 882). But ensuring that women are not "unsexed" does not mean that Eliot finds in women either a consoling fantasy or the kind of positive evidence of history that she requires. For that she turns to the Jews. They, like other "oriental peoples," are feminized in their otherness, but Eliot can make something of this difference. By idealizing the Jews, Eliot masculinizes them as historical subjects, thereby achieving the consolations of fetishism (the cover-up of difference). And by making the Jews into Israel, a world-historical nation, she confirms the truth of history.

*

Daniel Deronda is thus symptomatic, displaying the workings of a humanism which will do whatever is necessary to consolidate one norm, one standard, one reality, the humanity of western white bourgeois man. But the fetishism of the text and Eliot's troubles with women also show the difficulty of such complete totalization, because the harder Eliot tries to humanize the Jews, the more she draws attention to the Jews and Judaism as a troubling "problem," and the more she disciplines Gwendolen, the harder it is to believe in the "humanity" of the text. Judaism, when not assimilated to the categories of Christian metaphysics, is the ruin of idealist representation, and women are equally worrisome. Eliot's over-investment in the Jews and her punishing of women directs one to the limits of humanism, the text revealing in its insistence what must be denied, what must be excluded, where the lines must be drawn if man is to find his dwelling place in history.

Daniel Deronda is Eliot's last and most intentionally philosophical effort to reveal to her readers the saving grace of a history which is the realization of the human spirit. She prophetically declares in the Jewish half that those who have been most despised, who have been treated most inhumanely, incarnate this spirit most fully. And equally in the prophetic mode, she is willing to make sacrifices, to offer up women in Gwendolen's half, to guarantee man's place in history through Gwendolen's exclusion from the ideal. As the Prophetess of Humanity, Eliot had to rule women out. Edith Simcox, who adored Eliot, writes in her autobiography of a conversation they had:

> she said ... she had never all her life cared very much for women –
> it must seem monstrous to me. I said I had always known it. She
> went on to say, what I also knew, that she cared for the womanly

ideal, sympathized with women and liked them to come to her in their troubles, but while feeling near to them in one way, she felt far off in another; the friendship and intimacy of men was more to her.[56]

Feeling far off from women, Eliot identifies with men. One might ask her what Deronda's mother asks her son: " 'You speak as men do – as if you felt yourself wise. What does it all mean?' " (p. 726).

It means, in part at least, that George Eliot is a woman writer who is deeply identified with the idea of Man, whose writing displays the consequences of that incongruity. Always known by her masculine pseudonym, Eliot none the less is on the wrong side, as it were, of an asymmetrical difference crucial to the identity of man as a properly historical subject. She writes as a male *manqué*, to put it strongly, and her not quite right position helps to produce novels that show up the necessary costs of the anthropocentric historical project. One such cost is evident in the violence done to Gwendolen, who pays and pays for Deronda's transcendence; she is for all intents and purposes destroyed in order to be saved. "Pale as one of the sheeted dead" after the boating accident in which Grandcourt dies, she is never quite herself again. So, too, when Eliot assesses the value of the "spiritual products" of Jewish culture, she rates the Jews quite highly, but only in a philosophical economy which requires that Judaism be exchanged for something very like Christianity, a philosophy of presence, representation, incarnation. Eliot over-compensates in *Daniel Deronda*, raising up the Jews while dramatizing Gwendolen's fall, and in these extremes calls attention to the polarities of humanism, indeed, to the whole modern episteme of which humanism is one ideology. The demonstration that humanism is a matter as much of power as philosophy, of exclusion and forced assimilation, of ensuring law and order, is one of the most important lessons one can learn from the woman a West End clergyman called "that great teacher George Eliot."[57]

Chapter 2

Henry Esmond and the subject of history

Twenty-one years before Eliot began writing *Daniel Deronda*, William Makepeace Thackeray published *The History of Henry Esmond, Esq., A Colonel in the Service of Her Majesty Queen Anne, Written by Himself*, the most famous – one might say notorious – of his several historical novels. While Thackeray is far from a philosophical novelist (indeed, he declared that Eliot's novels left him mystified),[1] he is an acknowledged master of a genre which raises important questions about the relation of fact and fiction, of particular details and general historical truths. Historical novels enjoyed an unprecedented prestige in the early nineteenth century, as the career of Sir Walter Scott testifies. Yet by 1852, the genre's immense popularity was in a decline hastened by the rise of history-writing "proper," by the publication of works such as Macaulay's *History of England from the Accession of James II*. If in 1832 Carlyle could declare that Scott's novels "taught all men this truth ... that the bygone ages of the world were actually filled by living men, not by protocols, state-papers, controversies and abstractions of men.... History will henceforth have to take thought of it," by mid-century Macaulay set out to reclaim from the historical novel the narrative interest of fiction while writing history itself.[2] Indeed, he was determined "to produce something which shall for a few days supersede the last fashionable novel on the tables of young ladies."[3] Reading *The History of Henry Esmond* and *The History of England*, then, focuses attention on the development of history as a form of knowledge, a discourse, and an academic discipline, for both works – one a fictional, the other an historical narrative – represent the same crucial period in English history, the last years of the seventeenth century. Macaulay's *History*, published four years before *Esmond*, makes an argument for the glory of the revolution of 1688 that

Thackeray evidently repeats in *Esmond*. Yet for all their important similarities, *The History of Henry Esmond* stands as an ironic counter-text not only to Macaulay's *History*, although especially to that, but also to the whole nineteenth-century historical project. No wonder Eliot, with her profoundly historicizing imagination, found *Esmond* "the most uncomfortable book you could imagine."

As we have seen, "man," in the nineteenth century and since, is distinguished by his historicity, and can be understood fully only in the context of historical realities which are the preconditions of the present, the necessary foundation of both social and individual life. The priority accorded to the past, then, and to the forces of history, means that history is divided; "history" is both the general ground of human life and also an empirical science of events, the study and representation of the past. History writing thus must be pure of the "taint" of fiction, for, as a reviewer unhappy with Thackeray writes, "[history] requires absolute adherence to the truth and nothing but the truth."[4] History must be purged of fiction, must be objective and scientific in order to be truthful, for science, as the knowledge of positive realities, is the modern discourse of truth. The opposition of "history" to "fiction" is that of truth to falsehood, the exclusion of the latter guaranteeing the scientificity of the former. Or, as Michel de Certeau puts it, "historiography credits itself with having a special relationship to the 'real' because its contrary is posed as 'false.' "[5]

However, the objects of history ensure that the discipline of history can never successfully foreclose fiction, for fiction is the place not of falsehood, but of questions about the conditions of representation, the processes of signification, the constitution of the subject. Nineteenth-century fiction is increasingly about performance and production; towards the twentieth century, novelists address these problems more and more explicitly – this as history becomes increasingly positive, increasingly professional, one of the social sciences. Yet this separation of literary discourse and the discourse of history, while essential to the modern conception of history, is never complete, for, as Certeau points out,

> historiography is a science which lacks the means of being one. Its discourse undertakes to deal with what is most resistant to scientificity (the relation of the social to the event, to violence, to the past, to death), that is, those matters each scientific discipline must eliminate in order to be constituted as a science.[6]

"Fiction," then, always returns to haunt history, although the discipline has been largely successful in repressing the problems with which fiction engages. Fiction is thus imagined as other than – indeed, the opposite of – history.

For historians of the twentieth century, Macaulay's *History* is too fictional: too subjective, too dramatic, too highly plotted, and partisan. This is a frustration of Macaulay's hopes and expectations, for he wrote with "the year 2000 and even the year 3000 often in mind," and believed that his work would be read for its historical truth, while the literature of his time "should ... hardly ... be remembered in 1900."[7] For Macaulay, history is essentially different from and superior to fiction, even though, as he declares in an early essay in the *Edinburgh Review*, "the talent which is required to write history ... bears a considerable affinity to the talent of a great dramatist." The historian none the less has the advantage of the dramatist or novelist, for fiction is "essentially imitative": "In fiction the principles are given, to find the facts; in history, the facts are given, to find the principles."[8] That is, novelists begin from conventional assumptions about "the condition of society and the nature of man," while the historian is free to determine the truth about these things, the principles which the evidence of the past reveals. Macaulay believes that "the noblest earthy object of the contemplation of man is man himself," which means that the noblest discipline is history.

Thus he delighted in historical research, and reports in his journal that after a day spent "turn[ing] over 3 volumes of newspapers and tracts," he felt "transported back a century and a half. ... I begin to see the men, and understand all their difficulties and jealousies."[9] He is not alone in these pleasures, for a few years later, while doing the reading that would result in a series of biographical sketches and then in *Esmond*, Thackeray writes to his mother, "I have been living in the last century for weeks past – all day that is – going at night as usual into the present age; and Oxford and Bolingbroke interest me as much as Russell and Palmerstone – more very likely."[10] Both authors wish to "make the old times live again," as Thackeray says, and each is convinced that a truthful representation of the past must give an accurate account of the "manners and morals" of earlier times, what Macaulay calls "the domestic history of nations." Further, the histories that both write celebrate the progress of England from the time of James II to that of Queen Victoria, and each attributes this advance to the influence of the English gentleman of the middle class. Both historian and novelist find in history a confirmation of a particular class position, of laws both legal and moral, of "man" as an individual living in "society."

Yet even though their histories share these important similarities, which I will discuss in more detail, their writing has very different effects – effects produced by the relation in each of their texts of "history" and "fiction." Macaulay's *History of England* discovers in the men and events of the past a profound confirmation of man and society, both brought into being by the humanizing rule of law. Law, embodied in the English constitution, is what keeps man from the brutality of anarchy or despotism. Thackeray's novel, on the other hand, compromises every confirmation it offers, calls into question the whole idea that history reveals man to himself. For in Thackeray's text, fiction is not separate from history, but rather is all that history proper must not admit: the instability of identity, of subject and object, of time itself.[11]

*

While Macaulay's *History* was immediately an overwhelming success, *The History of Henry Esmond* was differently received. Thackeray's readers found the book unsettling – quite disturbing, in fact. As George Eliot writes to a friend after reading the novel, " 'Esmond' is the most uncomfortable book you can imagine. . . . The hero is in love with the daughter all through the book, and marries the mother at the end."[12] Indeed, the marriage of Henry Esmond and Rachel Castlewood is distressing not simply because the hero transfers his affections from daughter to mother, but also because Lady Castlewood has been a mother to none other than Henry himself. Mrs Oliphant refuses to countenance the ending, saying, "This error is monstrous and unredeemable. . . ."[13] So, too, John Forster declares that neither the stylistic beauties of the novel nor its evocation of character "[can] induce us to accept or tolerate such a set of incidences as these. The thing is incredible, and there an end on't. . . ."[14] And a writer in the *Eclectic Review* accused Thackeray of profanity.[15]

The shock which readers felt at the resolution of the novel is proportionate to the admiration they expressed for *Esmond*'s historical authenticity. If the novel had been less veracious, the ending would have been much easier to take. But Thackeray achieves in his imagined memoir "the best example of absolute reproduction which our literature possesses," as Mrs Oliphant declares. "Nothing can be more real or touching – more like a veritable page of biography. . . ."[16] No wonder she was "shocked" and "outraged" by the close. So, too, George Henry Lewes finds in the novel "so much the art and accent of the time, it would impose on us if presented as a veritable History of Colonel Esmond"; and Trollope, who regards the book "as the first and finest novel in the English language," praises it for the "completeness of historical plot, and an absence of that taint of unnatural life which blemishes, perhaps, all our other historical novels."[17]

To say that *Esmond* is an historical novel free of the "taint of unnatural life" is to claim for the book the truth of history – but what a history! The decisive events of 1688 and the years following are but the setting for the Castlewood family history, and a very disturbing history it is. For Esmond not only marries the woman he has regarded as a mother, he also is the unwitting cause of his adoptive father's death. A generation after Thackeray, Sigmund Freud will make this triad of father–mother–son the key to human psychic and cultural organization, and for we who read after Freud the Oedipal design of *Esmond* is insistently evident. But Esmond is Oedipus with a difference, since in his history there is no punishment, no prohibition, but rather the incessant production of desires. A family romance with no resolution, unconcerned with transgression, is even more disturbing than Oedipus proper, which offers, at a cost, the confirmation of identity.

The most evident effects of *Henry Esmond*, however, have to do not with Oedipus but with satire, for Thackeray, like the eighteenth-century wits he so admired, is a satirist, and the unease his text elicits is produced in part by Esmond's ironic and critical narrative. In his memoirs the Colonel sounds repeatedly the theme of the vanity of human wishes, and performs the classic gestures of satire, lifting the public mask, showing men divested of their periwigs and heels, women without their rouge and ornaments. Thus in his opening paragraph Esmond declares,

> I have seen in his very old age and decrepitude the old French King Lewis the Fourteenth, the type and model of kinghood ... who ... persist[ed] in acting through life the part of Hero; and, divested of poetry, this was but a little wrinkled old man, pock-marked, and with a great periwig and red heels to make him look tall – a hero for a book if you like, or for a brass statue or a painted ceiling, a god in a Roman shape, but what more than a man for Madame Maintenon, or the barber who shaved him, or Monsieur Fagon, his surgeon.[18]

Neither the Sun King nor any other man is immortal, but lives and dies in time – as his surgeon knows – nor is he the master of his desires – as his mistress knows – and his beard is not different from his barber's. So from the beginning to the end of his account, Esmond reverses the expected relation of public to private to demonstrate that the former is but show and acting, an illusion exposed as false and misleading when one goes behind the scenes where life is anything but heroic.

The whole book is organized, then, by the concept of unveiling, of exposing falsehood, determining the difference between authentic and inauthentic, between the legitimate and the spurious, truth and artifice. artifice. There are three distinct yet inseparable developments of this problem. First there is the matter of historical representation *per se* and the question of what makes a truthful history. Second, there is the issue of legitimate succession to the throne and lawful rule which is the basis of the story of political intrigue which makes up one of the major plots of the book. Third, there is a love story – the other major plot – in which Esmond is poised between two women and genuine worth is contrasted to brilliant but ultimately worthless allure.

The question of historical representation opens the novel, as Thackeray has Esmond declare in favor of "History familiar rather than heroic," arguing that history has been as artificially conventional and theatrical as classical tragedy:

> The Muse of History has encumbered herself with ceremony as well as her Sister of the Theatre. She too wears the mask and cothurnus, and speaks to measure. She, too, in our age, busies herself with the affairs only of kings; waiting on them obsequiously and stately as if she were but a mistress of court ceremonies. . . .
>
> (p. 11)

Just as Esmond will turn away at the end of his history from kings and courts, at the beginning he wishes that history would "cease to be court-ridden." Thus his *History* is not of political or military events, although Esmond and his family are actors in the revolution of 1688, in the Jacobite resistance to William III and his successors, and in the battles of Blenheim, Ramilles, and Malplaquet – decisive moments in the War of Spanish Succession. These crucial events in European history are subordinated to Esmond's account of his "private affairs," the family history he records for his descendants. Only such a record, Thackeray believes, can reveal the true and unheroic motives on which men act, or reconstruct the nuances of

"manners and morals" which characterize a past age. As he declares
in his biographical sketches of the four Georges, which begin where
Esmond's history comes to an end, he has no interest in "grave
historical treatises," but is devoted to "the humbler duty of Court
gossip."[19] For history, he holds, is but the aggregate of individual
lives, lives made up of the stuff of gossip: love affairs, family quarrels,
jealousies, secret ambitions, perverse fascinations. Echoing Esmond,
Thackeray writes in his essay on George I, "We are not the Historic
Muse, but her Ladyship's attendant, tale-bearer – valet de chambre –
for whom no man is a hero."[20] Certainly no king could be less heroic
than the Stuart Pretender, for whom the Castlewood family hazards
everything, and the question of political legitimacy, always linked
with the discussion of historical representation, is answered when
the truth about James is revealed. From the time of the Civil War
the family has favored the Stuarts, and Esmond is the instigator of
the last Castlewood plot in favor of the Jacobite cause. Esmond, of
course, is motivated not by political principle, but by his love for
Beatrix whom he wishes to please and impress; his desires, however,
are thwarted when he introduces the Pretender into his home. James
is smuggled into England disguised as Frank Castlewood, to wait in
London until Queen Anne dies, when he will present himself as the
legitimate heir to the throne. But he is more devoted to amorous
than to political conquest, and misses the main chance while pursuing
the fascinating Beatrix. In a masterful condensation of history and
symbol, Thackeray has Esmond discover their dalliance when a note
from Beatrix to her sovereign is found in the *Eikon Basilike*. This
book, furnished by Lady Castlewood for James's edification and
inspiration, is supposed to have been written by Charles I, the
Pretender's ancestor who lost his head to Cromwell: the "royal
image" is a spiritual autobiography published under the king's signature after his execution. But by 1852 it was known to be a forgery,
written by a bishop as political propaganda and passed off as the
king's own. This unauthentic image of royalty is a particularly appropriate vehicle of communication between Beatrix and the Prince, for
their sexual intrigue reveals to Esmond the falseness of them both.
It kills his long-standing passion for Beatrix: "it fell down dead on
the spot, at the Kensington tavern, where Frank brought him the
note out of 'Eikon Basilike.' " And, confronting James at Castlewood
hall, where the Pretender has pursued the luckless Beatrix, Esmond
renounces the king, breaks his sword, and burns the patent which
makes him a marquis. In the end, which follows quickly, he retires

with Rachel Castlewood to an exclusively private life in the new world of Virginia. Legitimacy, in this account of English history, is entirely on the side of the private gentleman, just as legitimate history – as opposed to the pretensions of the Historic Muse – is the history of private life.

Finally, the romantic plot of the novel repeats the political plot. It also is structured by the contrast of authentic to inauthentic, the private to the public. The two women Esmond loves, Beatrix Castlewood and her mother Rachel, represent in their contrasted characters the aristocratic world of Restoration England, absolute monarchy and the supremacy of the Court, versus the new world of parliamentary power, individual rights, and domesticity. Beatrix, allied with the old Viscountess Isabella who was once a mistress of Charles II, is all glitter and brilliance, as beautiful and hard as the diamonds she favors, as many-faceted and impenetrable. Rachel is pure, maternal, golden. Eclipsed by Beatrix for much of the novel, a disappearance Thackeray traces with a repeated pattern of astronomical imagery, Rachel finally reappears as Beatrix's reflected glory fades.[21] The young "Diana," who had seemed impervious to time, shows her age in the end: "The roses had shuddered out of her cheeks," Esmond writes. "Her eyes were glaring and she looked quite old" (p. 416). Here, then, is a characteristically Victorian division of the angelic and demonic woman, a split which emphasizes the difference between private and public. Rachel, who appears to Esmond in his youth as "a *Dea certe*," is throughout his memoirs a "saint," a "goddess," an "angel," and his love for her is a "sacred flame," whereas the worldly Beatrix is an "enchantress," a "leopard," a "siren," a "Circe" whose allure can be fatal. Her overthrow and flight from the Castlewood family inaugurate a new order of domestic security and tranquility.

Indeed, the new world in which Esmond is united with Rachel appears at the very end of his memoirs as a kind of achieved paradise just glimpsed by the reader, reached after the apocalyptic revelation of virtue and the expulsion of vice. For while the Pretender is off courting Beatrix, the queen dies, and Esmond returns with James to London just in time to hear the trumpets blow and the herald proclaim George, by grace of God, King of England. Esmond writes

With the sound of King George's trumpets all the vain hopes of the weak and foolish young Pretender were blown away; and with that music, too, I may say, the drama of my own life was ended. That happiness, which has subsequently crowned it, cannot be written in words; 'tis of its nature sacred and secret, and not to be spoken of, though the heart be ever so full of thankfulness, save to Heaven and the One Ear alone – to one fond being, the truest and tenderest and purest wife ever man was blessed was blessed with.

(p. 418)

Saints are separated from sinners, who are denied entrance to the new world, and in the last three paragraphs of the book – a kind of postscript to the *History* – Esmond marries Rachel and moves to Virginia. There the diamonds which once adorned Beatrix are exchanged for things of concrete value. They

are turned into ploughs and axes for our plantations; and into negroes ... and the only jewel by which my wife sets any store, and from which she hath never parted, is that gold button she took from my arm on the day when she visited me in prison, and which she wore ever after, as she told me, on the tenderest heart in the world.[22]

(p. 420)

This small object has made but one fleeting previous appearance, in the first chapter of book II, but it stands revealed at the end of Esmond's history as the emblem of the most profound truth of his life, the redeeming, sanctifying truth of love.

The close of Esmond's history, then, would seem to be the strongest confirmation of revealed truth, the reality of private life showing up the artifice of the public. For Juliet McMaster, the button is "the final clinching clue" that reveals *Esmond* to be "what careless readers missed – a record of the love story of Rachel and Henry Esmond."[23] This reading suggests that Esmond's history is structured by a dramatic irony which Esmond controls. Narrating retrospectively from his "summit of happiness," he distracts the reader from Rachel's love as he himself was distracted, leaving only clues in his account. However, as other readers have stressed, the irony of the text extends to Esmond himself.[24] For his apocalypse is premature, his celebration of Rachel as an angel evidently fantastic. Lady Castlewood, having harbored an adulterous, even incestuous passion for Henry from the time of his youth, is hardly the domestic angel he repeatedly declares her to be, and when it comes to love, Esmond is distinctly unreliable. If, as Esmond says at one point, his pen "cannot help writing" a

satire rather than a panegyric of the great world, Thackeray makes
sure that Esmond himself is ironically exposed as less heroic, and
much less wise than the colonel thinks himself.

This extension of the novel's irony, of the work of unmasking, is
most evident in the "Preface" Thackeray supplies to Esmond's memoirs. "Authored" by the daughter of Esmond and Rachel Castlewood some forty years after the events of the book, this fulsome
preface is evidence of a family life disturbed by jealousy and repressed
desires, the site of unsettling repetitions in which the daughter, named
after her mother, comes "to supply the place" quitted by Rachel
when she dies, a family in which Esmond's grandsons are divided by
"fatal differences" in political allegiance, and Esmond himself is
shown to be remote and unforgiving. Esmond's faults are, in fact,
evident from the beginning of his account, for he is rigid and unbend-
ing, all too ready to judge and condemn. Vanity, vanity, is Esmond's
cry, as when he observes of Lord Castlewood, "How well men
preach, and each is the example in his own sermon" (p. 117). But
Esmond himself preaches, judges, condemns, without ever acknowledging his own failings – his envy, his jealousy, his ambitions for
power and for the acclaim of others. Beatrix, to whom he proclaims
the virtues of modesty and humility with tiresome repetition, will
have none of it, and rebels against his authority, saying

> "of all the proud wretches in the world, Mr Esmond is the proud-
> est, let me tell him that. You never fall into a passion; but you
> never forgive, I think.... I won't worship you, and you'll never
> be happy except with a woman who will."
>
> (p. 329)

Rachel, of course, has already been on her knees to Esmond, and by
the end of the novel he has graciously accepted the homage, too, of
Frank Castlewood and of the royal Pretender – this in a book which
mocks all kings and derides absolutism.[25]

J. Hillis Miller, in an important essay on Thackeray's novel, has
argued that it, like the rest of his writing, "is nihilistic in the precise
sense in which the word is defined, for example by Friedrich Nietzsche, as the devaluation of all values and their reduction to nought,
nihil, nothing."[26] Certainly the irony of the preface and Esmond's
ironic limitations contest the apocalyptic revelation of a domestic
paradise on earth with which Esmond closes his history, and private
life, which is posed throughout *Esmond* as the locus of authenticity
and truth, the opposite of the theatricality and artifice of the public,

is shown to be a site of illusions and posturings as dramatic as any in public life. But this doesn't mean that public and private are, in the last analysis, the same for Thackeray, or that the private is without special value. The private is still the place of truth in *Esmond*, but a truth complicated by problems of knowledge, for, as we have seen, Esmond is caught up in the family romance of which he is the historian. Thackeray's satire is, in fact, thoroughly nineteenth-century in its structure, and its effects are more disturbing than a simple reversal of public and private, or a simple condemnation of both.

This is because by Queen Victoria's time the opposite of the public was a private sphere defined as the place of intimacy. As C. C. Harris writes, in the nineteenth century, "the intimate becomes the locus of one's true humanity and that locus is family and locality."[27] Thus Esmond's familiar history is familial history; thus some of the most evocative scenes of the novel are those in which Esmond recalls the sights and sounds of Castlewood Hall, the grey towers and the rooks cawing, the places of his childhood and youth with Lord and Lady Castlewood, Beatrix and Frank. Family and locale, however, are important not in themselves, but as the setting for the most intimate of matters, affairs of the heart. The intimate is not only set off from public life, but is also the place of one's deepest desires and the ground of one's most fundamental identity. To stress this, Thackeray almost perversely insists on the sexualization of the family, making Esmond in love first with the mother, then the daughter, then the mother again. Well might Esmond ask, "What is it? Where lies it? the secret which makes one little hand the dearest of all? Whoever can unriddle that mystery?" (p. 192). For in *The History of Henry Esmond* this mystery is the problematic ground of history itself. Acknowledging that "men have all sorts of motives which carry them onwards in life," Esmond none the less knows that every case is at bottom the same. "Why go on particularizing?" he writes.

> What can the sons of Adam and Eve expect, but to continue in that course of love and trouble their father and mother set out on? O my grandson! ... I say unto thee all my troubles and joys too, for that matter, have come from a woman; as thine will when thy destined course begins.
>
> (pp. 339–40)

*

In *Henry Esmond*, then, Thackeray poses a question as the ground of history, the question of desire. This is what makes Thackeray's text so different from Macaulay's, however similar their histories may be. *The History of Henry Esmond* is not part of a larger effort to make history a proper discipline. Although Thackeray is concerned with the problem of how to represent history, the questions his text raises concern the very things the discipline of history must exclude. True, Thackeray thinks of history as above all a matter of the individuals who make up the social whole, a common enough position, quite similar to Macaulay's, in fact. But when Thackeray tries to get to the heart of the matter he comes up with a riddle, a secret, a mystery, an ever-receding ground.

Macaulay, on the other hand, is quite sure of the organizing principle of history: it is law, the law which guarantees the social contract, the law which protects liberty and freedom, the law which humanizes man. Where Thackeray constructs Esmond's history around an unanswerable question, Macaulay organizes his narrative according to the immovable principle of the law. This conception of history determines the late seventeenth and early eighteenth centuries as Macaulay's subject, for the "preserving revolution" of 1688 is, for him, a glorious and originary moment, an event that secured liberty in a legal form appropriate for the modern nation. When William and Mary signed the settlement with Parliament, they laid the foundation for ministerial government, and preserved the freedom of the English from absolute power. These were, for Macaulay, heroic times, when men, most importantly William of Orange, risked everything for a principle and defended law, liberty, and freedom from the absolutism of James II, of France, and Rome.

In fact, all the dramatic scenes and lifelike characters which fill up the pages of Macaulay's work are developed with reference to the central point of law: the ill-conceived rebellion of Monmouth, the terrible Judge Jeffreys, the horrors of the Bloody Assizes held after Monmouth's failure; the striking vignettes of poor non-conformists persecuted for their faith; the dishonesty, weakness, and cowardice of James, who sought to concentrate all power in his royal hands, his hesitations and fears when confronted with the advancing William of Orange, his welcome in France by a king as insensible to liberties as himself – all these actors and scenes, and hundreds besides, have a wonderful coherence, lucidity, and power of persuasion. The clarity and narrative interest of these volumes is achieved by the power and simplicity of Macaulay's thesis, nowhere more clearly stated than in the closing paragraph of volume II. Writing in 1848, the year of European revolutions, he declares,

> It is because we had a preserving revolution in the seventeenth
> century that we have not had a destroying revolution in the nine-
> teenth. It is because we had freedom in the midst of servitude that
> we have order in the midst of anarchy. For the authority of law,
> for the security of property, for the peace of our streets, for the
> happiness of our homes, our gratitude is due, under Him who
> raises and pulls down nations at his pleasure, to the Long Parlia-
> ment, to the Convention, and to William of Orange.[28]

Here, compressed into a few sentences, are the essential premises
so effectively dramatized by Macaulay: the idea that the free individual is a legal subject, free by virtue of his subjection to an autonomous system of law; the idea that society is a contractual entity,
ordered by mutually constraining and protecting duties and rights.
Macaulay's skillful characterizations of historical figures and effective developments of scenes all depend on the moral drama of faith-
fulness to the law, or faithless treachery. Indeed, his mastery of what
he calls "the art of narration, the art of interesting the affections and
presenting pictures to the imagination"[29] depends on the founding
principle of the law, specifically the English constitution. The constitution is the origin of justice, of liberty and freedom; men and
events are significant in so far as they uphold or subvert the law.
This makes history a moral drama, a struggle of right against wrong,
in which events are historical to the extent that they have a legal and
moral dimension, and men are the agents of good or evil.[30] On these
grounds Macaulay claims to have a conception of history "more
just" than that of Hume, or Robertson, Voltaire, or Gibbon, a
conception by which men "will not merely be described, but will be
made intimately known to us."[31] He is thus one of the great historians
of agency, of the individual historical actors, this because of the
powerfully tautological conception which governs his *History*. In an
ideological move of admirable economy, the English constitution
becomes both the object of historical investigation and the principle
of historical interpretation.[32] Indeed, Macaulay's *History* is such a
great narrative precisely because of the priority he grants the law,
for narrative itself, the construction of a story with identifiable actors,
which progresses over time, which develops a conflict that comes to
a resolution, requires a concept of law. Hayden White makes this
case strongly when he argues that "narrativity ... presupposes the

existence of a legal system against or on behalf of which the typical agents of a narrative account militate."[33] The *History of England* is thus the story of the struggle for English liberty under the law, every incident and every actor of the voluminous account having some relation to that unquestioned principle. Indeed, God himself, as Macaulay sees it, approves of the Glorious Revolution, the constitution, private property, the prosperity of England and the loyal English subject.

The dramatic narration and intimate knowledge of men which Macaulay sets out to achieve in his history lead him to criticize other histories in terms very similar to the polemic which opens *Henry Esmond*. Where Esmond finds the Muse of History but "a mistress to court ceremonies," Macaulay chastises historians for having neglected the evidence of memoirs and other such materials for which, he says, they

> seem to entertain an aristocratic contempt.... They have imposed on themselves a code of conventional decencies as absurd as that which has been the bane of the French drama.... The majesty of history seems to resemble the majesty of the poor King of Spain, who died a martyr to ceremony because the proper dignitaries were not at hand to render him assistance.[34]

But for all his emphasis on "noiseless revolutions," the "moral changes which have gradually passed on the mass of the community,"[35] Macaulay's concept of historical truth is first and foremost political, legal, public – not at all what Thackeray calls "Court gossip," the intimate facts of familial relations, love affairs, desires satisfied or balked, private ambitions and jealousies, the kind of information a confidential servant would know. Macaulay can't abide gossip, for it confuses the trivial with the significant, and sacrifices objectivity to drama.

Of all the historians he discusses in his essay on history, Macaulay finds Herodotus the most guilty of these faults, and notes approvingly that after Herodotus history "became less gossiping and less picturesque; but more accurate, and somewhat more scientific." "The faults of Herodotus," he continues, "are the faults of a simple and imaginative mind. Children and servants are remarkably Herodotean in their style of narration. They tell everything dramatically. Their *says hes* and *says shes* are proverbial."[36] In fact, the Herodotean style confuses fact and fiction, since the narrator "tells the story as if he had been hid behind the royal bed at Windsor," and although not intending to deceive, embroiders the account with questionable details. History, Macaulay believes, requires a mature mind. Children and the lower classes don't have the discipline to distinguish what's trivial from what's significant, or rigorously to discriminate between fact and fiction. Their thinking is essentially unhistorical, because history is less a matter of facts than of principles; the historian must understand the general principles governing a series of events in order to represent the facts in the proper perspective.[37] Without the abstraction of principle from fact there is no history, only gossip more or less deceptive, more or less false.

The high office of historian is clearly marked in Macaulay's writing by class, and not surprisingly, also by gender. For continuing his discussion of the faults of simple and imaginative minds, he observes that

> the talent of deciding on the circumstances of a particular case is often possessed in the highest perfection by persons destitute of the power of generalization. Men skilled in the military tactics of civilized nations have been amazed at the far-sightedness which a Mohawk displays in concerting his strategems, or in discerning those of his enemies. In England, no class possesses so much of that particular ability which is required for constructing ingenious schemes, and for obviating remote difficulties, as the thieves and the thief-takers. Women have more of this dexterity then men. Lawyers have more of it than statesmen. . . . Indeed, the species of discipline by which this dexterity is acquired tends to contract the mind, and to render it incapable of abstract reasoning.[38]

Children, servants, savages, thieves, women, and lawyers all are unable to reason historically, for to understand history means to abstract an essential principle from contingent details. The principle is what counts, what makes the facts significant or insignificant; the principle is objective, and keeps the historian from fictional elaboration. The principle, as we have seen, is law, that which distinguishes men from beasts – or from Mohawks, or from women or children or thieves, all of whom are either before or beyond the law, not subject to it as are civilized men.[39] Only the men who are so subject can comprehend what makes human endeavors meaningful, what gives men and nations a history.

Macaulay has no doubts that England's history depends on the English constitution. The progress of the nation, meticulously detailed in the *History*, is the direct result of freedom and the rule of law. Above all, every detail, each actor, every scene has its significance in relation to this whole of English history. What, then, are we to make of the fact that *The History of Henry Esmond*, which is even more gossiping than Thackeray's historical essays, is none the less also explicitly about legal questions: Who is the legitimate sovereign? Who is the legitimate head of the Castlewood family, the real marquis? Who is true and who is false, according to what principle? When Esmond repudiates the Pretender, breaks his sword, and burns his patent, Thackeray ends his novel the same way he concludes his essays on the Hanovarian kings: in favor of the English gentleman, merit not rank, rights not hereditary privileges, Parliament not the king. Indeed, in his essay on the Elector of Hanover he sounds positively like Macaulay. "The days are over in England of that strange religion of king worship.... Mended morals and mended manners in Courts and people are among the priceless consequences of the freedom which George I came to rescue and secure."[40] So, too, Esmond, even when engaged with the Stuarts, is actually convinced that the Jacobite cause is wrong: "Were not his very sympathies and secret convictions on the other side – on the side of People, Parliament, Freedom?" (p. 381). Thackeray, it would seem, is of Macaulay's party, and *The History of Henry Esmond* as much a Whig history as *The History of England*.

Yet as he was finishing the novel Thackeray knew it was different. "I wish I had 6 months more to put into the novel," he writes in a letter.

> Now it's nearly done it's scarce more than a sketch and it might have been made a durable history: complete in its parts and its whole. But at the end of six months it would want another 6: it takes as much trouble as Macaulay's History almost and he has the vast advantage of remembering everything he has read, whilst everything but impressions I mean facts dates and so forth slip out of my head in which there's some great faculty lacking depend on it.[41]

Actually, there are abundant facts and dates in the novel, the result of Thackeray's own reading and the specific research tasks he set for his secretary, Eyre Crowe. The difference has to do not with historical specificity and accuracy, but with the relation of part to whole, for Thackeray is right: his is not a "durable history" like Macaulay's and the elements of Whig history in the text are actually emptied of significance. The originary, organizing principle of law, so strong in

Macaulay's work, is displaced in *Esmond* by "the secret which makes one little hand the dearest of all," and Esmond's intimate history of desire produces more questions than answers. Political legitimacy, legal right, and the moral order they guarantee are crucial thematically, but do not provide a definitive principle of organization and interpretation. *Henry Esmond* is not "complete in its parts and its whole" because Thackeray does not exercise the power of generalization, so indispensable to the proper historian as Macaulay points out. Indeed, as Bagehot writes in a retrospective essay on the novelist, he

> looked at everything ... from a *sensitive* aspect. His mind was, to some considerable extent, like a woman's mind. It could comprehend abstractions when they were unrolled and explained before it, but it never naturally created them; never of itself, and without external obligation, devoted itself to them.[42]

While other reviewers praised his "manly" style, and observed "the peculiarly masculine forms of [his] sentences," Thackeray none the less impressed his contemporaries with a kind of femininity: "One loved him almost as one loves a woman, tenderly and with thoughtfulness ... one loved him thus because his heart was tender, as is the heart of a woman."[43]

This feminizing of Thackeray has to do both with his subject and his treatment of it. First, there is his attention to emotions, to affections and antipathies, to the nuances of feelings, to "longing passion unfulfilled," to the question of desire.[44] For intimacy and the "inner life" it concerns are marked by gender, by femininity. Indeed, the construction of the intimate as the locus of identity is integrally linked with the nineteenth-century fascination with sexual categorization, "femininity" being everything that "masculinity" is not. Thus home and family, the places of intimate life, are set off from the public, political, properly historical world. Thus writing "familiar history" as familial history entails more than the ironic replacing of public by private life, for while public and private may be on the same plane, intimacy is a matter of depth, of enigmas, riddles: intimacy concerns women, "the sex," the effort of men to know what women want, the problem of identity. *The History of Henry Esmond* is thus "feminized" history, that is, a history which considers "matters where clear thinking is impossible," as one reviewer put it.[45] And feminized history contests disciplined history by focusing precisely on what the latter must eliminate.

Second, *Esmond* is most distinctly feminized in its lack of devotion to abstraction, the absence of general principles, the incommensurability of part to whole. While there is in *Esmond* a search for meaning in the past, the text provides no first or final principle of explanation. Thus the feminine matter of the text is not mastered, but displayed; exposed, not explicated. The fact that Thackeray offers no master narrative of the feminine is particularly important given that *Esmond*, published in 1852, is very near to what Certeau has called "the time of Freud (1856–1939)."[46] Thackeray's proximity to this time is suggested by the priority he gives to the determining and irrational force of desire, to the vividness and unreliability of memory, to the distortions of self-interest and vanity, to the difficulty, even impossibility of unmediated self-knowledge. These preoccupations, the preoccupations of the time of Freud, are indeed part of the great nineteenth-century concern with history as an epistemological ground: they are its other side. The latter part of the nineteenth century, then, is as much the time of psychoanalysis as it is of history. Both, for all their disciplinary differences, are historical projects, for Freud's work extends the field of history to encompass the unconscious, that which makes man subject in the most profound sense to the past. Indeed, just as *Esmond* is similar in important ways to Macaulay's Whig history while simultaneously going counter to the premises of history "proper," in its work of recollection the novel resembles psychoanalysis while refusing psychoanalytic explanation. The critical difference of Thackeray's text is that it fails to produce the "answers" psychoanalysis proposes to the question of desire and to the riddle of femininity. Where Freud will discover an unconscious organized by sexual difference, *Esmond* displays only the endless circulation of desire.

Still, the similarities between Thackeray's and Freud's work are striking, for in *Esmond* the present is inseparable from the past, and what lives on most vigorously are deeply felt desires. Recounting his long suit for Beatrix, Esmond writes,

Years after this passion hath been dead and buried ... he who felt it can recall it out of its grave.... I invoke that beautiful spirit from the shades and love her still; or rather I should say such a past is always present to a man; such a passion once felt forms a part of his whole being, and cannot be separated from it.... Our great thoughts, our great affections, the Truths of our life, never leave us.
(p. 347)

Passions once felt are indeed the materials of history in Thackeray's text, and if Esmond is an unreliable narrator, his failures of interpretation and awareness but confirm the degree to which the past always imposes on the present. Further, *Esmond* seems to prefigure in an almost uncanny way the story that – after Freud – we know by heart. Esmond kills his "father" and marries his "mother." So, too, he "breaks his head" on the riddle of desire and the enigma of Beatrix – he wonders what she wants:

> "If I do something you have at heart; something worthy of me and you; something that will make me a name with which to endow you; will you take it? ... If I come back to you and give you fame, will that please you?"
>
> (p. 359)

Beatrix, of course, remains mysterious, her "eyes wore that melancholy and inscrutable look which 'twas always impossible to sound" (p. 376). By focusing his history on the question of desire, Thackeray would seem to be working in the same direction as Freud to historicize the feminine, to discover the unconscious. This, of course, is the work of psychoanalysis, as Jacques Lacan declares: "What we teach the subject to recognize as his unconscious is his history – that is to say – we help him to perfect the present historization of the facts that have already determined his existence." Psychoanalysis is history; "its operations are those of history, in so far as history constitutes the emergence of the truth in the real."[47]

The truth which emerges is, for the analyst, the truth of sexual difference, the difference inaugurated by the phallus and institutionalized by the law of the father. Freud found the ancient tragedy of Oedipus to be the most economical dramatization of this humanizing law, for Oedipus unwittingly kills his own father and marries his mother, only to suffer blindness and exile when his true history is found out. Since Freud, his punishment has been known as the paradigmatic instance of castration, the lack of the phallus which is said to be the condition of humanized sexuality and human culture. Further, his story makes the past the inescapable condition of the present, for, as Schiller commented to Goethe, "that which has happened, in being unalterable, is naturally far more terrible [than a future event], and the fear that *something might have happened* affects the mind quite differently than the fear that something may happen."[48] The work of the analyst (and of the analysand), then, is historical work, the discovery of how the law of the father has borne down on the subject, what traces of that event are still present.

Thus both historian and analyst find in history evidence of man's humanity: the former finds the distinctly human features of a social contract and national life organized by law, and the latter discovers the humanizing effects of the law of the father. From his early interpretations of dreams to the masterfully told case histories, Freud constructs narratives of psychic development every bit as compelling as Macaulay's story of the progress of the nation. Further, both history and psychoanalysis aspire to be scientific discourses, and Freud, even though he is concerned with "feminine" matters, with childhood, the family, sexuality, and, of course, femininity itself, escapes the taint of femininity. When he asks questions, answers are forthcoming. What do women want, he wonders, and refers this question, as all others, to the law of the father. If women lack lack, and in their twice-removed relation to the phallus are for Freud an insoluble problem, the riddle of femininity still confirms the truth of sexual difference, the truth that women are different from men.[49]

In *Esmond*, the same questions are asked but with a quite different effect. The text is devoted to the most intimate of matters, is about unattainable desires, self-delusions, and the return of the repressed (that gold sleeve button), but is about these things without abstracting from them an origin, a principle which will make "the truth" emerge from "the real." *Esmond* thus makes history a problem, not a solution.

Consider the "resolution" of Esmond's history, the marriage of Henry with the woman who in his youth said to him, " 'I am your mother, you are my son, and I love you always' " (p. 228). Esmond has long since been the indirect cause of Lord Castlewood's death, for his patron lost his life in a duel with the dangerous Lord Mohun, with whom he had been gambling heavily in the hopes of recovering for Henry the family fortune – Esmond's patrimony – which he, his protector, has squandered. Lady Castlewood is ready to accuse Esmond, crying out when she first sees him after the duel, " 'Take back your hand – do not touch me with it! Look! there's blood on it!' " (p. 151). Yet after the downfall of Beatrix and the Pretender, she and her "son" leave England together, going first to Belgium where, as Esmond reports, "the great joy of my life was bestowed upon me, and ... my dear mistress became my wife." Then they receive from Frank the Virginia estate in the new world, where

Esmond enjoys "that happiness, which ... cannot be written in words" (p. 418). Esmond is Oedipus all right, but Oedipus with a happy ending.

An Oedipal plot which ends with the blissful union of mother and son cannot be construed as an originary instance of the law at work or as a model of the subject's subjection to a determining history. The relation of past to present is not that of the Oedipal drama, for while Oedipus finds his past weighing heavily and ominously, finally tragically, on the present, Esmond recalls the past from "the summit of happiness," his marriage to Rachel representing "the completion of hope." He kills his father, he marries his mother, but there is no retribution, no price to pay. There is also no closure, and no solution, for, as we have seen, the familial drama of the Castlewoods is unending, and the happy ending but the beginning of a new story of jealousy and desire.

In *Esmond*, the Oedipal plot serves to emphasize the proliferation of desire and the "affective intensification of the family space" which are such distinctive features of modern life.[50] These facts of life are part of what make the late nineteenth and the twentieth centuries "the time of Freud," but Thackeray's relation to these developments is quite different from Freud's. For the father of psychoanalysis finds in Oedipus the key to man's identity, the evidence of the law: he discovers an unconscious organized by the phallus. No matter, then, that identities are dispersed, that the subject is split, that consciousness is fictive, a matter of representation, for psychoanalysis finds in these very decentering processes a deeper, profounder ground for man's being. All the parts can be resolved into a whole again, the drama of Oedipus, the paradigmatic narrative of the constitution of the subject. The analyst, then, can reconstruct this drama from the fragmentary evidence of the present, working with the analysand to discover how the patient, too, is Oedipus, an actor in the drama of the unconscious which is played out no matter what he intends, without his knowledge. Here, perhaps, is the most striking contrast of Thackeray's "Oedipus" to Freud's, for while Oedipus pays dearly for his unknowing union with his mother, Esmond marries Rachel perfectly aware of who she is and what she has been to him, ending his history with the fulfillment of his dreams. Esmond thus differs from Oedipus in the most significant way: there is no deep structure to Esmond's history, no symptomatic expression of a determining law. His history is not his unconscious.

The difference of Esmond from Oedipus is evident in the design of the text. It is underlined by the brief appearance Oedipus makes *in propria persona*. In chapter III of book III, Jocasta and Oedipus both appear in a "parable" written by Esmond for Beatrix. On April Fools' day, he has his essay printed in the form of Steele's *Spectator* paper, imitating Steele's style and running it off on his press. This sham *Spectator* is in two parts, the first signed "Oedipus," the second a reply with the signature "Cymon Wyldoats." Oedipus's part is a question to Mr Spectator, an appeal for help. "Can you help us ... to read this riddle?" Oedipus asks, searching for the answer to a question plaguing Jocasta, a woman with numerous admirers who has inconveniently forgotten the name of one who has been especially attentive. Oedipus asks for help in determining the identity of the unknown man, help which is forthcoming in the second part. There Cymon Wyldoats, the nameless admirer, replies, writing that Jocasta is an artful flirt not worthy of his attention or affection, so quick is she to forget one on whom she turned her charms. This is, as Esmond explains, a parable, with Jocasta none other than Beatrix and Cymon representing Esmond, the whole "intended to convey to the young woman that she herself was a flirt, and the Cymon was a gentleman of honour and resolution, seeing all her faults, and determined to break the chains once and forever" (p. 317).

The appearance of Oedipus and Jocasta in *Esmond* has only a mocking relation to the ancient drama, and none at all to the "Oedipal" plot of the text. In the sham *Spectator*, Oedipus is a servant to Jocasta and confounded by a riddle, whereas in the classical account he is the King of Thebes and the husband of Jocasta by virtue of his ability to answer riddles, to reply to the Sphinx. As for the relation of this part of *Esmond* to the whole, Oedipus is not Esmond, for Esmond is in the part of Cymon Wyldoats, and Jocasta is not Rachel, but rather Beatrix, the daughter, not the mother. Indeed, Esmond's forged paper does more than distinguish Thackeray's Oedipus from that of Sophocles – or Freud – for it inevitably reminds one that *The History of Henry Esmond* is itself an imitation, originally printed in eighteenth-century type, written in eighteenth-century style, a book designed to impose upon its readers. But where Esmond helpfully "expounds" his "parable," explaining its real meaning, *Esmond* resists explication by confusing the relations of part to whole, original to representation, even while developing a thematics of exposure and the revelation of hidden truths.

One of the most striking instances of this confusion is the appearance in Esmond's *History* of the Pretender, an important figure in

English political, religious, and military history, a "world-historical" actor. In fiction, especially in historical novels, such persons are to make only brief appearances to authenticate the story; they then produce "superlative effects of the real," as Roland Barthes notes.[51] This effect is undone if fictional and historical characters mingle too promiscuously, which is exactly what happens in *Henry Esmond*. Not only does the Stuart prince lose his chance at the crown by dangling after Beatrix, his entire appearance in England under the protection of the Castlewoods inevitably calls attention to the fictiveness of the *History*, for no such episode was a part of the Jacobite resistance and the Pretender bore no resemblance to the fraudulent libertine of Esmond's memoirs. Other historical characters Esmond keeps company with appear much more briefly, but the scenes with the Pretender insist on the fictionality of *Esmond* as a whole.

By making over the events of the past to serve his novelistic ends, Thackeray stresses once again his skepticism about the truth of any "properly" historical narrative, holding that his fictive "reconstruction" of Colonel Esmond will be truer in spirit to the past than a history more accurate as to facts. But again *Esmond* does more than simply reverse the priority of history to fiction. By writing an historical novel that has no hermeneutic key, Thackeray engages with history without finding in it a confirmation of "man." *Esmond* in its fictiveness is an exemplary instance of the way fiction has become the place of that which history must eliminate, demonstrating

> the fact that identities of time, place, subject, and object assumed by classical historiography don't hold ... that they have been stirred by forces that trouble them.... But this is a part of historiography which is held to be shameful and illegitimate.[52]

So it is that *Henry Esmond* is a book "admirable and odious," as Charlotte Brontë put it; admirable in its historical authenticity, its veritable recreation of the past in Colonel Esmond's memoirs, and odious in its insistence on the instability of the subject, the conditions of representation, all of which trouble history as a discourse of truth. The incestuous marriage which ends the novel is actually only the most visible of the text's scandals. For *Esmond* brings together history and its others in a shocking union which collapses the difference between "truth" and "fiction."[53]

The History of Henry Esmond runs counter to the concept of a "continuous history" and its guarantees. Even psychoanalysis, which is directly concerned with the forces that trouble time, place, subject, and object, displaces these identities only to rediscover them at a greater depth through the analysis of the subject. *Esmond* offers no such deferred truths. The text is not only ironically compromised from beginning to end, it is also the scene of proliferating desires. Everybody wants somebody or something: Lady Castlewood wants Lord Castlewood, who is always off after the orange girl or Polly at Hexton; then Rachel wants Henry and my lord wants Rachel back, while Henry wants Beatrix; but Beatrix wants a duke, or a king, and so on. In this way *Esmond* is anti-Oedipus: a romance of ever-circulating desires but no prohibition, a text of parts without a whole, a text that is productive, not expressive.[54]

As feminized history, then, the text first challenges the concept of history as a positive record of men and events, then contests the idea that history is, in the final analysis, always going to reveal the truth of man. Like Macaulay, Thackeray is in favor of an authentic history which will make the men of the past "intimately known" to the reader, but where Macaulay finds all of history to be a confirmation of the grand principles of law embodied in the English constitution, for Thackeray authentic history is a matter of the secret which makes one little hand the dearest of all. *Esmond* does not unriddle this mystery and provides no master narrative of the inner life. And while Esmond may wonder what Beatrix wants, the text does not construe this question so as to affirm man's historical being, nor are the "feminine" matters of intimate life made to express a law even more profound than that of the constitution. *The History of Henry Esmond* really is scandalous, then, first raising questions that history proper must repress, then dispersing rather than consolidating man as the subject of history. How could Eliot not find *Esmond* distinctly uncomfortable!

Of course, both Eliot and Thackeray participate in the inescapable nineteenth-century fascination with and production of history. Thackeray's interests draw him to the convergence of national history and the deeply intimate histories of family life; Eliot, as the great Victorian expounder of humanism, is directly engaged and deeply invested in the consolidation of "man" as an historical subject. Unlike Eliot, however, Thackeray is not a believer, and his famous irony works in *Esmond* against the faith that history is man's salvation, "the guarantee that everything that has eluded him may be restored to him." The text is in no sense "outside history"; it depends entirely on the problematic of history, but, unlike many other texts, insists directly on the fact that history is a problem, a whole ideological–philosophical formation that is all too often taken for a solution. *Esmond* contests the grounds of history, does not honor its guarantee, and is, in that way, very uncomfortable indeed.

Chapter 3

History and the melodramatic fix

In December 1856, as his bleak representation of English government and English society in *Little Dorrit* was in the twelfth of sixteen numbers, Charles Dickens was staggering on to the stage at Tavistock House, transfixing a select audience of family and friends in the role of Wardour in Wilkie Collins's melodrama, *The Frozen Deep*. Over the summer and autumn Dickens had devoted much of his extraordinary energy to collaborating with his friend on the play, to transforming the schoolroom in his house into a theater (which could seat ninety-three), to overseeing the construction of sets (which produced admirably spectacular effects), to rehearsing his amateur cast. By all accounts the play was an unqualified success, leaving its audiences awash in tears. "I certainly have never seen people so strongly affected by theatrical means," Dickens wrote in January, and when he revived the play that summer in a series of charitable performances, the Manchester audiences, 2,000 each night, were overwhelmed: the reviewer for the *Leader* pronounced the play remarkable for "its power over the laughter, the tears and the interest of the audience."[1] Queen Victoria herself requested a private performance, and one of the stage carpenters declared to Dickens, "It's a universal observation in the profession, sir, that it was a great loss to the public when you took to writing books."[2]

Of course, Dickens's reputation for greatness depends not on his theatrical performances, but on his books, including *Little Dorrit*. *The Frozen Deep* is now buried in libraries, and Dickens's riveting performance is only to be imagined by the acclaim of contemporary accounts. Yet this melodrama which absorbed so much of Dickens's attention, and which moved its audiences so powerfully, actually has everything to do with the novel the author was writing at the same time. *Little Dorrit* is every bit as much a melodrama as Collins's play, is as fully nostalgic, as fully sentimental, as absolutely dependent on moving its audience for its effects. The novel, is, of course, a more complicated text than *The Frozen Deep*. While the play is a short three acts, *Little Dorrit* is seventy chapters long, complicated by multiple plots and scores of characters.[3] Further, the novel, unlike the play, develops an explicit satire of English politics and social life, a scathing criticism which Dickens enjoyed with a certain "grim pleasure."[4] Yet it is precisely because the novel is celebrated as such a powerful and complex instance of Dickens's social criticism that we must recognize and understand its melodramatic design. For the melodrama of *Little Dorrit* displays a particular complex of ideological commitments which together constitute "the social" as the opposite of politics, which separate private from public, women from men, which produce a "history" which is stunningly totalizing and ahistorical. All of this is crucial, indeed indispensable for the consolidation of the middle class, for the development of tutelary government and the fields of social science and social work, for the institutionalizing of modern forms of power.

If *The History of Henry Esmond* is a discomfiting text, as I believe it is in its refusal to make history produce the truth of man, the works of the "Other Author," as Thackeray called his rival Dickens, are a telling contrast. Dickens comforts his audience, makes his readers feel at home, secure. Given that I am going to stress the importance of the tears that Dickens's texts wring from one, this claim for the comfortableness, the homeliness, of his work may seem paradoxical. Not at all. Sentiment is Dickens's *forte*, and he uses it to manage history as effectively as Eliot uses speculative philosophy. That is to say, melodrama provides Dickens with a mode that is "historical" in its insistence on a past that is lost but not forgotten, that figures history as home.

THE FROZEN DEEP, OR, CAN THIS MAN BE SAVED?

As Laura Mulvey so rightly observes, "Ideological contradiction is the overt mainspring and specific content of melodrama, not a hidden, unconscious thread to be picked up only by special critical processes."[5] *The Frozen Deep*, a play so purely melodramatic that the script is, as its editor says, "skeletal," lays out its premises and elicits its responses in the most straightforward way imaginable.[6] It is an exemplary Victorian melodrama, turning as it does around the evils of being separated from home. Yet this absence, the home which is missing, also promises a presence, holds out the hope that if only events develop a certain way, happiness might be ours. Not that the audience identifies with the characters in the play as individuals; the drama is far too schematic. But the scheme turns around a lack that promises satisfaction, a lack associated in every way with home and all home represents, and in the process elicits from the audience the very desire it dramatizes: the desire for unconditional love, for the home, and the womanly presence that has been lost.

Act I opens at home, in an English drawing room, where Clara is tormented by the knowledge that the two men who love her are, by chance, on the same dangerous expedition to the frozen wastes of the Arctic. She fears for Frank, her fiancé, since Wardour, who has loved her from childhood and had assumed that Clara was his intended, is a disappointed and dangerous man. When she refused him, he vowed vengeance on any man who would think to marry her instead. Now all Clara can do is hope that neither discovers the other's identity, and that Frank will return home to her.

But in act II, set in the expedition's rough Arctic camp, Wardour accidentally discovers that Frank is engaged to Clara although Frank remains innocently ignorant of the danger he faces. Worse still, the expedition is out of supplies, and Wardour and Frank are chosen to set out together across the frozen deep in a last-ditch effort to find help. Will the expedition ever return home? Will Frank return to Clara? Or will Wardour fulfill his vow of vengeance and murder Frank out there in the wilderness of ice and snow?

Act III provides the answers. Clara and some others have gone to Greenland in hopes of discovering what has happened to the long-overdue expedition. All except Wardour and Frank have been discovered, and now Clara knows the worst: that those two went off together, Wardour aware that Frank was her beloved. She despairs. We despair. Then, when all seems lost, in stumbles Wardour, drawn and haggard. He says one word: " 'Found!' " and then turns away, only to re-enter staggering under the burden of Frank, whom he has saved from certain death. But in saving Frank, he has sacrificed himself. He dies, his head in Clara's lap, his virtue and his manhood fully acknowledged by all on stage and off.

Dickens's performance of Wardour was so affecting that the professional actress playing Clara in the Manchester theater bathed his face in uncontrolled tears, and the audiences wept as one. Every aspect of the play is directed to achieve this effect, these tears which bear witness to the power of women to humanize, indeed to sanctify men. For Wardour is saved, and saves Frank, because he loves Clara, loves her more than he desires revenge, loves her more than life itself. The single word, "Found!" sums it up: what was lost is found, what was missing is recovered. His desire is satisfied; there is a moment of perfect coincidence; and he dies. If only we, too, might experience such sanctification, such a reconciliation, such a home-coming. All eyes are on Wardour, for he is the one who was in danger of becoming truly evil, savage even, a murderer out there on the frozen deep. His heart was nearly frozen. But the memory of his childhood sweetheart saves him and his innocent companion, and on he struggles, always towards Clara, towards the light of home, towards the perfect union with the perfect woman.

Clearly, this union is a reunion; it requires an absence to work. Wardour must be divided from Clara, the men must be far from home, the howling wilderness of the Arctic must be set against the comforts and pleasures of the drawing room where the women wait. That is, at the center of the drama is the faraway home, the waiting women. Home and women-in-the-home together constitute an absent presence that may be recovered. It is absent in part because it recalls something that is "naturally" lost to a man, the "originary" union of mother and child. Yet the constructedness of this absence, its ideological character, is evident in the way it produces a presence, that of the Englishman to himself. Wardour is saved from savagery, from being a bestial murderer, by the recollection of Clara and his desire to be reconciled with her. He proves himself a true Englishman, proves that his early attachments guarantee his humanity under the most awful conditions.

The melodramatic articulation of presence and absence fore-grounds, as Mulvey says, certain ideological contradictions. A play such as *The Frozen Deep* shows explicitly how the ideology of domesticity works, how "women" are categorically marked as an absent presence. Robert Louis Brannan has demonstrated that Dickens actively intervened in the writing of *The Frozen Deep*, showing Collins how to shift the dramatic focus from the women waiting helplessly at home to the man out in the wilderness strug-gling to be a civilized Englishman. This is the aspect of Dickens's work that John Cordy Jeaffreson most appreciates. In his 1858 book *Novels and Novelists from Elizabeth to Victoria*, he puts the case well, calling Dickens "a divinely instructed writer" and crediting him with having elevated the moral standards of the nation.

Take any honest-hearted Englishman, and probe cunningly the depths of his nature to discover why it is that he would scorn to tell a lie, to desert a fallen friend, to reap benefit from a deed of shame? ... You will find the answer in his affections, in a chivalric belief in the excellence of women, and the dignity of honesty, in a strong love for the memory of a mother who first taught him to pray, or for the lisping babes of his own just learning to falter out accents of entreaty....[7]

Jeaffreson finds all these virtues admirably dramatized in "Boz's" writings, and his grateful admiration of Dickens, and of the "advances in our national morality" to which the author has contributed, is a widely-shared sentiment among Dickens's Victorian reviewers. Edwin P. Whipple considers that "[the] humanity, the wide-ranging and healthy sympathies ... so observable in the works of Dickens, are in a great degree characteristic of the age," and he admires "the sentiment of humanity" represented so well by the great novelist. So, too, in contrasting the "harsh unfeelingness" of the early nineteenth century to the liberality of 1858, Walter Bagehot proclaims Dickens the best representative of a "'sentimental radicalism'" which has rid the nation of inhumanely punitive laws and reformed its political administration as well.

The sentiment and sympathy which are produced by a properly private life, a life secure in the bosom of the family, have to do with the nation as a whole, the organization of English social life and the nature of its political order. A melodrama such as *The Frozen Deep* is doubly effective, for not only does it represent the humanizing effect of Home on Wardour, but it reproduces in the audience the sentiments acted out on stage. Clara's anxieties, her hopes and fears, are ours; but most of all Wardour's sufferings in the climactic last act are ours: our longing for home, our desire to recover what is lost, to have the purity of our hearts recognized and admired – all is encompassed in that final speech, "'Found!'" Melodrama creates this collective "we," an audience that bears witness by its tears to the truth of the representation before it. This power of captivating an audience is Dickens's great strength, on stage and on paper. For as Taine observed in 1856, "There is no writer who knows better how to touch and melt; he makes us weep, absolutely shed tears; before reading him we did not know there was so much pity in the heart."[8]

The fuller significance of this is evident in a sub-text to Collins's melodrama, the wide discussion in the English press of the fate of an expedition to the Arctic led by Sir John Franklin. As Brannan has noted in his scholarly edition of *The Frozen Deep*, during the 1850s Dickens ran six articles in *Household Words* on "the lost Arctic voyagers," all responding to the claim made by Dr John Rae in 1854 that the men on the expedition had all perished, but not before having been "driven to the last resource – cannibalism – as a means of prolonging existence."[9] This was a shocking claim, most shocking because, if true, it would show the Englishmen to be far more savage than the Eskimos who reported seeing evidence of the sorry end to which Franklin and his men had come. Dickens refuses to admit that the report could possibly be true, basing his argument on the opposed natures of the English and the Eskimos. The natives of the Arctic wilderness he knew to be "covetous, treacherous, and cruel," – savages, in short, and savages are natural liars. The English, on the other hand, were civilized men, educated, disciplined, religious. Thus "the noble conduct and example of such men, and of their great leader himself," especially as proven during the rigors of earlier expeditions, "outweighs by the whole weight of the universe the chatter of a gross handful of uncivilized people, with a domesticity of blood and blubber."[10]

Civilization itself depends on domesticity, home life of the sort that formed the heroic English, not some savage parody of the domestic. Cannibalism is the utter undoing of all social bonds; the feelings revolt, and it is the strength of the sentiments, in the end, that guarantee the English could not have eaten human flesh. Dickens knows this, he feels it in his heart. As he writes to Forster in 1856,

> Lady Franklin sent me the whole of that Richardson memoir; and I think Richardson's manly friendship, and love of Franklin, one of the best things I ever knew in my heart. It makes one's heart beat high, with a kind of sacred joy.[11]

Manly friendship and love – these are sacred things, the very stuff of social life, of civilization and order as opposed to savage anarchy. And, as *The Frozen Deep* clearly shows, a man is made a man, is socialized, humanized, civilized, at home by a woman – or, better, by the *memory* of a woman and by his desire to be fully in her presence again.[12]

*

Nostalgia, then, defines melodrama, the nostalgia which is "a longing for things, persons, or situations that are not present," "home-sickness."[13] The homesickness of nostalgia is a longing for the past, a desire to overcome the separation of past and present, a wish to return, to make past and present coincide. In this way, the "melo-dramatic imagination" is an extreme instance of the Victorian his-torical imagination, a conceptualizing of history as home, as the recoverable origin of man, something lost which can be found, which will in the finding reveal man to himself. History-as-home is, of course, profoundly ahistorical, as Foucault has observed in *The Archaelogy of Knowledge*:

> Continuous history is the indispensable correlative of the founding function of the subject: the guarantee that everything that has eluded him may be restored to him; the certainty that time will disperse nothing without restoring it in a reconstituted unity; the promise that one day the subject – in the form of historical consciousness – will once again be able to appropriate, to bring back under his sway, all those things that are kept at a distance by difference, and find in them what might be called his abode.[14]

We have seen how George Eliot, the masterful philosophical novelist, achieves this sort of appropriation in *Daniel Deronda*, a complex novel that requires devoted critical attention to understand how difference is dissimulated by an all-encompassing historical con-sciousness. Neither *The Frozen Deep* nor *Little Dorrit* may seem to have much to do with such complex philosophical matters, and in a sense that is true: melodrama is not philosophically complex. But in its simplicity melodrama foregrounds the logic so tortuously worked out by Eliot, displaying on the surface the ideological contradictions deeply embedded in more philosophical texts. History-as-home is such a contradiction.

Dickens is one of the major melodramatic novelists of mid-century, and *Little Dorrit* is a text which produces what I call the melo-dramatic fix, the repetitious, incessant effort to domesticate differ-ence, to display an over-arching moral order that informs all phenomena.[15] In *The Melodramatic Imagination*, Peter Brooks argues that melodrama is an exemplary modern genre which develops out of romanticism and the slow but definitive disappearance of God, a disappearance which gives rise to new ways of imagining ethical imperatives. The intensified polarities, hyperbolic exchanges, exaggerated conflicts, and charged settings of melodrama "may be made necessary," Brooks writes, "by the effort to perceive and image the spiritual in a world voided of its traditional Sacred, where the body of the ethical has become a sort of *deus absconditus* which must be sought for, postulated, brought into man's existence...."[16] The end of theology is the beginning of history, as Brooks and others have noted, and, in fact – although Brooks does not make the connection – the melodramatic imagination and the historical imagination are part of the same problematic. Reading melodrama, then, will help us understand the logic, or the ideology, of the Victorian obsession with history, the way both the historical and the melodramatic imagination produce the past as an origin which confirms the present.

As Brooks tells us,

[melodrama] comes into being in a world where the traditional imperatives of truth and ethics have been violently thrown into question, yet where the promulgation of truth and ethics, their instauration as a way of life, is of immediate, daily, political concern.[17]

Brooks is more attentive to ethics than to politics, but the "instauration" – which is to say the institutionalizing – of ethics and truth is fully political. It is an exercise of power which only *seems* to be free of politics and political institutions, which seems to be a matter not of power but of right and wrong, of truth and knowledge, of education and socialization, a matter of humanizing a world in danger of becoming inhuman. Ethics, then, and truth are to replace politics, which is very much what Dickens had in mind as he worked on *Little Dorrit*. Writing to a friend in 1855 he declares,

As to the suffrage, I have lost hope even in the ballot. We appear to me to have proved the failure of representative institutions without an educated and advanced people to support them. What with teaching people ... to go to the beer-shop, to go a-packing and go to the devil; what with having no such thing as a middle class (for though we are perpetually bragging of it as our safety, it is nothing but a poor fringe on the mantle of the upper); what with flunkyism, toadyism ... I do reluctantly believe that the English people are habitually consenting parties to the miserable imbecility into which we have fallen ... I have no present political faith or hope – not a grain.[18]

So when he was asked in the same year by the Metropolitan constituencies to stand for Parliament, he declined: "I declare that as to all matters on the face of this teeming earth, it appears to me that the House of Commons and Parliament altogether is become just the dreariest failure and nuisance that ever bothered this much-bothered world."[19] The nation needs an educated and advanced people, a real middle class free of the dehumanizing dissoluteness of the aristocracy and the even more inhuman brutality of the lower orders; education and social reform, then, must take the place of politics and political institutions, which are more noisome nuisances than the dust-heaps Parliament failed to regulate. Dickens's crusading for social reforms in his novels and in *Household Words*, and his service on the boards of innumerable associations and benevolent societies made the Metropolitan constituencies think of him as a political candidate, but Dickens was actually devoted to separating the social from the political.[20] Yet this separation is part of an institutionalizing of ethics which actually *is* political in that it is an exercise of power: it consolidates the middle class and generalizes its values, making bourgeois man the standard for Humanity and bourgeois values the highest instance of Truth and Justice.

This is politics without "politics," an exercise of power which depends on several distinctions. Just as the social is separated from the political, the intimacy of the private is differentiated from the public, and women are distinguished from men. Melodrama, as we have seen in *The Frozen Deep*, exaggerates these distinctions, turns them into polar oppositions, heightens and intensifies the difference between the terms, makes the differences elemental. Dickens's extraordinary success, his relationship to "the public" – "personally affectionate and like no other man's," as he put it – has to do with his ability to work up these elemental differences in his novels, to work them up so that the public feels the truth of the representation in the tears on their cheeks. As G. K. Chesterton knew, Dickens had a "deep and spiritual kinship [with] the community": "Dickens did not write what the people wanted. Dickens wanted what the people wanted."[21] Mrs Oliphant is more precise, writing in *Blackwood's Magazine* in 1855,

[W]e cannot but express our conviction that it is to the fact that he represents a class that he owes his speedy elevation to the top of the wave of popular favour.... [H]e is, perhaps more distinctly than any other author of the time, a *class* writer ... it is the air and the breath of middle class respectability which fills the books of Mr Dickens.

He is, she continues, "the historian of a class – the literary interpreter of those intelligent, sensible, warm-hearted households, which are the strength of our country...."[22] Dickens, then, sustains such an intimate relationship with his audience because he wants what they – what "we" of the middle class – want; his desires are ours. And our desires are, in part, elicited and directed by his representations, by the melodrama of longing for an absent home and the maternal presence, an always already absent presence. We long to say as Wardour does, "Found!"

In what follows, I read Dickens's melodramatic novel of imprisonment and liberation, of corruption and salvation, the story of Little Dorrit and "the ravishing little family history" of the Clennam household. Then I turn to the social historian so often linked to Dickens, Henry Mayhew, to see to what extent his "History of the People" (as he called his survey of "labour and the poor" in London) participates in the melodramatic fix. Given the way in which melodrama functions as the cultural imaginary of the Victorian middle class, recognizing otherness only to confirm the domestic, familial, homely identity of that class, and given that Mayhew, like Dickens, is a middle-class writer and reformer, it would seem inevitable that his "History" would be somehow melodramatic. And it is. But it is also true that in significant ways Mayhew's work is not melodramatic, and the history represented in his text often forecloses the consolations of home. Dickens's writing, on the other hand, is powerfully and exclusively melodramatic, and he is himself deeply invested in the melodramatic fix.

"ALWAYS LITTLE DORRIT"

A novel of the length and range of *Little Dorrit* may seem to exceed the simple and insistent polarizations which mark Collins's play so clearly as a melodrama. Some time ago Humphry House observed a change in Dickens's work which is now a critical commonplace, "a definite growth in his vision of society from the merely personal and domestic towards an understanding of the complicated interaction of countless social forces," an understanding which would seem to be incompatible with the simplicities and polarities of melodrama.[23] Indeed, John Holloway, in his introduction to the widely-distributed Penguin edition of the text, asserts that *Little Dorrit* is a fictional representation of "one of the great intellectual discoveries of the earlier nineteenth century. Dickens was registering, in fiction,

the emergence of the whole idea of society as a great unified fabric –
the emergence indeed of the social sciences themselves." Holloway
goes on to argue that the social sciences are unthinkable without
the corollary "discovery" of history as the condition of any social
organization, and declares that Dickens follows Carlyle's reasoning
in *Sartor Resartus*:

> Wondrous are the bonds that unite us one and all; whether by the
> soft binding of Love, or the iron chaining of Necessity ... if now
> an existing generation of men stand so woven together, not less
> indissolubly does generation with generation....[24]

Little Dorrit, then, is thought to be beyond melodrama, to be
closer to social science and history than to the simplicities of "the
merely personal and domestic." Actually, the text suggests how much
these great intellectual discoveries participate in the logic and repeat
the binary structures of melodrama. Dickens's novel does not so
much go beyond melodrama as demonstrate the impossibility of
such a move for the nineteenth-century middle-class imagination.
Neither the social sciences nor history can be fully separated from
"the merely personal and domestic," for the difference of the domestic is crucially important in the construction of "society" and
indeed of "history," too.

Dickens asks in the preface to the 1857 edition of *Little Dorrit*
that his readers look at the "weaving" of the book "in its completed
state, and with the pattern finished." This textile metaphor Holloway
cites as an apt figure for the general system of social relations just
being "discovered" at mid-century. But the interrelatedness to which
Dickens refers also establishes the melodramatic structure of the
novel, a totalizing system in which every element is invested with
ethical significance. This is true from the opening scene in the quarantine at Marseilles to the multiple connections of the denouement.
Dickens insists on the overall design of the text from the first, when
the cold and haughty Miss Wade says in the opening chapter,

> "In our course through life we shall meet the people who are
> coming to meet *us*, from many strange places and by many strange
> roads ... and what it is set to us to do to them, and what it is set
> to them to do to us, will all be done."

> (p. 63)

This ominous prophecy is repeated several numbers later, now in
connection with the hero's mother, Mrs Clennam. Arthur Clennam

is afraid that his father did some wrong in the past which should be righted, but Mrs Clennam, a hard and unrelenting woman, denies his suspicion, even though she has by her side the watch Arthur bore home at his dying father's wish, a watch engraved with "Do Not Forget." What it is that should be remembered remains to be discovered, and will be discovered, for although Mrs Clennam is an invalid confined to her room, those who are coming to meet her *will* come:

> Strange, if the little sick-room fire were in effect a beacon fire, summoning some one, and that the most unlikely some one in the world, to the spot that *must* be come to. Strange, if the little sick-room light were in effect a watch-light, burning in that place every night until an appointed event should be watched out! Which of the vast multitude of travellers, under the sun and the stars ... journeying by land and journeying by sea, coming and going so strangely, to meet and to react on one another; which of the host may, with no suspicion of the journey's end, be travelling surely hither?

> (p. 221)

Time will tell.

Time in this novel is nothing but the medium through which is revealed a truth already known, a circling around in the end to the beginning. For all the suspense of the mystery, the novel is designed above all to display ethical truths which are timeless, to reveal the pattern, the structure which subtends the surface of the social world and alone makes it meaningful. When Rigaud shows up at the end of the novel and forces Mrs Clennam to reveal the "ravishing little family history" of the Clennam household, the climax simply confirms the overall design which has been in place since the very beginning. The story may, indeed must, move through time, but only to show the elemental distinctions of a totalizing structure.

In fact, melodrama is mythologizing. That is, like "mythic thought" the melodramatic imagination "always progresses from awareness of oppositions towards their resolution."[25] Lévi-Strauss has analysed how myths formalize conflicts, creating a closed system of binary differences; melodrama does the same, exaggerating, intensifying, and polarizing oppositions. This Dickens does from the first in *Little Dorrit*. The novel as a whole is divided into two books, "Poverty" and "Riches," and we soon understand that these terms have to do with spiritual, not material wealth, with the purity or corruption of one's soul. Dickens insists on this moral dimension by inscribing it in nature itself. The opening paragraphs of the novel describe Marseilles as it "lay burning in the sun, one day":

> There was no wind to make a ripple on the foul water within the harbour, or on the beautiful sea without. The line of demarcation between the two colours, black and blue, showed the point which the pure sea would not pass; but it lay as quiet as the abominable pool, with which it never mixed.
>
> (p. 39)

This chapter, "Sun and Shadow," incessantly repeats the opposition of pure/impure, as the narration proceeds from the harbor to "a villainous prison" in the city:

> A prison taint was on everything there. The imprisoned air, the imprisoned light, the imprisoned damps, the imprisoned men [two of them], were all deteriorated by confinement. As the captive men were faded and haggard, so the iron was rusty, the stone was slimy, the wood was rotten, the air was faint, the light was dim. Like a well, like a vault, like a tomb, the prison had no knowledge of the brightness outside, and would have kept its polluted atmosphere intact in one of the spice islands of the Indian ocean.
>
> (pp. 40–1)

Light/dark, inside/outside, whole/corrupt, free/imprisoned – the text is saturated with these oppositions from the opening pages. The prisoners are the lively Signor John Baptist Caveletto and Monsieur Rigaud, the mustachioed villain: good/evil. The articulation of ethical difference by way of gender is not missing, either, for the prison-keeper appears with his little daughter, 3 or 4 years old. "The fair little face, touched with divine compassion, as it peeped shrinkingly through the grate, was like an angel's in the prison" (p. 43).

This fair little angel in the prison is, of course, repeated in Little Dorrit, as the Marseilles prison is repeated in the quarantine which detains the British travelers, in the Marshalsea, in Mrs Clennam's existence "in prison and in bonds," in Mr Merdle's unconscious habit of taking himself into custody by the wrists, "as if he were his own Police officer," in the endless rounds of the Circumlocution office, and so on and on. Indeed, the whole of the novel could be considered a repetition of oppositions which are already rhetorically repeated in the first chapter. Again Lévi-Strauss's analysis of myth is pertinent. "The question has often been raised why myths ... are so much addicted to duplication, triplication, or quadruplication of the same sequence. The function of repetition is to render the structure of the myth evident."[26] Therefore, he continues, the diachronic sequences of a myth "should be read synchronically," for only such a reading will adequately grasp the structure which the repetition is designed to bring to the fore.

Reading *Little Dorrit* one can hardly fail to recognize how the text repeats the oppositions so insistently set up in the first scene. Every instance is an outward and visible sign of moral failure, the concrete realization of an abstract, ethical state. In this Dickens is a master melodramatist, for melodrama is, as its critics have long recognized, a combination of realism and romance, "the effort being to achieve as realistic and spectacular a rendering of the romantic and melodramatic as possible."[27] In *Little Dorrit*, as in Dickens's novels in general, it is impossible to separate the proliferating realistic details of his scenes from the insistent exaggeration characteristic of melodrama, for, in fact, the details are melodramatic in their repetitious generation.[28] All phenomena are saturated with significance and work to realize, to make visible the oppositional structure which *is* the text.

This is evident throughout the book, even self-evident, making any explication rather redundant – which is the point of melodrama. Ethical truth is acted out, realized before one's very eyes. But to press my point, let me recall the scene of Clennam's return to London in chapter 3, entitled "Home." The first chapter was set in the Marseilles prison; the second in the Marseilles quarantine. Now we follow the protagonist as he returns home to a London which is "gloomy, close, and stale." It is Sunday evening. "In every thoroughfare, up almost every alley, and down almost every turning, some doleful bell was throbbing, jerking, tolling, as if the Plague were in the city and the dead-carts were going round." It is raining, which in the country would be refreshing and pleasant; "[i]n the city it developed only foul stale smells, and was a sickly, lukewarm, dirt-stained, wretched addition to the gutters." Going down an alley where "a wretched little bill, FOUND DROWNED, was weeping on the wet wall," Clennam comes home. The house he had sought is "so dingy as to be all but black," surrounded by rank grass and enclosed by rusty rails, and leaning to the side "on some half-dozen gigantic crutches ... weather-stained, smoke-blackened, and overgrown with weeds." He enters the house, and goes up to see his mother, finding her "on a black bier-like sofa ..., propped up behind with one great angular black bolster like the block at a state execution." Mrs Clennam, dressed in black, a woman of adamantine hardness, is paralyzed, in prison, and in bonds, as she puts it. This is Arthur's home; this is his mother (pp. 67–73).

Every detail of this scene, from the weeping bill to the crutches supporting the house, from the foul smells and dissonant sounds of the city to Arthur's funereal home, suggest a corruption at the heart of things. Arthur suspects something is wrong, that "in grasping at money and driving hard bargains" the Clennam house of business has incurred some debt, has committed some trespass that must be admitted and redressed. Of course he is right, but the debt has nothing to do with business; the debt is more moral than financial, and is revealed only at the climax of the novel when the blackmailing villain Rigaud begins to tell "[a] history of a strange marriage, and a strange mother, and a revenge, and a suppression" (p. 840). We then learn, from Mrs Clennam's own lips, that she is " 'Not Arthur's mother!'," a revelation perfectly consistent with the ethical economy of the book. For there is nothing maternal about her, nothing at all. She won't even remove to "a private dwelling" as Arthur urges when he returns to London, but insists on living in the house which is "a place of business," a house which can never be a home. Indeed, the lack of a mother and lack of a home are the absences which structure the whole text, are the origin of the disease and corruption which recur throughout the novel. And, in proper melodramatic fashion, these absences are repeated over and over in the course of the narrative.

No matter where the scene is set, the narrator describes a world which is fundamentally uncivilized. That the wealthiest parts of London are just as wild and barbaric as the poor, is evident in Dickens's description of the Park Lane neighborhood where the fabulously wealthy Merdles live. First of all, there is the Merdle name, which turns money into filth. Second, there is the setting:

> Wildernesses of corner houses, with barbarous old porticoes and appurtenances; horrors that came into existence under some wrong-headed person in some wrong-headed time, still demanding the blind admiration of all ensuing generations and determined to do so until they tumbled down, frowned upon the twilight. Parasite little tenements with the cramp in their whole frame ... made the

evening doleful. Rickety dwellings of undoubted fashion . . . looked like the last result of the great mansion's breeding in-and-in, and . . . seemed to be scrofulously resting upon crutches.

(p. 373)

These houses are not homes any more than Mrs Clennam's doleful house of business, and are equally empty of any woman with a heart, any maternal influence. Mr Merdle's mansion houses Mrs Merdle, The Bosom; "Mr Merdle wanted something to hang jewels upon, and he bought it for the purpose. Storr and Mortimer might have married on the same speculation" (p. 293). And Mr Merdle, who is later revealed as the origin of a "moral infection," a "Plague" of speculation which ruins thousands, is never at home, never at ease or at rest even within the walls of his house. "Let Mrs Merdle announce, with all her might, that she was at Home ever so many nights in a season, she could not announce more widely and unmistakably than Mr Merdle did that he was never at home" (p. 449).

Indeed, no one in this novel is at home. Little Dorrit, the heroine, was born in the Marshalsea debtor's prison, and has lived there with her brother, her sister, and her father all her life. Clennam, who wishes to aid and protect her, sensing that she may have something to do with the debt his family owes, is pained that she acknowledges the prison as home. " 'Don't call it home, my child!' he entreated. 'It is always painful to me to hear you call it home.' " Yet Little Dorrit has no other, as she says. " 'But it is home! What else can I call home? Why should I ever forget it for a single moment?' " Poor Little Dorrit! Not only is her mother dead, but her father has assumed an imaginary dignity as the Father of the Marshalsea on the strength of his long imprisonment, and, as the narrator comments, "a man so broken as to be the Father of the Marshalsea could be no father to his own children" (p. 112). He is "a captive with the jail-rot on him, and the impurity of his prison worn into his soul . . ." (p. 273).

The significance of home, or the lack of one, also explains the character of Miss Wade, a singularly unpleasant and perverse woman, who seems in many ways extraneous to the novel even though Dickens makes her a crucial element in the plot. She is given important functions simply to stress the evils which come of having no mother. As Pancks says,

"She is somebody's child – anybody's – nobody's. Put her in a room in London here with any six people old enough to be her parents, and her parents may be there for all she knows. She knows nothing about 'em. She knows nothing about any relative whatever. Never did. Never will."

(p. 595)

This accounts for her ostentatious solitude, her "unsubduable nature," and the "wasted look" that mars her beauty; melodrama requires no more complex motivation. Parentless, she is also homeless, moving about from place to place, unsettled in everything but her bitterness and ill will. Her perversity is repeated in Tattycorum, the young woman Mr and Mrs Meagles took in from an orphanage. Quick to anger, quick to harbor resentment, this distempered girl is like Miss Wade. The older woman has an evil influence over her, even stepping in as a kind of surrogate mother and luring Tattycorum away from her home, with the most unhappy consequences, as the poor girl comes to realize:

"I was afraid of her from the first time I saw her. I knew she had got a power over me through understanding what was bad in me so well. It was a madness in me and she could raise it whenever she liked."

(p. 880)

Thus the fundamental structure of the text is repeated again and again, is asserted at every point, and absence is written large. The presumably civilized world of London is no better than a howling wilderness, no more homely than the Arctic wastes where Wardour contends with his bad passions in *The Frozen Deep*. Indeed, the English are no better than savages, worshipping Merdle for his money, bowing down before that idol. As the narrator says, they "prostrated themselves before him, more degradedly and less excusably than the darkest savage creeps out of his hole in the ground to propitiate, in some log or reptile, the Deity of his benighted soul" (p. 611). This is strong indeed, for, as we have seen in Dickens's *Household Words* essay on the lost Arctic voyagers, he "knows" that savages are "covetous, treacherous and cruel," "uncivilised people" with repulsive domestic arrangements. Yet Dickens gives us reason to hope, just as Collins does in his play, for the repetition of absence in the novel also repeatedly calls up its opposite, presence; the text painfully, but pleasurably, promises that absence will be overcome. Remember the "fair little face, touched with divine compassion ... [which] was like an angel's in the prison"? She is a promise of things to come.

Little Dorrit, the title character of the novel, repeats and fulfills that promise. "[T]he least, the quietest, the weakest of Heaven's creatures," she is fully angelic. The narrator, and therefore the audience, recognize her virtues, her self-sacrificing loving kindness, her care for her family, her humility, her unshakable attachments. In short, we recognize in her the maternal presence everywhere else absent in the text. Yet no character in the novel sees her as completely as we do. Her family, for instance, hardly acknowledges her virtue at all, as Clennam knows:

> It was not that they stinted her praises, or were insensible to what she did for them; but that they were lazily habituated to her, as they were to all the rest of their condition. . . . He fancied that they viewed her not as having risen away from the prison atmosphere, but appertaining to it; as being vaguely what they had a right to expect, and nothing more.
>
> (p. 134)

And Clennam, though he sees more than Little Dorrit's father, sister, and brother, is none the less blind to her in a very crucial way. For Little Dorrit falls in love with him, and recognizes in him what he refuses to acknowledge in himself, his capacity for love, his longing to marry, to have a home. But poor Little Dorrit! Clennam has no idea.

> He never thought that she saw in him what no one else could see. He never thought that in the whole world there were no other eyes that looked upon him with the same light and strength as hers. . . . O! If he had known, if he had known!

But he doesn't know, and he unwittingly tells her just what she can hardly bear to hear: that he has loved another and lost, and now will love no more. "If he could have seen the dagger in his hand, and the cruel wounds it struck in the faithful bleeding breast of his Little Dorrit!" (p. 432–3).

If only, if only: this is the classic melodramatic fix, which suggests both the pain of non-coincidence, the discrepancy between desire and satisfaction which gives melodrama its characteristic pathos, and the pleasure of hope, the possibility that happiness, union, completeness is within grasp – if only! Franco Moretti has argued in an analysis of "moving" literature that the structure of "if only" suggests the irreversibility of time, and the impossibility of human intervention in a time which is past. Our tears come, he says, when we recognize "that it is clear how the present state of things should be changed – and that this change is impossible."[29] It is always too late. However, others have pointed out that "if only" is not only negative, for it also holds out the possibility of overcoming the pathetic discrepancy, closing the gap, becoming one with the object of desire. If we cry, it is because we have no power as spectators actually to intervene, even though we know more than the characters. But this crying is pleasurable because we can *imagine* satisfaction, even if the narrative withholds it from us.[30]

Little Dorrit certainly delays final satisfaction; Book the First has thirty-six chapters, and Book the Second thirty-four, after all. None the less, the text offers us the painful pleasures of melodrama from beginning to end, most strikingly in a tableau which is repeated several times in the course of the novel. Each time it appears it promises redemption from the evils of separation. Its elements are established in the opening scene in the dungeon of the Marseilles prison when the fair young daughter of the prison-keeper comes like an angel and reaches through the bars to feed Rigaud and Caveletto who are languishing in the dungeon. Later in the novel the scene is repeated and amplified in Mr Dorrit's room in the Marshalsea, for there Little Dorrit comes every evening to prepare her father's supper. She makes his shabby room a home, cooking, cleaning, and sewing, nourishing him body and soul. That we should see clearly not only the facts of the matter, but what those facts stand for, Dickens writes a scene that fixes Little Dorrit and her father in relation to one another, stopping the action to show him degraded, needy, degenerate and her loving, faithful, nurturing. As he is eating the supper she has prepared for him – her own food, which she forgoes so that he can eat – he has one of his bursts of degenerate self-pity. It is her office to embrace him, to soothe him, and, when he is quiet, she "prepared the remains of his supper afresh, and, sitting by his side, rejoiced to see him eat and drink" (p. 274). This is, as the narrator is at pains to tell us, "a serious picture . . . in the obscure gallery of the Marshalsea," a picture the narrator glosses with a reference to *Caritas Romana*, the much-painted and dramatized scene of a Roman daughter who saved her imprisoned and starving father by nursing him at her own breast. As the narrator says,

There was a classical daughter once – perhaps – who ministered to her father in his prison as her mother had ministered to her. Little Dorrit, though of the unheroic modern stock and mere

English, did much more, in comforting her father's wasted heart upon her innocent breast, and turning to it a fountain of love and fidelity that never ran dry or waned throughout all his years of famine.

(p. 274)

Martin Meisel has argued in his study of Victorian art that the picture of "Roman Charity" offered Dickens "an image of sublime symbiosis, of paradoxical physical inversion but moral and spiritual release from the debt of time."[31] Stopping the action of the narrative, Dickens stresses this release, the release which comes with the full presence of the maternal, the recovery of unconditional, unending love.

Of course, Little Dorrit as the realization of the maternal presence is fully idealized, fully spiritualized, the angel of the house. This is crucial, for the extremities of incarceration could lead not to salvation through the transcending of "nature," but to the barbarity of cannibalism, a collapse into nature in which the stronger feed off the weaker. Meisel has pointed out that Dante's account of Count Ugolino's imprisonment in the Tower of Famine with his children (he was tempted to eat his sons) held a fascination for the Victorians, as did the subject of cannibalism in general, for it establishes the limit of civilization. Dickens's investment in the subject is clear in his defense of Sir John and the men of his Arctic expedition, and is no less evident, though in a sublimated form, in the novel he was writing at the same time. For in *Little Dorrit* that which could be the ultimate horror – Mr Dorrit does, after all, feed off his daughter – is transformed into a saving grace, the maternal presence which guarantees social life, which is at the beginning and the end of history.

The "picture" in the Marshalsea is presented to us, then, and interpreted by the narrator in a way that allows the audience fully to recognize the heroine's virtue, to know that she *is* full presence, but to know, too, that no one else knows, not her father, nor her sister, nor her brother, nor Clennam. Only Young John Chivery, the turnkey's son, has an impossible, chivalric love for Little Dorrit, fulfilling the melodramatic convention of comic commentary (*he* recognizes her virtue) and comic relief. If only! if only Clennam would see how she is the one for him, the presence that has always been lacking in his life, daughter–mother–wife. This revelation is delayed until Arthur himself is jailed for debt, held in the Marshalsea in the same little room where Little Dorrit's father wasted away so many years. Then, "light of head with want of sleep and want of food," Clennam sees Little Dorrit. She seems like a vision, but he can read in her face

> as in a mirror, how changed he was ... and with her knees upon the floor at his feet, and with her lips raised up to kiss him, and with her tears dropping down upon him as the rain from Heaven had dropped upon the flowers, Little Dorrit, a living presence, called him by his name.

The scene repeats the earlier picture, the melodramatic tableau which freezes the actors in symbolic relation to each other. There Little Dorrit was a mother to her father; here she is a mother to Clennam:

> drawing an arm softly round his neck, [she] laid his head upon her bosom, put a hand upon his head, and resting her cheek upon that hand, nursed him as lovingly, and GOD knows as innocently, as she had nursed her father in that room when she had been but a baby ...

> (p. 825)

She has come back to the old room, in her old dress, a living presence who transcends time, who returns Clennam to himself and makes of him a proper man. She reads to him, and he hears in her voice

> all that great Nature was doing, heard in it all the soothing songs she sings to man. At no Mother's knee but hers had he ever dwelt in his youth on hopeful promises ... in the tones of the voice that read to him, there were memories of an old feeling of such things. ...

> (p. 884)

Motherless except for Mother Nature, Clennam has been in need of the living presence of the maternal to make him truly a man, a manly man with a heart and a soul and a will to live and work. He begins the book confessing that he "has no will," and is now free to address himself to the business of life, to share with his wife "a modest life of usefulness and happiness."

Before the constructed absence of the maternal can become a living presence, however, Clennam must learn to see what he's missing, must learn, in short, what the reader has known all along: that everything refers to Little Dorrit. "Little Dorrit, Little Dorrit. Again, for hours. Always Little Dorrit." Finally Clennam's point of view is merging with the narrator's and with the reader's:

> Looking back upon his own poor story, she was its vanishing-point. Every thing in its perspective led to her innocent figure. He had travelled thousands of miles towards it; previous unquiet hopes and doubts had worked themselves out before it; it was the centre of the interest of his life; it was the termination of everything that was good and pleasant in it; beyond there was nothing but mere waste and darkened sky.
>
> (p. 801–2)

No where does this melodramatic text display more clearly the contradictions of domestic ideology, an ideology which posits that women must be absent in order to be present; must be the center of interest of a man's life and of his story but must in the process disappear into infinity. This vanishing-point, then, brings all the plot lines of the novel into relation with one another, makes possible a sense of perspective, of progress, of space, and of time, but does this by fixing all the elements of the text in a totalizing design. The many roads which are travelled by the many characters all disappear into the timeless, infinite vanishing-point of the maternal. All contradiction vanishes there, too.

A VERY SACRED BUSINESS

This resolution confirms the mythologizing effects of melodrama since, as Lévi-Strauss has made clear, "the purpose of myth is to provide a logical model capable of overcoming a contradiction (an impossible achievement if, as it happens, the contradiction is real)...."[32] This impossibility is the melodramatic fix, since melodrama produces a resolution which is not a resolution, which generates further repetitions of melodramatic logic. Just as myths repeat the same sequence to emphasize their structural logic, and just as a myth is repeated with variations "until the intellectual impulse which has produced it is exhausted," melodrama produces the same nostalgic fix over and over. To say that melodrama cannot overcome real contradictions is not, however, to say that its effects are not real. Dickens has been characterized by some as a hopeless sentimentalist whose ideological commitments keep him from engaging with the real conflicts, the real political and economic struggles of his time, and the resolution of *Little Dorrit* would certainly seem to support this view. But the melodramatic fantasy is fully political and really productive; it helps to produce particular desires, it helps to order social life according to the logic of separate spheres, it transforms bourgeois culture into universal nature.[33] Those are material effects, for the social relations of the middle class and the social policies they promulgate repeat this melodramatic order.

The achievement of melodrama is thus very real indeed, for it helps to produce not only the Victorian middle-class family, its structure and its practices, but also other institutions dedicated to the formation of the properly socialized individual. The "instauration of ethics" which Brooks sees as simply an inevitable modern development compensating for the disappearance of God is in fact the institutionalizing of a modern form of power. In this sense Dickens is fully engaged with politics, not in spite of, but because of the sentimentalism and melodrama of his writing. This engagement is perhaps most evident in the pages of *Household Words* in articles which discuss the social issues of the 1850s: sanitation, education, housing, poverty, crime, prostitution, poor-relief and forms of private charity, and so on. The key distinction of Victorian middle-class reformers between the "deserving" and the "undeserving" poor is at work in these articles, a categorization that depends on domestic ideology: the deserving poor are men who are trying to provide for their families, women trying to provide for their children, children whose future depends on the success or failure of their parents in these efforts. The undeserving poor are parents who ignore or exploit their children, who are lazy and deceitful, criminal in intent and act, heartless and beyond reform. The deserving poor are members of families that are distorted by external pressures sometimes exerted by the very institutions intended to safeguard social life; the undeserving poor threaten all social institutions, including the family.

In his novel, Dickens characterizes the residents of Bleeding Heart Yard as the deserving poor, and makes Mr Plornish, an unemployed plasterer, their spokesman. His family is "uncommon hard up," as Mr Plornish puts it, and he goes on to say,

> There was people of pretty well all sorts of trades you could name, all wanting to work, and yet not able to get it. There was old people, after working all their lives, going and being shut up in the workhouse. . . . Why, a man didn't know where to turn himself for a crumb of comfort.

(p. 184)

In fact, Mr Plornish's own father-in-law is one of the old people locked up in the workhouse; Mr Nandy is separated from his daughter and her family because they cannot afford to keep him. It is the poor in this character that Dickens contrasts with begging-letter writers in a scathing article in *Household Words*. He despises the "set of lazy vagabonds" (who lived off charity gained under false pretenses) for criminally manipulating the sympathy properly evoked for the deserving poor:

> many who sought to do some little to repair the social wrongs inflicted in the way of preventable sickness and death upon the poor, were strengthening those wrongs, however innocently, by wasting money on pestilent knaves cumbering society ... what will not content a Begging-letter Writer for a week, would educate a score of children for a year.... [L]et us give and do, with a high purpose; not to endow the scum of the earth to its own greater corruption, with the offals of our duty.[34]

It is to protect the deserving from the undeserving, and the home (whether poor or rich) from those who have no home and wish for none, that Dickens inveighs against the begging-letter writers.

He is equally harsh in his judgment of the men and boys sleeping in a low-life lodging house, the "Rat's Castle," which he enters in the company of Inspector Fields of the Metropolitan Police. Celebrating the inspector's "individual energy and keenness" and the "organised and steady system" of the police, Dickens praises their power to control wholly undomesticated men:

> Halloa here! Come! let us see you! Shew your face! Pilot Parker goes from bed to bed and turns their slumbering heads towards us, as a salesman might turn a sheep. Some wake up with an execration and a threat – What! who spoke? O! If it's the accursed glaring light that fixes me, go where I will, I am helpless.

So Dickens proceeds with the inspector "through a labyrinth of airless rooms, each man responding like a wild beast, to the keeper who has tamed him, and who goes into his cage."[35] Those who have not been properly socialized, who are wild and savage, who are thus a threat to society can none the less be controlled, fixed, and rendered helpless by the police.

Yet, as Dickens argues in another article on "The Metropolitan Protectives," this sort of policing is not enough:

> Excellent method, carefully administered, vigilant in all respects

except this main one: – prevention of ignorance, remedy for unnatural neglect of children, punishment of wicked parents, interposition of the State, as a measure of human policy, if not of human pity and accountability, at the very source of crime.[36]

The family is the origin of social life and its end; society must therefore institutionalize the family to ensure that every individual will be socialized. Thus Dickens supports Ragged Schools and Pauper Schools and Industrial Schools, all of which have "humanizing influences." When on duty with the Metropolitan Protectives, he observed a poor woman and her child come into the police station to ask for relief. She was admitted to the workhouse; her child was taken from her, as stipulated by the Poor Laws. "The wretched urchin parts from his mother without a look," Dickens reports, "and trots away with the constable. There would be no very strong ties to break here if the constable were taking him to an industrial school." Indeed, an article on "London Pauper Children" published in *Household Words* describes the institution where some small number of such children are sent when their parents claim relief:

> The Pauper School at Norwood ... may be called a factory for making harmless, if not useful subjects of the very worst of human material – a place for converting those who would otherwise certainly be miserable, and most likely vicious, into rational, reasonable, and often very useful members of society; – in short, a house for training a large and wretched class in habits of decency, regularity, and order, and leading a pitiable section of the great two-million-strong family of London from the road to crime into that of honest industry and self-respect.[37]

This house, in short, is the home every individual requires.

Thus, when necessary, the state must interpose itself between an "unfit" mother and her innocent child, must, in fact, assume the maternal function, an intervention made both possible and necessary by the fact that society is but an extension of the family. Conversely, decent, regular, and orderly families must be protected against incursions from the public world, from institutional pressures like the Poor Law which legislates the break-up of the Plornish family by requiring that Mr Nandy be incarcerated in the poorhouse, since to claim relief is to be offered the House – which in this case is distinctly *not* a home.[38] Either way, everyone, particularly every child, must be guaranteed a proper home which will be the source of all the social virtues. "[S]uch a cause as this must be approached, worked in, and carried out in a far higher spirit than that in which most of what is called 'reform' is undertaken," we learn from *Household Words*. "It is a very sacred business, this!"[39]

Indeed it is, for it makes the home both paradise lost and paradise regained; it is the means for converting savages, for humanizing otherwise perishing and dangerous souls. Further, this business of reform *creates* the very souls it saves, for to be saved is to have a soul – or a heart. Both the middle class and "the poor" are sanctified by this work, confirmed in an individuality which is separate from yet inseparably attached to society. Reform is a business – as the Norwood Pauper School is a factory – which works up individuals and works on them so that they have the right desires and the right discipline to be social subjects.

*

A reviewer for *Bentley's* magazine said of Dickens that "his greatest triumph is to take the world captive in spite of [his] accumulated heresies against nature and against art."[40] These "heresies" are, of course, the sentimentalism and melodrama of Dickens's writing and are, in fact, not heretical at all. They are the means by which he conducts the orthodox business of reform, as Dickens knows. He reports in a letter to Wilkie Collins,

> I made a speech last night [at the first anniversary dinner for the Royal Hospital for Incurables], at the end of which all the company sat holding their napkins to their eyes with one hand, and putting the other into their pockets. A hundred people or so contributed £900 then and there![41]

Yet Dickens is not fully in control of this business, regardless of his boast to Collins. Or, perhaps it would be better to say that because of this boast and many others of a similar sort, we can see how Dickens is too deeply invested in the business of sentiment ever to get out.

Dickens could captivate nearly any audience, and throughout his career he relished this power. "It's a great sensation to have an audience in one's hand," he wrote to Miss Coutts about his triumph as Wardour.[42] Indeed, so great was the thrill that he went public with *The Frozen Deep* at the first opportunity, performing this originally private play as a charitable enterprise to raise money for the family of his friend Douglas Jerrold, who had died unexpectedly. And the degree to which Dickens desired the sensation of holding an audience in his hand became increasingly evident after *The Frozen Deep* was a thing of the past. *Little Dorrit* was finished, too, so he went off on a walking tour of the lake country with Collins, but he was still restless. Then he was on stage again, this time reading *A Christmas Carol* in a benefit performance for the Child's Hospital. What began as charity soon became a second career. For the rest of his life he toured Britain and America – he even contemplated going to Australia – performing in front of hundreds of audiences, year after year. And they couldn't resist him. Whether he was reading the pathetic scene of little Paul Dombey's death (at which men cried openly, "certainly more than the women"), or the horrific murder of Nancy by Sikes (which more than once set off "a contagion of fainting"), Dickens, being a master melodramatist, could do with his audience what he would.[43]

That he was in a sense equally mastered *by* the sensation of performing as his audiences were by the performance is only right, given that "he wanted what the people wanted." Dickens wore himself out traveling, reading night after night to sustain his relationship with the public. He would, for the moment, become one with the house, as when he read in Belfast. After the pathos of the death scene from *Dombey and Son*, Dickens read some comic selections: "As to the Boots at night and Mrs Gamp too, it was just one roar with me and them, for they made me laugh so that sometimes I could not compose my face to go on."[44] But the union, and the thrill, was over when he walked off stage, and therefore had to be repeated again and again.

As an author and performer, then, Dickens acted out the drama of middle-class subjectivity, was taken captive by its rigors and its impossibilities. Always longing for something he didn't have, he separated from his wife of twenty years to be with an actress who had played in *The Frozen Deep*, yet was of course unable to attain the perfect union he realizes so fully in *Little Dorrit*; he celebrated perfect domesticity while driven away from home, on to the stage, out into the streets of London where he would obsessively walk hour after hour. Indeed, Dickens's famous energy and restlessness and enormous productivity, the qualities which have marked him as quintessentially "Victorian," are evidence of the power of the melodramatic fix to structure desires around an absence and the fantasy of presence, to keep one always at it. Thus Dickens writes to Forster in 1856,

However strange it is to be never at rest, and never satisfied, and ever trying after something that is never reached, and to be always laden with plot and plan and care and worry, how clear it is that it must be, and that one is driven by an irresistible might until the journey is worked out! ... As to repose – for some men there's no such thing in life. ... I find that the skeleton in my domestic closet is becoming a pretty big one.[45]

Dickens can articulate his culture's fantasy of satisfaction, directing Clennam's journey so that it ends in the living presence of Little Dorrit. But the point is really to construct a desire that cannot be satisfied, that will keep men always "in harness," as Dickens says, always at work, and women always in the home.

THE HISTORY OF THE PEOPLE

In *Little Dorrit*, then, and in *Household Words* and his correspondence, Dickens represents the social in profoundly nostalgic terms, creating a melodramatic, mythological system in which "history" is a matter of loss and gain, of absence and presence, as in the history of the Clennam household which organizes the multiple plots of the novel. Yet, as we have seen, Dickens has been read as a social historian of sorts, a novelist whose work is related to both the emergent social sciences and to history as the newly acknowledged ground of social life. In fact, the melodramatic fix, which depends on the constructed absence of the maternal, is an exaggerated and intensified version of the nineteenth-century fix on history, which constructs the past as the ever receding ground of the present. Melodrama, then, is in Victorian England much more than a set of literary conventions; it is a way of construing "society" and "history" that consolidates the middle class, its identity and its values.

The range of melodrama is suggested by a comparison of Dickens's writing with the series of articles on "labour and the poor" which Henry Mayhew wrote for the *Morning Chronicle* newspaper. Dickens and Mayhew are often paired, Mayhew's non-fictional writing being taken as the historical proof of Dickens's novelistic representations of the urban poor. In such readings, Dickens is said to achieve a heightened, generalized symbolic representation, while Mayhew, as a "systematic empirical investigator," is thought to produce work that is unmarked by melodrama, that records the historical truth of life in the East End of London.[46] Yet Mayhew's work, while usually

not very melodramatic in form, is none the less inescapably melodramatic in its conception. How could it be otherwise when his
subject is the lower classes in London, the people whose lives are so
far from the middle-class ideal, yet who live in families and are "like
us"? It is this poignant resemblance which Thackeray responds to in
Mayhew's "Letters." Writing in *Punch* as Mayhew was publishing
in the *Chronicle*, he declares,

> What a confession it is that we have all of us been obliged to make!
> A clever and earnest-minded writer gets a commission from the
> *Morning Chronicle* newspaper, and reports upon the state of our
> poor in London: he goes amongst labouring people and poor of
> all kinds – and brings back what? A picture of human life so
> wonderful, so awful, so piteous and pathetic, so exciting and
> terrible, that readers of romances own they never read anything
> like to it....[47]

Mayhew claimed that his survey was "the first real History of the
People that has ever been attempted in any country whatsoever," but
Thackeray reads it as romance. Indeed, he even sees a melodramatic
tableau, a sensational and sentimental "picture of human life" that
reveals the hidden humanity of "our poor."

When Mayhew most assiduously frames and composes his letters
he does produce a wonderful, awful, piteous, exciting, and terrible
picture of human life. Such conventionally melodramatic tableaux,
though more the exception than the rule in the *Morning Chronicle*
series, suggest when they do appear how Mayhew was drawn to the
devices of melodrama to represent (and contain) the poverty and
destitution he witnessed. A particularly compelling instance is part
of his letter of 4 December 1849. While working on the history of
the street-sellers of various goods, Mayhew has come to a new
"class" of workers, "the hucksters of tape and cotton." He says these
"are usually elderly females," and proceeds to give an account of a
woman who has been nine years in the trade. He begins

> I was given to understand that the woman was in deep distress,
> and that she had long been supporting a sick husband by her little
> trade; but I was wholly unprepared for a scene of such startling
> misery, sublimed by untiring affection and pious resignation, as I
> there discovered.[48]

Mayhew provides a sentimental moral frame for his interview with
the old woman and her dying husband, his commentary highlighting

the extremes of the sight before him. Directed to their apartment, "'the two-pair back,'" he opens the door only to be "terrified by the misery before me." An old man lies "in almost the last extremity of weakness" on a "wretched bed," being spoon-fed warm sugar and water flavored with cinnamon (all they could afford) by his elderly and crippled wife.

What particularly distinguishes this scene of misery from hundreds of other instances of destitution in the letters is its pure *domesticity*. That is what Mayhew remarks, that is what the interview emphasizes:

> "We have lived like children together," said the old woman, as her eyes flooded with tears; "never had no dispute.... After I put my hip out, I couldn't get my living as I'd been used to do.... So I got a little stall, and sat at the end of the alley here, with a few laces and tapes and things.... He's been an ailing man these many years. He used to go on errands for me, buy my little things for me, on account of my being lame.... My husband would have the kettle always boiling for me against I'd come in. He used to sit here, reading his book ... he was so sober and quiet...."

She continues in this way until her husband speaks up.

> "She's been stopping by me, minding me here night and day ...," mumbled the old man, who now for the first time opened his grey glassy eyes, and turned towards me to bear, as it were, a last tribute to his wife's incessant affection. "She has been most kind to me. Her tenderness and care has been such that man never knew from woman before.... I've made up my mind that I must soon change this tabernacle; and my last wish is that the good people of the world will increase her little stock for her.... If the kind hearts would give her but a little stock more, it would keep her old age from want, as she has kept mine. Indeed, indeed, she does deserve it. But the Lord, I know, will reward her for all she has done to me."
>
> (vol. 2, pp. 45–47)

Mayhew knows just how to resolve this death-bed scene, saying simply,

> I told the kind-hearted old dame that some benevolent people had placed certain funds at my disposal for the relief of such distress as hers; and I assured her that neither she nor her husband should want for anything that might ease their sufferings.
>
> (vol. 2, p. 48)

Thus the picture of pious domesticity, fully realized in the words of the old woman and her dying husband, is framed by the benevolent middle-class investigator who recognizes and rewards virtue when he sees it. These are "our poor"; like "us," they are deserving by virtue of their homeliness. "Found!" we say, quickly followed by "if only!," for if only the "kind hearts" had known sooner, maybe the old man wouldn't have to die. " 'If God takes him, I know he'll sleep in Heaven. I know the life he's spent, and I'm not afraid; but no one else shall [take] him from me – nothing shall part us but death in this world.' " He will get his reward in Heaven, as will she, but, as an angel in the house, the old woman will also be rewarded on earth – "neither she nor her husband should want for anything that might ease their sufferings." This letter is indeed a wonderful and awful, a painful and pleasurable confirmation of an over-arching moral order. Mayhew thus draws on the conventions of melodrama to transform the elderly huckster into The Virtuous Woman and to ensure that the scene will be one of perfect coincidence: all eyes are on her, all attest to her perfect faith and unconditional love. Moved by the scene, we are all members of the family of man.

Although Mayhew is clearly capable, then, of a sensational, sentimental realization of piety and resignation, more often than not the melodrama of his text is at a remove, embedded. His work is marked by melodrama on the conceptual level, and even when he forgoes melodramatic devices his letters are composed so as to produce a sense of unity and coherence among all – "the poor" whose words appear in his pages are men and women just like the readers who regard their histories with fascination. Most notable is the format he developed for his letters: in them he elides the questions he asks of his informants, while recording their words with remarkable precision. The informant then seems to speak directly to the reader. This makes Mayhew's "History" a series of "vivid individual autobiographical histories," as Peter Razzell writes in the introduction to the collected *Morning Chronicle* pieces.[49] "People could identify for the first time with the poor," Razzell declares, "not just as depicted in a novel, but through the words of individuals whose lives were being laid out before the reader." The voice of the investigator disappears into that of the object of the investigation, who thereby becomes its subject. The erasure of Mayhew's questions means that the individual seems to speak directly to the reader. In this way, oral history tends to reinforce a cultural imaginary which takes differences as evidence of coherence and wholeness, for the reader is quick to identify with the speaker.

In an essay titled "Human Values in Oral History" James Bennett makes this perfectly, if uncritically, clear. As he argues, the apparently unmediated character of oral history allows the reader to identify with the speaking subject: when history is recorded in the first person, "the reading I merges with the grammatical I," establishing a "personal contact [which] may be pleasant (even when it is painful)...."[50] Oral histories "give representations of human experience in times and places unfamiliar to a reader," and while that experience may be one of hardship and suffering, the identification is none the less rewarding. Indeed, such an identification is, according to Bennett, a way to overcome the pain of history *per se*: oral histories "[exhibit] our capacity to escape in some way from the captivity and defeat that time and therefore history itself impose on us." Reading Mayhew to hear the "voices of the poor" virtually guarantees that one will see as Thackeray did "a picture of human life" which rivals romance, which is the concrete realization of a transcendent, all-inclusive humanity.[51] As Bennett righteously declares, "Perhaps oral history should be called *moral history*."

To the extent that Mayhew's "History of the People" solicits such identifications it indeed contributes to the melodramatic fix, to the nostalgia for a whole and unalienated humanity. This is true even though many of the letters are not conventionally melodramatic in form, even though Mayhew imagined his work not as melodrama but as science. He thought of his survey in terms of scientific study, saying in 1850,

> I made up my mind to deal with human nature as a natural philosopher or a chemist deals with any material object; and, as a man who had devoted some little of his time to physical and metaphysical science, I must say I did most heartily rejoice that it should have been left to me to apply the laws of the inductive philosophy for the first time, I believe, in the world to the abstract questions of political economy.[52]

Yet the science which he pursued is but the other side of melodrama, and the "objectivity" of this work, his commitment to "inductive philosophy," cannot be separated from the decidedly speculative operations of the melodramatic imagination any more than his oral histories in their compelling specificity can be separated from the universal humanity that specificity evokes.

As must be the case, Mayhew's empiricism and objectivity is the other, complementary side of the transcendental universality of melodrama, and his objective gathering of evidence is controlled by the way his object of study is defined. "The poor," as Thackeray knew, are "our poor," whose destitution is dangerous and threatening to the social health and wholeness of England. Their condition cannot be accounted for according to the received ideas of political economy, so a new science – "social science" – is required, a discipline that will objectively study the society in which all are necessarily included, examining individual men and women in order to arrive at a picture of the whole.[53] Thus, the empiricism which marks Mayhew's work, his "objective" recording of hundreds of interviews, is conceivable only *after* society has been defined as the condition of possibility for the individual, his ground and his limit. That is, social science, seemingly so far from melodrama, actually assumes what melodrama hyperbolically dramatizes, a (feminized) "social" which brings man into being, which is his past, and which must be reformed if he is to have a future. The same imaginary relations which are realized in melodrama are at work in oral history and, more generally, in social science. The example of Mayhew suggests that the melodramatic imagination is a particular inflection of a nineteenth-century historical imagination that manages to discover the unity of man even under the most trying conditions. What is self-evident in all of Dickens's writing is at work in Mayhew, too. Not only does Mayhew's survey confirm in detail Dickens's novelistic representations of the London poor; Mayhew also contributes to the myth of the family of man – not despite his science, but because of it.

However, to stop here would be too easy an assessment of Mayhew's "History," for his work is not simply a social scientific instance of the melodramatic fix. His letters also break, unpredictably and intermittently, yet forcefully, with the unities produced by the melodramatic imagination. While Dickens is singularly consistent in his adherence to melodrama, Mayhew is not, and the difference has to do precisely with Mayhew's aspirations to the scientific. We have seen that the empirical investigation of "society" is by no means conceptually antithetical to melodrama, no matter how different its methods and conventions. None the less, Mayhew's commitment to gathering evidence and his effort objectively to record what "the people" said produce material which overwhelms the definitions with which he begins. In fact, we see in his text a different kind of history:

not a demonstration of the ultimate sameness of all people, but a record of irresolvable conflict and struggle. In some important ways, Mayhew's "History of the People" shows "labour and the poor" to be effects of intersecting but non-congruent systems – the economic system, the gender system, the system of social administration, to name three of the most prominent.

Mayhew's commitment to gathering evidence led him away from his original plan for the survey, a plan based on neat classifications and categories. Indeed, he worried about the "erratic and imme-thodic nature of [his] communications," but defended his procedure on the grounds of necessity:

> [An] unsystematic mode of treating the subject is almost a necess-ary evil attendant upon the nature of the investigation. In the course of my inquiries into the earnings and condition of one class of people, sources of information respecting the habits and incomings of another are opened up to me, of which, for several reasons, I am glad to avail myself at the immediate moment, rather than defer making use of them until a more fitting and orderly occasion.
>
> (vol. 1, p. 248)

In fact, his "inquiries" soon led him to abandon his original classi-fications, which were pure middle-class orthodoxy. In his first letter he proposed dividing his subject into

> two distinct classes, viz., the *honest* and *dishonest* poor; and the first of these I propose sub-dividing into the *striving* and the *disabled* – or in other words, I shall consider the whole of the metropolitan poor under three separate phases, according as they *will* work, they *can't* work, and they *won't* work.
>
> (vol. 1, p. 40)

But these categories soon give way under the pressure of testimony such as this by a handloom weaver who can't survive on the price his cloth will bring:

> "The prices of weaving is so low, that we're ashamed to say what it is, because it's the means of pulling down other poor men's wages and other trades ... it's the competitive system; that's what the Government ought to put a stop to.... The people is a-being

brought to that state of destitution, that many say it's a blessing from the Almighty that takes 'em from the world. They lose all love of country – yes, and all hopes; and they prays to be tortured no longer.... oh, it's a shocking scene! I can't say what I thinks about the young uns. Why you loses your nat'ral affection for 'em ... civil society with us is all at an end. Everybody is becoming brutal – unnatural."

(vol. 1, pp. 61–62)

As he continued his investigation of the many London trades, constructing general histories of wages and conditions of employment from government records and group meetings with the workers themselves, and then conducting as many interviews as he could with individuals, Mayhew's own evidence challenged the categories of "honest" and "dishonest" poor. He began to argue that the wretched condition of so many workers was not the inevitable result of an oversupply of labor in a free market and the dissolute character of the workers, as the political economists of the time argued. Rather, the suffering was the result of "the competitive system" which enabled employers to increase their profits either by reducing wages or by increasing hours, or both. Mayhew became more and more concerned with wages and the social relations of production – the sweating system (whereby workers were paid by the piece, not by the day, and had to go through a middleman to get work) and the strapping system (whereby hours were increased, the shop was strictly supervised, and higher productivity demanded) – until, as Eileen Yeo says, "under the general concept of forced productivity, or what he later called 'economy of labor,' [he] was eventually able to group the seemingly endless variety of patterns for organizing labor which he discovered in the London slop trades."[54]

This emphasis on a system which produces poverty for some and wealth for others is particularly clear in letter VIII, part of Mayhew's investigation of the London "slop" trade, the sewing of ready-made clothes at a piece-rate. In this letter Mayhew turns his attention to poor needlewomen, specifically those who sew the uniforms for the army. By the time he wrote in 1849, the "distressed needlewoman" was a melodramatic icon for the Victorians, the symbol of innocent womanhood doomed to corruption by working for a wage. As is only natural, her wages are very low, for she should be under the care of a husband or father, her earnings only a supplement to the family income. Out of the house and on her own, she is all too likely to turn to prostitution, first as a way to get easy money, and then, as she is increasingly degraded, as a means of gratifying her vanity.[55] The cultural availability and power of this icon is suggested by Dickens's use of it in *Little Dorrit*, for to stress the vulnerability of his heroine, Dickens makes her a seamstress: "Little Dorrit let herself out to do needlework. At so much a day – or at so little – from eight to eight, Little Dorrit was to be hired" (p. 93) But Little Dorrit is in no danger of "falling" – her innate virtue protects her as Dickens makes emphatically clear when she and Maggie (the retarded young woman who calls her "little Mother") have to walk the streets all night. Rough men give way before them, and Little Dorrit is explicitly contrasted to a prostitute, a " 'poor lost creature,' " as she calls herself, who meets them just before dawn (p. 217).

In the beginning of letter VIII it looks as though Mayhew is going to offer a predictably sensational and sentimental view of needlewomen. He opens with a conventional melodramatic claim, worthy of Dickens:

> The facts that I have to set before the public in my present communication are of so awful and tragic a character that I shall not even attempt to comment upon them. The miseries they reveal are so intense and overwhelming that, as with all deep emotions, they are beyond words.

Mayhew thus evokes that which can't be said, which can only be shown in a dramatic tableau. Yet immediately after this opening statement, he turns not to the awful fact of prostitution, but to the history of the manufacture of uniforms. We do not see a tableau of misery, but rather several tables of figures derived from government reports. These show the rates fixed to clothe the men in a regiment, the sums paid to and the profits taken by the colonels of those regiments. Their profits are enormous, for they get the uniforms made for much less than the fixed rate by subcontracting to sweaters in the East End. The reader's attention, then, is directed first to lists of rates and profits, then to another table showing the cost of a suit of clothing for a soldier (including the cap) from 1792 to 1812, and finally to the overall system of production of this clothing before there is any personal testimony from the women who do the work. The melodramatic conventions disappear, giving way to a very different representation of the subject.

Moreover, the personal histories which come after the history of the trade do not represent prostitution as a tragic fall, but as a compelling necessity. The sheer proliferation of specific information about wages, rents, the cost of food and clothing, inescapable indebtedness, pregnancies, child care, the whole daily reproduction of life further distinguishes this letter from the simple verities of conventional middle-class wisdom about this "great social evil," as prostitution was called. First Mayhew interviews a young woman who earns 3s. a week sewing trousers. She supports her widowed mother (who can earn 1s. 6d. a week by scrubbing pots), and pays 1s. a week for rent. Together they spend between 3s. 6d. to 4s. on food and clothing. " 'There isn't one young girl as can get her living by slop work,' " she says.

> "It stands to reason that no one can live, and pay rent, and find clothes, upon 3s. a week ... I've heard of numbers who have gone from slop work to the streets altogether for a living, and I shall be obligated to do the same myself, unless something better turns up for me."

She is pregnant, and says,

> "I know how horrible all this is. It would have been much better for me to have subsisted upon a dry crust and water rather than be as I am now. But no one knows the temptations of us poor girls in want.... If I had been better paid I should have done better."
>
> (vol. 1, p. 161)[56]

Her personal history is repeated, with variations, three more times in the same letter, as Mayhew records three more interviews with slop-workers who " 'have resorted to the streets for money,' " as one puts it. Unlike the repetitions of melodrama which make evident the overriding truth of a (mythological) moral order, the repetitions in letter VIII stress the multiple forces pressing on these women and their strategies for survival. Each woman in turn condemns the competitive system and emphasizes the injuries of class, but that is not all. These interviews also insist on the injuries of gender, since these women are responsible not only for themselves, but for feeding and clothing and caring for their elderly parents and their children, yet their wages are set on the assumption that they are being supported. Further, they suffer from the sexual double standard in losing their "characters" and being forced from respectable shops, and by having sole care for the children born of illegitimate unions. Finally, an intrusive and punitive Poor Law figures in these interviews, showing social administration as yet another force to contend with.

Letter VIII is thus not melodramatic in its effects, even in those sections where Mayhew's commentary is conventionally melodramatic in form. He introduces the last interview by declaring,

> The story which follows is perhaps one of the most tragic and touching romances ever read. I must confess that to myself the mental and bodily agony of the poor Magdalene who related it was quite overpowering.... She told her tale with her face hidden in her hands, and sobbing so loud that it was with difficulty I could catch her words.
>
> (vol. 1, p. 165)

Our tears do not come, however, for despite Mayhew's claim, her history is not a romance and she is no "Magdalene," a fallen woman whose virtue is recognized and who is thereby redeemed. She says a "Christian gentleman" has been her "salvation," giving her a character so that she could go into service and get off the streets, saving her after thirteen years of slop work, of prostitution and destitution, of living in and out of the workhouse. But she was never "fallen," just poor, and that hasn't changed. Her sisters, who make waistcoats, are still starving, and one is "suffering from cancers brought on by poor living." Her son is in the workhouse, her wages are so low that she can't get him out. There is no salvation here, no home prefiguring Heaven, as in the letter about the elderly woman who sold tape and cotton and tended her dying husband. Here the history of the people thwarts identification and breaks the melodramatic fix.

Mayhew's work differs significantly from that of Dickens and other middle-class social reformers. The melodrama of his letters is not sustained; the people he interviews, and even Mayhew himself, speak in terms of "the competitive system" and exploitation, of being worked to death. For E. P. Thompson and Eileen Yeo, Mayhew's work in the *Morning Chronicle* is not only far from sentimental reformism, but close to the analysis of capitalism Marx was developing. As Yeo writes, "like Marx, Mayhew saw exploitation in terms of the appropriation by the capitalist of the surplus value created by the worker."[57] In her marxist reading of Mayhew, the economic system accounts for the culture of poverty his work so compellingly represents. "Mayhew's ability to see poverty in the round, as the product of an economic system, with devastating moral and social consequences and yet varied cultural manifestations, amounted to a unique and short-lived moment in middle-class consciousness," she declares.[58]

Reading Mayhew in these marxist terms is indeed a sharp break with the moralizing logic of "reform" and of the melodramatic fix, and rightly stresses how Mayhew's "History of the People" does much more than show a wonderful, awful, piteous, and pathetic picture of human life, as Thackeray would have it. Yet in seeing the economic system as the motor of history, as a first cause from which everything else follows, Thompson and Yeo must overlook what Mayhew's letters in fact insist upon, the multiple determinants of the "devastating moral and social consequences" there represented. In the narratives which Mayhew records, sexual categorization has its own logic and force, and is more than an effect of capitalism, though economic and sexual exploitation interact. So, too, the Poor Law, the workhouse, and the police function *with* the systematic exploitation of capitalism; to read these institutions as functions *of* the economic system is again to miss the specificity of their forms and their effects, a specificity suggested by the detailed accounts which make up the *Chronicle* letters.

Still, the relation which Thompson and Yeo see between Marx and Mayhew is important, for the break with a middle-class discourse of history is very real. This suggests that a more theoretical marxism, one which takes up the concept of "history" as a theoretical problem, may be more productive. In *The Political Unconscious*, Fredric Jameson declares that "History is what hurts," and surely this is the case in Mayhew's work, where history is nothing if not the struggle to survive. Jameson argues that History is the pressure of a Necessity which will impose itself regardless of our understanding of it. "History is the experience of Necessity," he writes.

> Necessity is not in that sense a type of content, but rather the inexorable *form* of events.... History is what hurts, it is what refuses desire and sets inexorable limits to individual as well as collective praxis.... History as ground and untranscendable horizon needs no particular theoretical justification: we may be sure that its alienating necessities will not forget us, however much we might prefer to ignore them.[59]

In another formulation of the same problem, Jameson says that History is an "absent cause," knowable only through its effects.[60] If in Mayhew history "is what hurts," does that mean that history becomes History, absent but inescapably present in the cultural forms, social institutions, and modes of production which are its effects; absent but always felt? Mayhew's text actually resists such a reading, just as it exceeds the structures of melodrama, and for the same reasons. That is, Jameson's order of absence/presence is surprisingly like the order of melodrama: an absent cause orders the whole structure; everything is a realization of this absence; History waits to be read in its inevitable effects. Not surprisingly, such a theory not only has its melodramatic moments, but inevitably produces a homogeneous whole. So Jameson declares,

> Only Marxism can give us an adequate account of the essential *mystery* of the cultural past, which, like Tiresias drinking the blood, is momentarily returned to life and warmth and allowed once more to speak, and to deliver its long-forgotten message in surroundings utterly alien to it. This mystery can be reenacted only if the human adventure is one; ... a single great collective story ... sharing a fundamental theme – for Marxism, the collective struggle to wrest a realm of Freedom from a realm of Necessity....[61]

For Jameson, then, the hurt of history holds a utopian promise, the promise not only of reviving the past, but of meeting the future, at least in imagination – a future in which History, and its pain, will come to an end. Such a conception is all too much of the order of melodrama, and like melodrama ensures that only one story can be told.

The history which "hurts" in Mayhew is different, more what Foucault has called "the always open and hazardous reality of conflict"[62] than Jameson's "single great collective story"; Mayhew's "History of the People" promises no salvation, even as it insists on the necessity of resisting the system of sweating and strapping, even as it emphasizes the injustice of the sexual double standard, even as the distinction between the "deserving" and the "undeserving" poor collapses before one's eyes. This is the interest of Mayhew's work, that it breaks in these ways with a melodramatic discourse in which history is fundamentally consoling, and that the history it produces is *not* totalizing, does not assimilate all conflict into a dialectical logic of contradiction. In so doing, Mayhew's *Morning Chronicle* letters not only break the melodramatic fix, but suggest the need for an anti-capitalist, feminist theory of history, a theory which will produce something other than a singular History, which will tell something other than the story of the same.

DICKENS, ALWAYS DICKENS

Mayhew does not himself provide this theory – far from it. Indeed, with his commitment to "inductive philosophy" and his bourgeois class interests, he does little with his work for the *Chronicle*. While in 1850 he was introduced to a public meeting of London tailors as Mr Mayhew, "our able and distinguished advocate . . . the champion of the working classes," by 1856 he was dramatizing some of his interviews under the title of *How We Live in London*, and took to the stage himself to imitate various street people and sing comic songs.[63] Shades of Dickens. Melodrama takes over as Mayhew moves on to the stage and away from any sustained effort to conceptualize history differently. Yet the unconsoling history represented in Mayhew's *Morning Chronicle* letters remains, a reminder of why the melodramatic fix is so crucial to middle-class hegemony.

If history is what hurts, fix it – stabilize it, adjust it, frame it, again and again. The Victorians, painfully aware of conflict, are addicted to melodrama, as are we who follow them. We can't get enough of it, for it saves us from thinking of the openness and hazards of history. Let Anatole Broyard, an editor of *The New York Times Book Review*, attest to that. On 15 May 1988, he writes:

> What does Dickens have that I need so badly? I would say that it is *coziness*, a feeling of being secure on every side. There is no womb like the works of Dickens. More than any other author, he *grasps* you and offers you an image of salvation. He proposes a "radiant idleness," as Orwell observed, a theatrical domesticity. It's a rather empty salvation, but perhaps all salvations are empty. Dickens's version is like a childish, vulgarized heaven, and that's why its appeal is so powerful. He is incomparable at persuading us to regress, at making us feel that the mawkish, even the maudlin, are deep inexpugnable human instincts. We defend him as we defend our children and our own childhood.[64]

Chapter 4

Villette and the end of history

No one, I believe, would argue that Charlotte Brontë's last novel is "cozy." To the contrary: although *Villette* is a text of extremes and intensities, it offers nothing like the melodramatic fix. As Brontë herself declared, she makes no effort to represent the social issues of mid-century. Nor does she engage in the philosophical-historical speculations which characterize Eliot's writing, and her style has none of the subtle and elegant irony of Thackeray's representation of history. Yet this novel, which is compelling by virtue of its representation of the trials and sufferings of a single woman, is nonetheless as inextricably involved with the historical problematic as all the other texts I have considered, its narration of a solitary woman's life bound up with theological and aesthetic inflections of "history."

In the fifth chapter of *Villette*, the heroine and first-person narrator Lucy Snowe arrives alone in London, "a Babylon and a wilderness," where she has come to begin a new life. Poor and plain, without family or friends, she sits in her inn deeply troubled:

All at once my position rose on me like a ghost. Anomalous, desolate, almost blank of hope, it stood. What was I doing here alone in great London? What should I do on the morrow? What prospects had I in life? What friends had I on earth? Whence did I come? Whither should I go? What should I do?[1]

Haunted by the specter of her friendless condition, having lost the protection of her godmother, Mrs Bretton of "the clean and ancient town" of Bretton, Lucy Snowe is solitary and homeless and is overcome by "a terrible oppression."

"What should I do?" This is the question Lucy asks in her desolation in the wilderness of a great city, and is the same question that an earlier pilgrim, Christian, asked in the city of Destruction. Weeping and trembling (Bunyan tells us), "he brake out with a lamentable cry, 'What shall I do?'" and, shortly thereafter, still "greatly distressed in his mind," cried out, "'What shall I do to be saved?'"[2] *The Pilgrim's Progress* answers that question by showing Christian's pilgrimage to Zion, a journey that follows in the steps of biblical characters who have gone before, and which anticipates the path of Christians to come.[3] Christian is thus a type, his true progress intelligible only with reference to the divine dispensation, his pilgrimage a representative part of the whole of human history.

Charlotte Brontë's many allusions to Bunyan's text, and even more importantly, her extensive references to the Bible, mark *Villette* as allegorical and Lucy Snowe as typical. Yet the intense individuality of the heroine, her "shades of peculiarity," as she calls them, "born in and with me, and no more to be parted with than my identity," make Lucy Snowe an eccentric, even perverse character, unreliable and odd (p. 102). Brontë's publishers were concerned enough about the character – who, in the first-person autobiographical form of *Villette*, virtually *is* the novel – to suggest some changes, to which the author replied,

> You say that she may be thought morbid and weak, unless the history of her life be more fully given. I consider that she *is* both morbid and weak at times; her character sets up no pretensions to unmixed strength, and anybody living her life would necessarily become morbid. . . . If, however, the book does not express all this, there must be a great fault somewhere. I might explain away a few . . . points, but it would be too much like drawing a picture and then writing underneath the name of the object intended to be represented.[4]

So *Villette* was published unrevised.

In fact, as her publishers had feared, the novel was read as a record of "subjective misery" that is "almost intolerably painful," from which the author "allows us no respite," an obsessive representation which is too singular to be "a true presentment of any large portion of life and experience."[5] Harriet Martineau forfeited Charlotte Brontë's friendship by that review, but her opinion is hardly unique. She is seconded by the *Guardian*, which declares that the novel "is too uniformly painful, and too little genial, to be accepted by the generality as unmingled truth."[6] Thackeray, in a private letter, is more blunt: "That's a plaguey book that *Villette*. How clever it is – and how I don't like the heroine."[7] But the most revealing comment comes from Matthew Arnold, also in private correspondence. *Villette* is, he writes, "a hideous undelightful convulsed constricted novel," the product of a mind "entirely ... a fire without aliment – one of the most distressing and barren sights one can witness."[8] For him, the book is entirely and intolerably solipsistic, or, as he puts it to another correspondent, "Why is *Villette* disagreeable? Because the writer's mind contains nothing but hunger, rebellion, and rage, and therefore that is all she can, in fact, put in her book."[9] This is worse, much worse, than "morbid and weak," but logically consistent with the first critical opinion Brontë heard from her publishers. For all these readers, Lucy Snowe is aberrant, her story bizarre and unrepresentative, the author obsessively narrow in her concerns. This is a far cry from Lucy as a typical pilgrim, "the object intended to be represented."

Even the defenders of the novel concentrated on the individuality of the heroine and of the author. As the reviewer for the *Athenaeum* wrote,

> A burning heart glows throughout it, and one brilliantly distinct character keeps it alive – the oldest man, the sternest and most scientific, who is a genuine novel-reader, will find it hard to get out of Madame Beck's school when he has once entered there with Lucy Snowe....[10]

After the publication of Mrs Gaskell's *Life* (which came out in 1857, four years after *Villette*) readers were able to refer to the tragic circumstances of the author's life to explain the irresistible interest of the novel – for even those who hated the novel responded strongly to it. "It is well that the thoughtless critics, who spoke of the sad and gloomy views of life presented by the Brontës in their tales, should know how such words were wrung out of them by the living recollection of the agony they suffered," Mrs Gaskell admonished.[11]

This, indeed, is the thesis of the biography, and its effectiveness is immediately evident. Caroline Fox, for instance, writes in her journal after reading the *Life*,

> [Brontë] is intensely true, and draws from actual life, cost what it may ... facts come to light of a frightful unmitigated force; events accompanied them, burning with lurid glow and setting [the sisters'] very hearts on fire. She is like her books and her life explains much in them which needs explanation.[12]

By 1877, twenty-four years after the publication of *Villette* and twenty-two after Brontë's death, the author is so fully identified with her novels that Leslie Stephen declares flatly,

> The most obvious of all remarks about Miss Brontë is the close connection between her life and her writings. In no books is the author more completely incarnated. She is the heroine of her two most powerful novels.... Her powers of observation, though restricted by circumstances and narrowed by limitations of her intellect, showed amazing penetration within her proper province.[13]

And yet, this "proper province" is surely more restricted than that claimed by Brontë herself, more limited than the typicality she intends. Is there, in fact, "a great fault somewhere"?

It is true that Brontë deliberately restricts her scope, as she says frankly in writing to her publishers about *Villette*: "You will see that [it] touches on no matter of public interest. I cannot write books handling the topics of the day; it is no use trying."[14] But she invests the "mere domestic novel" (as she called her earlier *Jane Eyre*) with a significance which belies her own limiting phrase, and she designs *Villette* so as to place Lucy Snowe and her narrative in an overarching historical scheme: no less than the divine dispensation which begins "in the beginning" and ends with the end of all human time. George Eliot, writing to a friend in 1853, bears witness to the effects of this strategy: "I am only just returned to a sense of the real world about me, for I have been reading *Villette*, a still more wonderful book than *Jane Eyre*. There is something almost preternatural in its power."[15] Indeed there is, and it has to do with the insistent figuration of the text, a constant metaphorical elaboration which transports significance from one level to another, a typological design which informs the whole novel and opens Lucy Snowe's narrative to a "universal history." In fact, the typological dimension of the text, evident in both the rhetoric and the plot, explicitly prepares the novel for several levels of interpretation, and does so according to a traditional exegetical procedure well-known and widely practised in Victorian England.

Typology is a hermeneutical theory and method of scriptural interpretation developed by the early Christian Fathers and elaborated in the medieval period, a theory of history to which Evangelical English clergymen turned in the desire to develop a theologically based historicism. As an exegetical method, typology takes the events and characters, laws and rituals, prophecies and histories of the Old Testament to be divinely ordained prefigurations of the New, anticipations of Christ, His sacrifice and resurrection, and God's new covenant with man. As Patrick Fairbairn writes in *The Typology of Scripture, Viewed in Connection with the Whole Series of the Divine Dispensations,*

> History is also prophecy. The past unfolds in the future as a germ, and at certain points, discernible by the eye of the mind. The greater may be imagined in the smaller, the internal in the external, the present or future in the past.[16]

That is, the "historical transactions" of the Old Testament "bear a prospective reference to the scheme of grace unfolded in the Gospel. For what is this scheme itself, in its fundamental character, but a grand historical development?" Thus the Old Testament anticipates the Gospel, and the Gospel itself is prospective, prefiguring the second coming of Christ, the Kingdom of Heaven on earth, the end of time, and ushering in of eternity.

The typological scheme thus yields four distinct levels of interpretation, each one encompassing and transcending the one which comes before. First is the literal: for instance, the historical fact of animal sacrifices as a ritual expiation for sin, an ancient Judaic practice. Second is the allegorical level: the sacrifice of Christ, also a "literal fact," but with a much higher spiritual significance. Third is the moral: the salvation of each individual Christian who accepts Christ as his savior. Fourth and last is the anagogical: the coming of the Kingdom of God when all shall put off mortality for immortality. Each level concerns the same thing, salvation, or, as Fairbairn writes with emphasis: *"The typical is not properly a different or a higher sense, but a different or higher application of the same sense."*[17] The old is both canceled and preserved in the new. Past, present, and future are one.

Villette invites a typological reading; its sustained biblical intertextuality and insistently figurative style call for an informed interpretation. The "preternatural" power of the text owes much to its figures which make poor, plain, and perverse Lucy Snowe a type, which involve the reader in an analogical relationship with her, and which open the text and the reader to the higher truths of history. Brontë believed fervently that the mundane real – the literal – contains higher truths, that the external may reveal a higher inner meaning, but only through the medium of what she calls "poetry." Thus she writes to G. H. Lewes, taking issue with his recommendation to her of Jane Austen as a great artist:

> Can there be a great artist without poetry? What I call – what I will bend to as a great artist, then – cannot be destitute of the divine gift.... Miss Austen ... maybe is sensible, real (more *real* than *true*), but she cannot be great.[18]

In *Villette*, then, Brontë strives to be *true*, to make the merely sensible truly intelligible, to transfigure the real – hence the figurative insistence of the text, its plentitude of tropes.

As we have seen, however, not every reader follows every transport of meaning, and some critics took issue specifically with Brontë's style, with the figures of the text. The *Spectator* praises the general "clearness and power" of *Villette*, but with this exception:

> When the style becomes less pleasing, it is from an attempt to paint by highly figurative language the violent emotions of the heart. This is sometimes done at such length, and with so much obscurity from straining after figure and allusion, as to become tedious and induce skipping.[19]

The *Examiner* objects to "needlessly tragical apostrophes" and recommends that they be "expunged," along with various extended metaphors, warning that readers will surely skip them "after experience of one or two."[20] Another declares that "the personifications of passion are unnatural and clumsily patched upon the tale," and finds them very disagreeable.

Here, then, is a problem, for the figures are the key to *Villette*'s "higher meaning" and must be understood if one is to move beyond the literal and allegorical levels – that is, beyond reading the novel only as an allegory of the author's inner life. But where – again – lies the fault? Some recent feminist criticism has suggested that the true meaning of *Villette* in fact *can* be reached through the apostrophes, the extended metaphors, and the personifications of the text, and that negative criticism of the novel is symptomatic of a refusal to recognize or accept the more profound meaning of the book. Thus Kate Millett writes in *Sexual Politics* that *Villette* is "a book too subversive to be popular," and praises "the astonishing degree of consciousness one finds in the work...."[21] Several years later Sandra Gilbert and Susan Gubar make a similar point, arguing that "the very erratic way Lucy tells the story of her own life illustrates how Brontë produces not a literary object but a literature of consciousness." That is, "the object intended" which Brontë refuses to explain further to her publishers is, in Gilbert and Gubar's reading, "the interiority of the Other."[22] Negative responses to the text like Matthew Arnold's violent dismissal or Leslie Stephen's more urbane depreciation are further evidence of this truth. According to these critics, then, the "great fault" lies with unwilling or hostile readers, readers who claim that the text is obscure or idiosyncratic to avoid seeing the way Lucy Snowe is not just a representation of Charlotte Brontë, but of any woman, of Everywoman. Lucy is far from marginal and eccentric in such feminist interpretations; indeed, marginality and eccentricity become the condition of being a woman in Victorian England, or in any patriarchal culture, including our own.

These interpretations engage with the explicitly analogical dimension of the text and make a great deal of sense, for the novel is designed to elicit a fourfold totalizing reading. And typology is nothing if not totalizing; it is, as Jameson calls it, "Christian historicism," a system in which all issues from and returns to Spirit, to God.[23] History, then, is the progressive revelation of God, each stage in human history bringing man closer to his Creator, making him more conscious of the God in whose image he is made. Brontë secularizes this scheme in writing Lucy's narrative so that Spirit becomes consciousness; when inflected through feminism, the consciousness of Lucy Snowe, so strikingly represented in the first-person narrative, becomes the consciousness of women in general, "the interiority of the Other," to return to Gilbert and Gubar's phrase. In such readings, women are alienated from any self-evident subjectivity by virtue of their Otherness, but none the less can comprehend and master their condition. Consciousness is thus always historical, and just as man finds himself in and through history, so does woman. Her identity is as fully a matter of consciousness as his, and she is equally a subject of history.

The interpretive coherence of this feminist analysis is very persuasive, and, as we will soon see in more detail, is confirmed by the logic of Brontë's secularized typology. Yet when one reads the text closely, the figures which some reviewers found obscure, strained, and disagreeable are undeniably problematic. That is, the whole structure of analogical extension rests on tropes which have no firm foundation. There are moments when the logic of the text gives way, undone by figures which produce no proper meaning, which not only disrupt the line of the narrative by deviating far from the story, but also break down the logic of metaphorical resemblance. *Villette*'s style actually violates the novel's own order of intelligibility and evades the rule of metaphor. In so doing, the text calls into question its own constructions of consciousness and identity, its own sublimation of the material to the spiritual, the outer to the inner, the other to the same. That is, the rhetoric constitutes a fundamental challenge to the historical consciousness the novel itself works to develop. In the process, the text reveals the limits of a "history" which is wholly inscribed in the economy of the same. The "fault" of *Villette*, then, is foundational; like a fault line, the style of the text renders an apparently secure foundation unstable and shatters any confidence one might wish to repose in a totalized "history" or a coherent "consciousness" – and above all in history as consciousness.

*

The implications of the rhetorical instability of the text can best be gauged by considering more fully the typological structure of the text, so before attending to the details of Brontë's rhetoric, I will turn back to this important system of interpretation.

As the daughter of a moderately Evangelical Anglican clergyman, Charlotte Brontë was brought up believing that the Bible is the literal word of God and the highest source of truth. Her father had been influenced by the Wesleys in his youth, and while firmly within the pale of the Established Church all his adult life, he always preached the scripture as revealed truth and emphasized the concepts of faith, sin, grace, redemption, salvation, and eternal punishment.[24] While typology was used by non-Evangelical ministers and theologians in sermons and exegetical works, Evangelicals were most familiar with its principles and most attached to its results, for typological exegesis proves that the Scriptures are a "perfect whole ... a matchless, regular account of God's dealings with man through every age of the world, from the commencement to the end of time, even to the consummation of all things," as Patrick Fairbairn asserts in his *Hermeneutical Manual*.[25] He goes on:

> The adversaries of the faith in every age have well understood this; and hence, from the Manicheans of early times to the infidels and rationalistic writers of the present day, they have ever sought to overthrow the foundations of Divine truth by playing off one part of Scripture against another – exposing what they deemed the

contrarieties between things established in the Old, and things taught in the New Testament. . . ."[26]

Typology meant Evangelicalism needed concede nothing to the German "rationalistic" historical criticism of the Bible so influential in nineteenth-century theology, a "Higher Criticism" which analyzes Christianity as but one religious myth among others, historically specific and secular in origin. For the typologist makes his own historical claims, as Fairbairn does when he bases his hermeneutical principles on the founding premise of the unity of the book of God's revelation, "as well as in respect to words as to ideas": the New is fulfilled in the Old, the Old prefigures the New, down to the smallest and apparently most insignificant detail.[27]

This Evangelical emphasis on the whole of the Bible had its effects on Brontë, for, as her friend Ellen Nussey reports,

no girl in the school was equal to Charlotte in Sunday lessons. Her acquaintance with Holy Writ surpassed others in this as everything else. She was very familiar with all the sublimest passages, especially those in Isaiah in which she took great delight.[28]

Brontë's preference for Isaiah, the prophetic book in which Immanuel is promised to the Israelites in a sublime synthesis of Old and New, suggests that she learned her lessons well, learned to read the foundations of Divine truth in the unity of Scripture, and learned that the Gospel truths both rest on and transfigure the Old Dispensation. As for her acquaintance with Holy Writ, any reader of her novels can attest to that, so fully intertextual is her writing.

Further, in all of her writing – her correspondence and her novels – Brontë declares her faith in divine providence, God's over-arching plan. This she affirms just after Anne's death (having already buried Branwell and Emily in the space of half a year): "Why life is so blank, brief, and bitter I do not know. Why younger and far better than I are snatched from it with projects unfulfilled I cannot comprehend, but I believe God is wise – perfect – merciful."[29] And so she writes again, three years later, when what she has lost forever is even more evident to her:

. . . I felt such a craving for support and companionship as I cannot express. Sleepless, I lay awake night after night; weak and unable to occupy myself I sat in my chair day after day, the saddest memories my only company. It was a time I shall never forget, but God sent it and it must have been for the best.[30]

Of course, such a faith in Providence requires no acquaintance with the exegetical studies which demonstrate that (as Fairbairn writes) "one grand idea pervades all" – all the scriptures, and all of God's dealings with man.[31] But for Evangelical Victorians, the typological proofs for such a faith were close to hand.

Brontë does not claim to comprehend the mysterious ways of God or the ways in which her suffering is a part of His plan, for the divine can be seen but through a glass darkly. Yet she is sure the events of her life are significant, evidence of a wisdom which passes understanding. Indeed, Victorians schooled in Evangelicalism read and interpreted more than the Bible in their search for enlightenment, for the whole world around them could yield divine significance. For just as the events, people, laws, and prophecies of ancient Israel prefigured the coming of Christ and God's new covenant with man, that new covenant will be fulfilled only when His Kingdom comes on earth, when human history is at an end. The nineteenth-century Christian is poised between a past which has prefigured the present, and a future which may be anticipated in the here and now. The material, natural world is charged with significance, as is each individual life. All must be interpreted as the outward and visible signs of invisible truths.

Indeed, the typological and providential scheme, as promulgated in the nineteenth century, is a clearly theological instance of the Romantic faith in an over-arching and underlying order to which everything ultimately refers. Typological exegesis *per se* is wholly orthodox, whereas romanticism tends towards natural supernaturalism, but typology was by no means confined to hermeneutical manuals or the pulpit. As several recent critical studies have demonstrated, typology was widely generalized in Britain during the Victorian period.[32] It is a specific instance of romantic idealism, in which types and shadows rather than elective affinities or correspondences are significant; it is a transcendental historicism. The *locus classicus* of the generalized discourse of typology is Carlyle, whose early religious training is evident in all his work, even when his idealism is, in its philosophical principles, more German than Presbyterian. Thus in his essay "On History" he calls "the Past" a

complex Manuscript ... nay ... a *Palimpsest* [which] had once prophetic writing, still dimly legible there, – some letters, some words, may be deciphered, here and there an intelligible precept ... be gathered: well understanding, in the mean while, that it is only a little portion we have deciphered; that much still remains to be interpreted; that History is a real Prophetic Manuscript, and can be fully interpreted by no man.[33]

Furthermore, not only the past, but the present must be read, as Teufelsdrockh declares in *Sartor Resartus*: " 'Rightly viewed no meanest object is insignificant; all objects are as windows, through which the philosophic eye looks into Infinitude itself.' " Hence, "all visible things are emblems."[34]

Similarly, in *Modern Painters*, John Ruskin writes that the world is full of "types and shadows [of] things to the heavenly region belonging."[35] Generalized typology is the basis of his aesthetics:

[I]f we wish, without reference to beauty of composition, or any other interfering circumstances, to form a judgment of the truth of painting, perhaps the very first thing we should look for, whether in one thing or another – foliage, or clouds, or waves – should be the expression of infinity always and everywhere, in all parts and divisions of parts. For we may be sure that what is not infinite, cannot be true.... [I]t is impossible for mortal mind to compose an infinity of any kind for itself, or to form an idea of perpetual variation, and avoid all repetition.... The moment that we trust to ourselves, we repeat ourselves....

The way to the infinite, to truth, is through particularity, which is to say through history: "It ought further to be observed respecting truths in general, that those are always more valuable which are most historical, that is, which tell us most about the past and future states of the object to which they belong;" for instance, the painter should represent the details of a tree "which [indicate] growth and life ... [which] tell us tales about the tree, about what it has been, and will be ...."[36] Ruskin's aesthetics are, like Carlyle's history, an instance of generalized typology, participating in and contributing to that discourse. Ruskin sees infinity in the bole of a tree, just as the exegete attends to every detail of scripture, for divine truths may be revealed where one least suspects; Carlyle claims that "History is a real prophetic manuscript," even as Fairbairn says that "History is also prophecy." Both aesthetician and historian declare that truth is visible to those with eyes to see.

Charlotte Brontë was well-prepared to hear these latter-day preachers. "Carlyle's 'Miscellanies' interest me greatly," she wrote in 1849, but her highest praise is given to the author of *Modern Painters* and *The Stones of Venice*: "Mr Ruskin seems to me one of the few genuine writers, as distinguished from book-makers, of this age.... He writes like a consecrated priest of the Abstract and Ideal."[37] Yet she herself had felt a similar vocation before she knew anything of Ruskin, as she revealed in her early correspondence with W. S. Williams (her reader in George Smith's publishing house):

> The first duty of an author is, I conceive, a faithful allegiance to Truth and Nature; his second, such a conscientious study of Art as shall enable him to interpret eloquently and effectively the oracles delivered by those two great deities.[38]

For Brontë as well as for Ruskin, Art is a matter of types and shadows, and she finds the discourse of prefiguration and fulfillment to be the most effective means of interpreting Truth and Nature, since it is the nature of truth to be veiled and oracular.

In the nineteenth century, then, typology is far more than a method of biblical interpretation; it is a part of the romantic and Victorian fascination with the Abstract and Ideal, one of the figurative modes for representing a supersensory reality. Any artist who would be (in Brontë's words) "more true than real" must have "the divine gift" of poetry, since only poetic language is properly symbolic. As Paul de Man explains, in the rhetoric of romanticism "the symbol is founded on an intimate unity between the image that rises up before the senses and the supersensory totality that the image suggests."[39] This transformation of the sensible world is obviously what Brontë aspires to, the apprehension of a supersensory totality that can only be achieved through "poetry," which is to say through the symbol. Yet typology, which is such an important figurative element in her writing, is more allegorical than symbolic, a system of one-to-one correspondences between Old and New rather than the wholistic revelation of an "intimate unity" of sensible image and supersensory totality. And allegory is generally decried in the nineteenth century precisely on the grounds that its correspondences are one-dimensional and artificial, not a properly symbolic discovery of the True in the real.

The stakes are quite high in these aesthetic matters, as the vigorous debates in the nineteenth century about the relation of allegory to symbol suggest. The dominant position (then as now) privileges metaphor (or symbol).[40] In Paul Ricoeur's words, metaphor is a matter of both "poetics and ontology," far more than one trope among others. It is, he says, "the central act of discourse, namely, predication."[41] In metaphor, this *is that*; identity is discovered where there had been only difference. The metaphoric process is a conceptual one, mental, not material, as becomes evident when one compares metaphor with other tropes like synecdoche (connection, part for whole) or metonymy (contiguous correspondence). "[C]onnection and correspondence are primarily relationships between objects," Ricoeur writes, "while resemblance is principally a relationship between ideas."[42] Or as Derrida says, "to take an interest in metaphor ... is above all to take an interest in semantic 'depth,' in the magnetic attraction of the similar, rather than in positional combinations, which we may call metonymic. ..."[43] Metonymic combinations are a matter of chance; they are contingent, whereas metaphor is thought to be a matter of necessity: the resemblance metaphor brings to light is an *essential* correspondence which gives one a glimpse of the supersensory totality which sponsors all seemingly different and discrete phenomena. It is thus that metaphor can be seen as a movement of idealization, a movement through the material to the ideal, a process in which concrete difference is both cancelled and preserved in a higher unity. That is, metaphor is the *aufhebung* at work, the dialectical process of working through apparent contradiction to achieve synthesis, of moving through material difference to an intelligible unity.

When metaphor is so valorized, other figures, but especially allegory, are correspondingly depreciated. In the economy of the same, allegorical difference is too intrusive. Allegory, like all figurative modes, is under the rule of metaphor, but fails to achieve the unity which metaphor produces. For in allegory, predication is a matter of artifice, not necessity, and allegorical resemblance is arbitrary, a sense imposed by the author, not an essence which becomes intelligible through the figurative process. Proper metaphor requires that "the sense aimed at through [the] figures is an essence rigorously independent of that which transports it," as Derrida writes. But in allegory, the figures turn not to an independent essence, but to another system of signs; it is a mode of closed repetition rather than a movement to the infinity of the ideal.

How, then, is one to explain the Victorian fascination with typology? For typology is, as the theologian Horne explains, "*Mystical Allegory*, in which a double meaning is couched under the same words ...," in which the Old simply refers to the New.[44] It is a closed and repetitive system, "dryly rational and dogmatic in its reference to a meaning that it does not itself constitute" – as de Man says in summarizing the charges against allegory in general.[45] Yet when Ruskin bases his aesthetics on "types and shadows [of] things to the heavenly region belonging," and envisions a nature vitally charged with a higher significance, he argues for infinity, not repetition, as we have seen: "It is impossible for mortal mind to compose an infinity of any kind for itself.... The moment that we trust to ourselves, we repeat ourselves." In his theory and practice typology is no predictable or dogmatic mode, for infinity manifests itself in an infinite variety of ways.

Generalized typology, then, can be understood to be not so much mystical allegory as "historicized" metaphor, a figurative mode which stresses the dialectical process of representation, emphasizes the fact that the ideal can be approached only through the material, insists that the highest truths can be realized only when embodied, and declares that infinity can be reached only through history. Typology focuses attention on historical specificity, particularity, mutability, and also on Eternity, Spirit, and divine Truth; and when generalized beyond a strictly allegorical interpretation of Scripture, it is not a failure of metaphor, but a complement to it. This is clearly evident in Wordsworth's famous poetic description in *The Prelude* of the descent of the Simplon pass. There he writes that the concrete, natural world of woods and waterfalls, rocks and sky, "Were all like workings of one mind, the features/ Of the same face, blossoms upon one tree;/ Characters of the great Apocalypse,/ The types and symbols of Eternity,/ Of first, and last, and midst, and without end."[46]

"The types and symbols of Eternity" are what the poet sees and the status to which his poetic language aspires: his readers are to experience the same revelation, to read the characters of the Apocalypse in his poem. The movement is from nature to spirit, and promises implicitly a moment when nature will be completely absorbed by spirit, when all will be immediately intelligible and types and symbols a thing of the past. As Ruskin writes,

[T]here will come a time when the service of God shall be the beholding of him; and though in these stormy seas, where we are now driven up and down, his Spirit is dimly seen on the face of the waters, and we are left to cast anchors out of the stern, and wish for the day, that day will come, when, with the evangelists on the crystal and stable sea, all the creatures of God shall be full of eyes within, and there shall be "no more curse, but his servants shall serve him, and shall see his face."[47]

That day is far off for Lucy, for in one of the first extended metaphors of the text Lucy recounts certain cataclysmic events of her youth, saying,

> I too well remember a time – a long time – of cold, of danger, of contention.... [T]here was a storm, and that not of one hour nor one day. For many days and nights neither sun nor stars appeared; we cast with our own hands the tackling out of the ship; a heavy tempest lay on us; all hope that we should be saved was taken away.
>
> (p. 30)

Brontë, with her romantic faith in the transfiguring power of "poetry" and her Evangelical training in Holy Writ, develops a generalized typological scheme to mark Lucy's narrative as typical and to produce semantic depth. When Lucy languishes alone in Madame Beck's pensionnat over the long vacation, solitary and unloved, she finds her life

> to be but a hopeless desert; tawny sands, with no green fields, no palm-tree, no well in view ... I did not in my heart arraign the mercy or justice of God for this; I concluded it to be part of His great plan that some must deeply suffer while they live, and I thrilled in the certainty that of this number I was one.
>
> (p. 151)

*

With Lucy, readers of her narrative must ask, " 'of what are these things the signs and tokens?' "

As we have seen, for many readers these are the signs of Lucy's inner life, of her consciousness, that secularized version of the soul. The "burning heart [of] one brilliantly distinct character" – to recall the words of the *Athenaeum* – has long been acknowledged as the center of interest in the novel, compelling by virtue of the figures which make it intelligible. The exaggeration of the rhetoric, the excessiveness of Brontë's style, are either condemned as missing the mark (as when the *Spectator* reviewer objects to Brontë's "straining after figure and allusion" in "an attempt to paint by highly figurative language the violent emotions of the heart"), or praised as the only possible way to represent Lucy's consciousness (as when Gilbert and

Gubar declare that "her story is perhaps the most moving and terrifying account of female deprivation ever written").[48] But the extraordinary profusion of figures in *Villette* is not only a matter of making concrete and comprehensible the abstraction of heart or soul or consciousness. Brontë's style is also explicitly typological, her figures designed to represent her heroine's consciousness in "universal" terms, marking her as a "type" and her experience as "typical," placing Lucy in the all-inclusive sweep of providential "history."

One effect of the profuse rhetoric of the text is to call attention to Lucy's narrative *as* a text which requires interpretation. Readers of *Villette* must be in an exegetical frame of mind. The hermeneutical principles enunciated by theologians like Fairbairn and widely disseminated in the nineteenth century through sermons, hymns, and other literature both secular and sacred, are – if not *the* interpretive key to the text – an evidently important part of its design. Much of *Villette* rests on the fundamental typological principle that the Old Testament is material, whereas the New is spiritual; that, as Fairbairn puts it, "the carnal and earthly nature of the Old" is transfigured into the spiritual realities of the Gospel.[49] The Mosaic law of the "old economy," with its ritual sacrifice and burnt offerings; the "Old Dispensation" in which the Promised Land was all too earthly and material; the Old Testament, whose prophets foresaw a higher order to come – all are but the preparation for a higher and better order, a necessary moment in human history, but one which has been superseded by a "new economy" in which law is sublimated into grace, sacrifice into salvation, blood into eternal life.

Throughout most of the novel Lucy resembles the Israelites in the wilderness. Solitary in Madame Beck's school, feeling her life to be a "hopeless desert," she finds "more firmly than ever fastened into [her] soul the conviction that Fate was of stone, and Hope a false idol – blind, bloodless, and of granite core" (p. 154). Not only is she living without grace, she is even tempted to worship false gods. Lucy is drawn to Dr John, the son of Mrs Bretton and the object of her unrequited affection even when she visited her godmother as a young girl. Older now, yet still as plain and even more unobtrusive, she falls in love with the golden-haired and handsome Englishman; she idolizes him, for as she says, his "beamy head" shining in the sunlight drives her thoughts "to . . .the 'golden image' which Nebuchadnezzar the king had set up" (p. 92). She tries to keep the faith, to resist worshipping this image, as Brontë makes clear in a turn to Exodus and Deuteronomy: Lucy makes for herself some imperious rules ... commanding a patient journeying through the wilderness of the present, enjoining a reliance on faith – a watching of cloud and pillar which subdue while they guide ... – hushing the impulse to fond idolatry, checking the longing outlook for a far-off promised land whose rivers are, perhaps, never to be reached save in dying dreams, whose sweet pastures are to be viewed but from the desolate and sepulchral summit of a Nebo.

(p. 224)

Of Brontë's extensive citations of the Old Testament – and the Old Testament figures far more prominently than the New in *Villette* – this reference is one of the most obviously typological, for the death of Moses within sight of the Promised Land was a famous type, easily recognized by many Victorians.[50] As Henry Melvill, a famous Evangelical Anglican preacher, explained in a sermon, Moses died outside Canaan because "he was but the representative of the law, and ... the law itself can never lead us into heavenly places...."[51] Only Christ can lead man into Paradise, and the Old Testament bears witness to this Gospel truth.

Villette, in its own way, also testifies to this truth, for not until Lucy comes to love Paul Carl David Emmanuel can she overcome her alienation, the perverse projections of herself on to others, the fragmentation of her self. This is, of course, a secular salvation, more mental and emotional than spiritual, a matter of Lucy's consciousness, not of her soul. Yet Lucy is changed, and Monsieur Emmanuel's part in her transformation is evident enough in his name; one need not be initiated into the hermeneutical principles of typology to recognize that he is invested with special powers in *Villette*. In fact, the new world Lucy enters into under his protection is a promised land, and though not heaven, is more spiritual than carnal. The school that Lucy opens, the "stewardship" of Paul's investment that she undertakes (recalling the New Testament parable of the talents), are all of this world. But the real victory at the end of the novel is not simply material: it is, as many readers have recognized, Lucy's achievement of integration, a synthesis of her divided self, of passion and reason, of heart and mind, of the sensible (sensual) and the intelligible.

Indeed, this is said to be Brontë's own achievement, too, in writing *Villette*. As G. H. Lewes declares in his review of the novel, "In Passion and Power – those noble twins of Genius – Currer Bell has no living rival, except George Sand. Here is the passionate heart to feel, and the powerful brain to give feeling shape...."[52] In this synthesis of heart and brain, reason makes feeling intelligible, shapes it, gives it significance, reveals its otherwise incomprehensible essence. Lewes does not hesitate to acknowledge Brontë's writing as sublime (he compares reading *Villette* with "wander[ing] delighted among the craggy clefts and snowy solitudes of the Alps"), which suggests that she has succeeded in investing typology with symbolic power and properly metaphoric resonance, while retaining the typological emphasis on the literal and material.

She unquestionably emphasizes the concrete and material, but only to stress that such a coming to consciousness as Lucy suffers is achieved through contradiction and struggle – or, in typological terms, by moving through the carnality of the Old into the spirituality of the New. This movement – from material to beyond – helps to account for the extreme physicality of so many of the metaphors in *Villette*, the violent images of physical suffering and pain. Lucy is not only subject to trials of storm and desert pilgrimage; strikingly material figures of torture, hunger, and thirst make her pilgrim's progress vividly concrete. When she is left entirely alone in the Rue Fossette over the long vacation, she suffers terribly. As Lucy reports, "A goad thrust me on, a fever forbade me to rest; a want of companionship maintained in my soul the cravings of a most deadly famine" (p. 152). The text is replete with such tactile images, often brutal, always strikingly corporeal, and frequently developed in conjunction with a specific citation of the Old Testament.

When Lucy receives a letter from Dr John, her false god, she describes her ecstasy by saying,

> I held in my hand a morsel of real solid joy.... [I]t was the wild, savoury mess of the hunter, nourishing and salubrious meat, forest-fed or desert-reared, fresh, healthful, and life-sustaining. It was what the old dying patriarch demanded of his son Esau, promising in requital the blessing of his last breath.
>
> (p. 232)

She calls it a "godsend." But, as all good students of their Sunday lessons know, Esau was cheated out of his blessing by his younger brother Jacob, who made up the savory meat his father desired by slaughtering two goats from the flock, and so, too, is Lucy's letter a cheat.[53] She saves it all day, hoarding it to read alone in the evening, and when she does, she finds it "a bubble – but a sweet bubble – of real honey dew" (p. 237). That is, it is manna, where she thought it was meat, manna "which at first melts on the lips with an unspeakable and preternatural sweetness, but which, in the end, our souls full surely loathe ..." (p. 232). Before too long Dr John forgets her and no more letters come. Her "morsel of real solid joy" was no such thing, and she is thrown back on her own resources, as she reports:

> I commenced an elaborate piece of lace work, I studied German pretty hard, I undertook a course of regular reading ... in all my efforts I was as orthodox as I knew how to be. Was there error somewhere? very likely. I only know the result was as if I had gnawed a file to satisfy hunger, or drank brine to quench thirst.
>
> (p. 260)

And she despairs, saying, "I suppose animals kept in cages, and so scantily fed as to be always upon the verge of famine, await their food as I awaited a letter" (p. 261).

Dr John, a golden idol, cannot quench her thirst or satisfy her hunger. Even manna, which was God's sustaining gift to the Israelites wandering in the wilderness, cannot save Lucy, a nineteenth-century Christian. For the Old has been superseded by the New; the old time is past, its work is done, and to live in the present under the Old Dispensation – as Lucy does through much of her narrative – is to live without the "living water" that Christ promises in the Gospel, "a well of water springing up into everlasting life." For, as Jesus says, "God *is* a Spirit: and they that worship him must worship *him* in spirit and in truth" (John 4: 10–13; 24). In the typological scheme of *Villette*, Lucy must wait for Paul Emmanuel to come into her life to lift her from the material into the spiritual – that is, into a fully realized consciousness of herself. The "three happiest years of [her] life" she spends not in Paul's company, but sustained by his letters. From across the seas he writes, and "there was no sham and no cheat, and no hollow unreal in him ... his letters were real food that nourished, living water that refreshed" (p. 479).

The extraordinarily physical figures evoking Lucy's mental and emotional sufferings thereby stress her need for salvation, for the grace which will lift the "earthly and carnal" into the spiritual. A similar effect is achieved by the personifications which proliferate throughout the text, from brief phrases to figures that extend for a paragraph or more. These personifications, which are a distinctive and often intrusive element of Brontë's style, have been read as signs of Lucy's emotional conflict, projections of a war within, an important aspect of Brontë's "literature of consciousness."[53] Like the figures of physical deprivation, the personifications render abstractions in concrete terms and mark Lucy's experience in terms of the Old Dispensation, not the New. This typological scheme is most evident in personifications which are also citations of scriptural texts, though such passages are precisely those singled out by *Villette*'s reviewers as "unnatural and clumsily patched upon the tale," and sure to "induce skipping." Indeed, the *Examiner* recommends that Brontë "expunge" "all passages written in the same key as the following":

> This longing [for a fuller life], and all of a similar kind, it was necessary to knock on the head; which I did, figuratively, after the manner of Jael to Sisera, driving a nail through their temples. Unlike Sisera, they did not die: they were but transiently stunned, and at intervals would turn on the nail with a rebellious wrench: then did the temples bleed, and the brain thrill to its core.
>
> To-night, I was not so mutinous nor so miserable. My Sisera lay quiet in the tent, slumbering; and if his pain ached through his slumbers, something like an angel – the ideal – knelt near, dropping balm on the soothed temples, holding before the sealed eyes a magic glass, of which the sweet, solemn visions were repeated in dreams, and shedding a reflex from her moonlit wings and robe over the transfixed sleeper, over the tent threshold, over all the landscape lying without. Jael, the stern woman, sat apart, relenting somewhat over her captive; but more prone to dwell on the faithful expectation of Heber coming home. By which words I mean that the cool peace and dewy sweetness of the night filled me with a mood of hope: not hope on any definite point, but a general sense of encouragement and heart-ease.
>
> (p. 104)

The passage describes Lucy's reverie as she sits in the garden of the pensionnat, meditating on her life and on her longing for a change. It is, to say the least, a problematic sequence, one which many readers have undoubtedly skipped in their eagerness to get on with the story. Yet one could argue, as some have quite persuasively, that its very excessiveness is adequate to the terrifying deprivation Lucy suffers. In such an interpretation the figure of Jael and Sisera would be a proper romantic image, a symbol in Coleridge's sense: "such as the life is, such is the form."[55] Skipping the passage, then, would amount to averting one's eyes from the truth represented by the text.

The typological dimension of the figure, its turn to the Old Testament, would thus complement its symbolic significance. In the fourth chapter of Judges, the scripture recounts how "the Lord discomfited Sisera . . . and all his host, with the edge of the sword." This is a strong instance of the "old economy" of blood and divine vengeance: Jael, who "smote the nail into [Sisera's] temples, and fastened it into the ground," is "blessed . . . above women in the tent."[56] Brontë makes Lucy's violent repression of her longings into a kind of antitype (the later fulfillment on a higher level) of this "literal," "historical" event, her mental agony a more sublime instance of the physical pain Sisera suffered. Brontë's typology thus positions Lucy in universal history; she is no longer marginal and eccentric in the violence of her emotions, but typical. Moreover, that she should be suffering even more than Sisera, that her agonies are greater than his, stresses how desperately she needs the spiritual guidance that Paul Emmanuel will provide.

No one else in the novel can help. Dr John, while a good upright Englishman, is limited by his "dry materialist views" and utterly misapprehends Lucy, seeing in her only an "inoffensive shadow." The other English characters are little better, and those who are native to *Villette* are Roman Catholic, represented by Brontë as slaves to a ritual religion, materialists, and sensualists. In fact, the diatribes against "Popery" and "Romanism" in Lucy's narrative are yet another instance of excess in the text, as disruptive and "disagreeable" as the extended personifications. Yet, once again, the anti-Catholicism is an aspect of Brontë's emphasis on the primacy of consciousness and of the self, and, like many an English person prejudiced against "Rome," Brontë makes the Roman Church represent a deadening of the spirit and Protestantism its wakening to life. And, again, this aspect of Brontë's "literature of consciousness" has a typological "proof."

"Romanism" in *Villette* is fully identified with the Old Economy, entirely of the carnal and earthly. Madame Beck and her "junta" – the "crafty Jesuit" Père Silas and Madame Walravens, "hunchbacked, dwarfish, . . . adorned like a barbarian queen" – are the most important representatives of this life-denying economy, along with the ghostly nun which appears to Lucy several times in the course of the novel. Lucy's exorcizing of the nun, her discovery that it is no specter, but simply a disguise assumed by the Count de Hammal to gain access to the pensionnat as he courted one of the girls, signals her victory over the Old and readiness for the New. Coming on the disguise, she boldly goes forward:

> nothing leaped out, or sprung, or stirred; all the movement was mine, so was all the life, the reality, the substance, the force, as my instinct felt. I tore her up – the incubus! I held her on high – the goblin! I shook her loose – the mystery! And down she fell – down all around me – down in shreds and fragments – and I trode upon her.
>
> (pp. 456–7)

This climax prepares for the denouement, wherein Lucy is saved from Madame Beck by Paul, liberated from the pensionnat (which had once been a convent), established in her own house with her own school. This is a victory for life and reality and substance, a synthesis of material and spiritual, Lucy's salvation. And to emphasize that salvation, Brontë makes the Roman Catholics no better than heathens and infidels.

We learn of Madame Beck that "no force or mass of suffering concentrated in one heart had power to pierce hers. Not the agony in Gethsemane, not the death on Calvary, could have wrung from her eyes one tear" (p. 69). Madame Walravens and Pere Silas live on the Rue des Mages, and when Lucy is sent there on an errand by Madame Beck, a storm is approaching which will "transform ... Villette into ... Tadmor" (p. 376; II Chronicles, 8:4). The references to the Old Testament multiply: "[the] church, whose dark, half-ruinous turrets overlooked the square, was the venerable and formerly opulent shrine of the Magii ... three mystic sages of a dead and dark art" (pp. 376, 378). In *Villette*, then, "Romanism" is no better than the Judaism of typology; both have been superseded by a "New Economy." When Lucy is taken by Pere Silas to see "the pomp of Rome," she found "the Papal ritual and ceremony ... grossly material, not poetically spiritual" (p. 409). She continues more fervently (in a passage which runs to four full paragraphs),

> A thousand ways were opened with pain, with blood-sweats, with lavishing of life ... and all for what? That a Priesthood might march straight on and straight upward to an all-dominating eminence, whence they might at last stretch the scepter of their Moloch "Church." ... God is not with Rome, and, were human sorrows still for the Son of God, would He not mourn over her cruelties

and ambitions, as once He mourned over the crimes and woes of doomed Jerusalem?

(p. 409)

Brontë here assumes a perfectly orthodox (Orientalist and anti-Semitic) typological position, one which Fairbairn teaches in his *Hermeneutical Manual*. There he writes that the apostles clearly prove that the New Dispensation is spiritual where the old was material: "they show conclusively, that the external forms of the ancient worship, its visible temple, aaronic priesthood, fleshly sacrifices, stated festivals, and corporeal ablutions, were no longer binding on the conscience, and naturally led, if perpetuated, to carnalize the Gospel." But, Fairbairn warns, the old "Judaizing tendency" of the early church reappears in Roman Catholicism,

bringing in a train of forms and ceremonies, purgations and sacrifices, feasts and solemnities which differ only in name from those of the Old Economy; and a Christian priesthood established itself ... [which has its] recognized place now, much as in ancient Israel. To such a mournful extent has Christianity been Judaized.[57]

No wonder Madame Beck becomes "Appolyon," blocking Emmanuel's way to Lucy, "straddl[ing] across it, breathing flames" (p. 433). But how can Paul, Jesuit-trained and a devout Catholic, be Lucy's "Greatheart," her guide to salvation? As is necessary for the logic of the book, Emmanuel joins Old and New, a union symbolized in the "David" and the "Paul" of his name, and in that synthesis, the Old is both cancelled and preserved, lifted up to a more fully spiritual truth. Thus when speaking with Lucy on theological subjects he concludes,

"How seem in the eyes of ... God ... the differences of man? But as Time is not for God, nor Space, so neither is Measure, nor Comparison. We abase ourselves in our littleness, and we do right; yet it may be that the constancy of one heart, the truth and faith of one mind according to the light He has appointed, import as much to Him as the just motion of satellites about their planets, of planets about their suns, of suns around that mighty unseen centre incomprehensible, unrealizable, with strange mental effort only divined."

(pp. 410–11)

The carnal and earthly are here left behind: mind and light remain.

And the novel ends with mind and light, with consciousness and enlightenment. Lucy and Paul have one evening together in paradise under "such moonlight as fell on Eden – shining through the shades of the Great Garden, and haply gilding a path glorious for a step divine – a Presence nameless" (p. 476).

Paul believes, as he tells Lucy (quoting without attribution the First Epistle of Paul to the Corinthians, 15:54), that " 'in the future time will be a resurrection ... but all will then be changed – form and feeling: the mortal will have put on immortality ...' " (p. 335). But that time is not yet, and Paul must therefore be sacrificed, as he is by "the destroying angel of tempest" (p. 480). The day has not yet come "when, with the evangelists on the crystal and stable sea, all the creatures of God shall be full of eyes within, and there shall be 'no more curse, but his servants shall serve him, and shall see his face.' " In a fallen, historical world, "consciousness" must be painful, and synthesis achieved through the struggle of contradiction. In *Villette*, Brontë testifies to this truth.

*

Villette is thus a testament of faith, but of a distinctly modern faith in interpretation and representation, in the difficult achievement of subjectivity. This achievement, in its very difficulty, has been claimed as a universal necessity, the condition of being human. As Peter Brooks argues in his work on plot, "reading the signs of intention in life's actions is the central act of existence," an especially pressing exigency "in the absence or silence of divine masterplots."[58] For Brontë, of course, the Bible is not silent: for her it is the living word, evidence of God's plan for all time, even to eternity. None the less, in *Villette* her most pressing concern is not the state of her heroine's soul, but the state of her mind. She may have said, as Mrs Gaskell reports, "I trust God will take from me whatever power of invention or expression I may have, before He lets me become blind to the sense of what is fitting or unfitting to be said," but her text exceeds her intention in several respects.[59]

The biblical intertextuality is, strictly speaking, improper, for as the *Christian Rembrancer* reviewer declares,

> the mind here pictured ... rejects all guide but her Bible, and at the same time constantly quotes and plays with its sacred pages, as though they had been given to the world for no better purpose than to point a witticism or furnish an ingenious illustration.[60]

Brontë dismissed this attack as a predictable part of current religious controversy, High Anglicanism offended by her criticism of church ritual in *Villette* and Lucy's staunch Evangelical Protestantism. But the *Christian Rembrancer* has a point. The intertextuality of the novel is illustrative, and not of divine truths. Rather, *Villette*, with its typological design, may be read as an exemplary (if eccentric) instance of narrative in general, a striking example of the narrative of self-discovery and consciousness which is such a crucial part of nineteenth- and twentieth-century Anglo-European life. Brooks declares that interpreting the events of one's life, thus transforming them into a narrative, is the central act of existence, which means that representation is distinctively human, a way of making sense out of what is otherwise unintelligible. Or, as Derrida summarizes the cardinal rule of a long-standing philosophical tradition, "Mimesis is proper to man.... The power of truth, as the unveiling of nature (physis) by mimesis, congenitally belongs to the physics of man, to anthropophysics."[61]

The intensely figurative text of *Villette* would seem to bear this out – albeit paradoxically in that Brontë is a woman writer, marked by her gender, and *Villette* a highly, even overly-wrought representation. Brooks argues that in fact there is a place for paradox, that narrative is itself paradoxical, constituted in the tension between resemblance and difference, between metaphor (the figure of essential sameness) and metonymy (the figure of contingent combination):

> The energy generated by deviance, extravagance, excess maintains the plot in its movement through the vacillating play of the middle ... toward recognition and the retrospective illumination that will allow us to grasp the text as total metaphor, but not therefore to discount the metonymies that have led to it.[62]

Metonymy, contingent and arbitrary, gives way to the necessity of metaphor, but not before generating the differences which will be overcome in the discovery of unexpected resemblances. In fact, the more excessive, extravagant, and deviant the middle, the more satisfying and enlightening the final resolution of the text into an intelligible whole.

Read this way, *Villette* is a prime instance of the revelation of meaning and necessity in apparently arbitrary deviance and excess. Errancy is the condition of the text both stylistically and thematically. That is, the text itself, with its many extended figures, is often in "a state ... of going astray" – the first definition of errancy; and Lucy Snowe's state for much of the narrative meets the second definition –

"the condition of being in doctrinal error." She wanders in the wilderness of the Old Economy, she succumbs to the temptations of idolatry, she adheres to a harsh and unforgiving law; her errancy is represented in figures which deviate from the narrative line, which are extravagantly long and excessively painful, which seem to have a logic of their own. Yet both the rhetorical excessiveness and the theological wanderings fall into place when considered as parts of a whole – the whole being the text as metaphor for knowledge, for consciousness, for the act of interpretation; in other words, a metaphor for representation itself. An "enlightened" interpretation, then, one carried out in the "retrospective illumination" of the resolution of the novel, would see that *Villette* is about "anthropophysics."

In this reading, the text is a metaphor for consciousness, for the process of coming-to-consciousness through negativity. Brontë writes within a novelistic tradition of self-discovery through social and romantic conflict; Brooks is working within a psychoanalytic tradition that understands subjectivity as the effect of repressions and substitutions, the negativity which is a necessary condition for representation and thus for consciousness itself. If one follows Brooks, one understands that to be a subject, to be conscious, is to narrate, to make the merely material and sensible properly intelligible. Extravagant, excessive difference resolves into resemblance, into an order of necessary correspondences. This is an historical and teleological process of interpretation, a matter of reading the events of the past (in Brooks's words) as " 'promises and annunciations' of final coherence."[63] It is also exegetical, but a hermeneutics without God. The power of truth is transferred from God to man, from theology to a history that is none the less deeply theological in its concepts. It would seem that *Villette*, a text by a woman, about a woman's progress, participates fully in this New Economy, making it an exemplary modern narrative, a mimesis of consciousness, a representation of representation, of that which is proper to man.

There is another reading of *Villette*. In rereading the text, one is confronted again by those figures which "induce skipping," the extended personifications which deviate so remarkably from the narrative line. In this rereading, errancy is not contained and the illumination which should reveal sameness in difference is absorbed by the figures of the text – or, better, refracted and splintered by them. If the truth of the text (the truth of consciousness) is produced through the figures of the text (those wandering, errant figures), if the truth of truth is representation (man's need to make the sensible intelligible, which is in his very nature), then something is amiss in *Villette*. In it there is something "unnatural," which is to say, different from anthropophysics. Doubtless Brontë intended nothing improper, but the style of *Villette* produces differences without similarity, metonymies too excessive and deviant to be resolved into a total metaphor. Indeed, her text is an instance of a failure of metaphor, for her figures are more allegorical than metaphoric, governed less by necessary resemblance than by arbitrary correspondence; and as Naomi Schor has said (following de Man), "allegory is the failure of the resemblance which founds metaphor."[64] In *Villette*, typology is allegory, and wildly excessive allegory at that. Here, then, is a "great fault."

The passage in which Lucy evokes Jael and Sisera as a type of her mental sufferings is an instance of this stylistic subversion of the principles of representation in which Brontë has such faith. As we have seen, in the generalized typological scheme of *Villette*, Sisera impaled with a nail prefigures Lucy's repressed inner life, the "dead trace," as she says, "in which I studiously held the quick of my nature" (p. 103). The first paragraph of the two which make up this figure is orthodox enough: an essential similarity – agony – is evoked in an unexpected resemblance between an English teacher in Madame Beck's pensionnat and a captain who commanded 900 chariots of iron, dying in ancient Canaan.[65] Here the necessary resemblance is simply given extra force and historical resonance by the addition of a typological dimension. But the second paragraph takes liberties with the biblical text which Brontë cites to characterize the extent of Lucy's mental suffering. For in the second part of this extended figure, Sisera is not dead, though the nail is driven through his temples; an angel, "the ideal," soothes him with a "magic glass"; Jael sits apart, anticipating the return of her husband. With this the text wanders off, thoroughly destabilizing the metaphoric economy with arbitrary and strained "correspondences" which emphasize not resemblance but the discontinuity of the signifying system.

The figure has several turns. It begins with an awkward analogy: "This longing, and all of a similar kind, it was necessary to knock on the head, which I did, figuratively, after the manner of Jael to Sisera, driving a nail through their temples." The analogy is immediately qualified – "Unlike Sisera, they did not die" – setting up a fanciful extension: "To-night I was not so mutinous or miserable. My Sisera lay quiet in the tent...." The passage becomes a strange little allegorical narrative which entirely displaces the original reference to Judges on which the metaphor was predicated, leaving behind the supposedly literal, historical event that was to define and characterize Lucy's suffering.

The extension of the passage is quite detailed, as is any allegory. For in the figurative mode of allegory, details have a signifying vocation marking the text as a sign which needs to be read, and establishing the many one-to-one correspondences which make up an allegorical system. But, as readers of *Villette* can see, in that text the details proliferate according to a logic of their own, and it is only with real difficulty that they are made to correspond to Lucy's inner life. No wonder Brontë has abruptly to break off this passage with an intrusive effort to make it all make sense. As Jael is "dwell[ing] on the faithful expectation of Heber coming home," Lucy suddenly interrupts, saying, "By which words I mean that the cool peace and dewy sweetness of the night filled me with a mood of hope ..." and we return to the garden of the pensionnat. Yet even this intervention cannot account for the bizarre story the passage tells, cannot make its every detail correspond to the "higher meaning" of Lucy's "inner self" – which here is simultaneously a man, a woman, and an angel in a tent, with Heber waiting in the wings. The correspondences here are arbitrary and forced, so arbitrary that they call for explanation "in other words." Such a supplementary explanation is exactly what Brontë *refused* to include when her publishers complained that Lucy's narrative was hard to understand. "It would be too much like drawing a picture and then writing underneath the name of the object intended to be represented," she said. Yet after the Jael and Sisera interlude, that is indeed what she must do.

The Jael and Sisera passage is certainly not the way to a supersensory totality. Nor does the passage lead to the divinely ordained history of typology, for it is no more properly typological than it is properly symbolic. It indulges in what Fairbairn characterizes as "allegorical license," a perversion of proper typology in which the type becomes nothing but an "ostensible representation" which is then used "simply as a cover for the higher sense, which may refer to things ever so remote from those immediately described." In allegory, "the Bible [can] be made to reflect every hue of fancy ... it would be turned into one vast sea of uncertainty and confusion."[66] Such is the case in *Villette*, for the text from Judges, cited as a type for Lucy's sufferings, is simply cancelled, left behind in the reference to "things ever so remote." Far from establishing the narrative on the firm ground of divinely ordained history, *Villette* is cast adrift.

In the forty-two chapters of *Villette*, there are twenty-five wildly allegorical passages, ranging from several sentences to several pages in length. Most have some element of religious intertextuality, referring either to the Bible or to *The Pilgrim's Progress*, and yet the typological dimension simply contributes to the ruin of representation one witnesses in *Villette*. For no single coherent meaning can be assigned to these figures (if one reads them carefully, without skipping), and, as Derrida observes in a reading of the "law" said to govern signification, "Univocity is the essence, or better, the *telos* of language.... What is proper to man is doubtless the capacity to make metaphors, but in order to mean some thing, and only one."[67] While Derrida evokes this law to question the grounds of its authority, Brooks's theory of narrative – the "central act of existence" – abides by it, making narrative depend on differences only to reveal in the end a more profound order of resemblance, a resolution into "total metaphor." *Villette*, however, deviates markedly from the way to singular, resolved meaning. For the extended allegorical figures display the failure of resemblance, both in the highly artificial and largely unsuccessful system of correspondences they establish, and in the uncontrollable metonymic sequences which generate the allegorical details.

This is true of the Jael and Sisera passage, and even more so of the extended figure in which Lucy responds to Monsieur Emmanuel's decision that she should participate in a public examination and improvise a composition in French:

I knew what the result of such an experiment would be. I, to whom nature had denied the impromptu faculty; who, in public, was by nature a cypher; whose time of mental activity, even when alone, was not under the meridian sun; who needed the fresh silence of morning, or the recluse peace of evening, to win from the Creative Impulse one evidence of his presence, one proof of his force; I, with whom that Impulse was the most intractable, the most capricious, the most maddening of masters (him before me always excepted) – a deity which sometimes, under circumstances apparently propitious, would not speak when questioned, would not hear when appealed to, would not, when sought, be found; but would stand, all cold, all indurated, all granite, a dark Baal with carven lips and blank eye-balls, and breast like the stone face of a tomb; and again, suddenly, at some turn, some sound, some long-trembling sob of the wind, at some rushing past of an unseen stream of electricity, the irrational demon would wake unsolicited, would stir strangely alive, would rush from its pedestal like a perturbed Dagon, calling to its votary for a sacrifice, whatever the hour – to its victim for some blood or some breath, whatever the circumstance or scene – rousing its priest, treacherously promising vaticination, perhaps filling its temple with a strange hum of oracles, but sure to give half the significance to fateful winds, and grudging to the desperate listener even a miserable remnant – yielding it sordidly, as though each word had been a drop of the deathless ichor of its own dark veins. And this tyrant I was to compel into bondage, and make it improvise a theme, on a school estrade. . . .

(p. 346)

In a letter to G. H. Lewes, Brontë uses a more measured version of the same figure to characterize her relation to creative inspiration. She declares,

When authors write best, or, at least, when they write most fluently, an influence seems to waken in them, which becomes their master – which will have its own way – putting out of view all behests but its own, dictating certain words, and insisting on their being used, whether vehement or measured in their nature. . . .[68]

This is the power of poetry, of a spirit which moves the author to represent the truth regardless of the artificial constraints of convention. It is a higher power, a breath of the divine moving on the earth through the inspired writers. The extended figure with which Lucy represents the Creative Impulse seems to have been written under such an influence, which dictates these vehement words to represent the most profound truth of the narrative: the truth of representation, of the complexities of consciousness itself. So this passage, representing the process of representation, needs to be especially intelligible.

It is not. The rhetorical turns of the passage begin with the mundane and "literal" fact of writing a composition but leave it far behind, cancelling without preserving it in some higher meaning. In the place of Lucy on the school estrade, improvising a theme, stand strikingly concrete details produced by metonymic association – a "carven" granite idol, lips and eyeballs, the stone face of a tomb, some sob of the wind, a stream of electricity, a votary, a sacrifice, blood and breath, the hum of oracles, a drop of ichor, dark veins. Relationships of contiguous association move the text from granite to stone; from wind to electricity; from votary to sacrifice to blood and breath; from priest to temple to oracle, and so on. This passage is not governed by the principle of resemblance, but by the pure contingency of metonymy, each instance of metonymic contact simply leading to the next, composing a sequence of associations that has its own mechanical logic, but none of the revered analogical, integrating, conceptual force of metaphor.[69] The figure of the Creative Impulse never approaches such a luminous truth, although in personifying this Impulse and transforming it into a deity, Brontë is at least establishing allegorical correspondences, however awkward and disruptive. Once she arrives at that deity, however, the metonymic sequence takes off, and all possibility of resemblance disappears in the welter of details.

Any hope for identity disappears, too. The details make up a series of relative clauses which begin by modifying the "I" that starts the passage; this series goes on and on, abandoning its initial subject until it finally comes to a full stop – without ever having reached a predicate. If, as Ricoeur claims, "the central act of discourse [is] predication," an act which is in itself the metaphoric process, then this fragment is rigorously disqualified from that high function. The sentence is grammatically incomplete and logically incoherent, and the "I," that representative in language of subject and consciousness, is fragmented, endlessly modified until it is completely displaced.

The details in this allegorical rendering of the Creative Impulse thus violate the rule of metaphor, the process of making total sense which is thought to be in the nature of man. There is no necessary relation of part to whole, no synthesis of sensible and intelligible, no achieved totality in this passage, nor in the other extended figures which are such a characteristic aspect of *Villette*. The "immediate unity" of the symbolic is an impossibility: partly because allegory is constituted in an "unnatural" relation of sign to sign, an infinitely repeatable relation which never reaches a final synthesis; and also because the allegorical passages of *Villette*, already compromised by their failure to achieve resemblance, are further undone by a wild metonymy that is equally unstoppable, automatic, and governed by no "higher" necessity. Brontë's intensely figurative style promises semantic depth, but delivers an excess of signification not controlled by a rigorously independent essence. In so doing, it insists on difference and repetition rather than resemblance and closure, and undoes the order of intelligibility on which any totalizing system depends.[70]

*

Brontë's avowed intent is clear enough: to serve Truth and Nature by interpreting eloquently and effectively the oracles delivered by those two great deities. This is, in the nineteenth century, a project with a necessarily, explicitly historical dimension, for Victorian poets, novelists, philosophers, and theologians approached the Abstract and Ideal through the concrete and particular, through a material world which is also temporal, existing in both space and time. Thus the power of typology, which insists on the reality of the historical past (and also of a present soon to be history) while reading in it signs of an order which transcends all time. Brontë's secularization of the typological scheme, her move from the Divine Spirit to spirit as consciousness, does not disturb the theological structure in any important way, for consciousness remains that which creates meaning out of chaos, resemblance out of difference, intelligibility out of the purely sensual and material. And, as is evident from many careful and persuasive readings of her novel, *Villette* is generally considered successful to the degree that it represents this most fundamentally human attribute.[71]

However, her textual practice is another story, for it disturbs the very foundations of the analogical system of representation in which differences exist only to reveal a more profound unity. How the text does this is clear enough, but the question remains, why? To suggest an answer, it may be helpful to recall George Eliot's practice in *Daniel Deronda*, but not before turning for a moment back to Derrida, to his reading of the "law" which determines the "being" of man: man is said to be man in so far as he can make metaphors, can achieve a mimesis of the sensible world. In the economy of the same, as Derrida says, mimesis is proper to man, is of his nature. Further, in this economy, metaphor, although working through difference, must achieve synthesis; univocity is the end of language, the goal to which it aspires. So Derrida writes, "In this sense, the philosopher, who ever has but one thing to say, is the man of men."[72]

We have seen the economy of the same powerfully at work in George Eliot's writing, for *Daniel Deronda* is masterfully narrated and says one thing, the truth of man. As a philosophical novelist, Eliot aspires to be the man of men, dramatizing the truth of the dialectic, the workings of the "ideal forces" of history which cancel and preserve all difference, slowly and inexorably lifting the peoples of the world into an all-inclusive humanity. Her voice is magisterial, authoritative, wise, and her narrative an exemplary instance of the ordering power of resemblance, for there differences are evoked in order to produce the totality in which they are subsumed. Yet Eliot cannot be the man of men, for in proving the identity of man through the difference of women and the difference of the Jews, her text stresses how coercive, even violent that project must be. She thereby tells a different truth of man from the humanist story of progress and enlightenment, tells the truth that man's identity is predicated on violent exclusions and suppressions.

Villette, it seems, couldn't be further from *Daniel Deronda* both in terms of form and content. One is a "mere domestic novel," the representation of a solitary woman's struggle to self-consciousness, the other a "world-historical" philosophical novel which represents a history that stretches back to ancient Israel and forward to Zionism. Eliot aspires to be a philosopher; Brontë has no such aspirations. Yet both write texts in which "consciousness" is imagined in an integral relation to "history," and both texts are in fact riven by the differences they produce. Eliot's dialectical representation of differences moves towards a unifying vision of history as totality, towards a secular apocalypse of transcendental significance, Mordecai's vision of the Spirit embodied in the state: she aspires to a full *consciousness* of History. Yet as a woman writer who is subject to the Victorian system of sexual categorization, Eliot writes not as the man of men in the univocal voice to which philosophy aspires, but as Man *manqué*: her text coerces recalcitrant differences into a dialectical synthesis which reveals the costs of its production. In *Villette*, the inner life of Lucy Snowe – individual, even eccentric and idiosyncratic – is represented as typical in a discourse which makes consciousness itself the most salient historical fact. Yet "a great fault" opens up *Villette*, dividing the object from its representation, displacing the anthropomorphic relations of sensible and intelligible, the order on which history as consciousness necessarily rests.

These novels by two of the most prominent Victorian women writers thus emphasize the contradictions inherent in the regime of truth which constitutes man as the subject of history, which helps to consolidate the middle-class family, the bourgeois state, and the English empire. To show how *Daniel Deronda* reveals the high costs of these political projects, and how *Villette* brings to an impasse the philosophical-aesthetic operations of this problematic, is not to claim that these texts in and of themselves "subvert" the order in which they were written and read. However, it is to suggest that neither the univocity of philosophy nor the hegemony of the English patriarchal middle class are ever finally achieved, once and for all. History becomes, then, the possibility of reading the impossibility of totality, an impossibility in which "history" is necessarily inscribed.

Conclusion: The high cost of history

Where does one find history in Victorian Britain? Not only where one would expect to, in the British encounter with the *Philosophy of History* and Hegelianism in general, in Macaulay's *History of England* and Thackeray's historical novel. As my readings suggest, history is everywhere in the nineteenth century. It is integral to the design of Collins's three-act melodrama and to Dickens's melo-dramatic *Little Dorrit*, it is indispensable to Ruskin's aesthetics and to Brontë's representation of the solitary Lucy Snowe. History, then, appears in the least likely places, for in the nineteenth century history is the necessary condition for thought and saturates the field of knowledge.

It is generally held that the disappearance of God issued in the "discovery" of the historical, but it is less often observed that history itself is conceptualized in profoundly theological ways, imagined as the alpha and the omega of human life. This is a particular conception of history: "history" as the revelation of meaning, of truth, the revelation of the meaning and truth of humanity. To think his-torically in these terms is to comprehend, after the fact, the sig-nificance of the fact, to reconstruct, as best one can, the historical event, to grasp how it emerged from the past and how it carries within it the germ of the future. This is to dream of one day seeing history "itself."

Moreover, given this concept of history it becomes logically impossible to see anything but history, think anything but history; thus Carlyle's question, "[S]trictly considered, what is all Knowledge too but recorded Experience, and product of History," a question which presupposes its own answer in the ultimate identity of know-ledge and experience, concept and phenomena, subject and object. To read history otherwise – to find history in the texts of Victorian

Britain without discovering, with Carlyle, that it is the origin and end, world without end – requires posing different questions about history.

To ask "what is history?" yields little, for as Ellen Rooney and others have pointed out, that question is idealizing in its assumption that history is some thing in itself, that it is substantive, unified, to be known through its attributes.[1] The question presupposes its answer. But to ask "how is the concept of history produced?" shifts the focus to the ways in which "history" comes into being. And this leads to related questions: what are the limits of a particular text's historical field, and what is necessarily excluded to produce an historical understanding proper to the concept? What does "history" guarantee, and at what cost?

The guarantees are generally much more evident than the costs, which become visible only when one looks beyond the concept of "history" to the process by which it is produced. In the nineteenth century, "history" above all promises unity: the unity of humanity, the unity of time, the unity of meaning. Thus, in *Daniel Deronda*, history is taken to guarantee the unity of all men, and in Hegelian philosophy to ensure the ultimate identity of Spirit and phenomena, the concept and the real. In Macaulay's *History of England*, history is believed to guarantee the moral and material progress of the nation, and in *The History of Henry Esmond* the unity of the individual who is made up by the memory of his desires – though in *Esmond* this guarantee is voided by the irony of the text, its repetitions and unsettling reversals. Both *The Frozen Deep* and *Little Dorrit* offer their readers the melodramatic fix, the assurance that the past will be recovered in the future, the certainty that the pain of absence is inseparable from the pleasure of presence. Finally, typology, whether Fairbairn's biblical exegesis or Brontë's story of Lucy Snowe, envisions the past as an anticipation of the future, and history is the Word, promising that the sensible will be intelligible in the fullness of time – a promise *Villette* both makes and breaks as the figures of the text run wild.

It is just the guarantee of unity, however, which is so costly. Indeed, as these texts demonstrate, the effect of unity is achieved through systematic repressions, denials, and exclusions, operations which are necessarily invisible from within the totalizing field of foundational, sacred history. Thus Eliot cannot see the difference of Judaism, evoking the "superlative peculiarity" of the Jews only to sublate them into the higher unity of Humanity; she sees the difference of women, but only as a difference from men. These oversights are the price of recognizing history as the realization of Man, the blindness which allows Eliot to see history as a unified field.

To read *Daniel Deronda* differently – indeed, to read the differences in *Daniel Deronda* – is to reconfigure the field so as to see its construction of history as a coercive process rather than as a revelation of truth. It is to see that the "refractory" Gwendolen is "reduced to a mere speck" to pay for Deronda's transcendence. Further, if the one thing Eliot has to say is "history," the other is "women." That the first is predicated on the second is a difference internal to the supposed unity and totality of history "itself," and has consequences legible in all of the texts I have read. Beatrix, easily as refractory as Gwendolen, is banished to secure a new domestic and political order in Henry Esmond's narrative. Little Dorrit, angelic rather than demonic, vanishes to enable Clennam's self-realization. And Lucy Snowe, wandering in the wilderness, must have faith in Paul Emmanuel, who teaches her that "Time is not for God, nor Space."

Women are thus either rendered invisible or seen only as the immanent matrix of historical progress and fulfillment. In their exile from history, "women" confirm its truth. Furthermore, certain other collectivities which attain a notable prominence in Victorian thought, "savages" and the "lower orders," are equally, though differently, crucial to "history." The cunning Mohawk of Macaulay's essay on history, the treacherous Eskimos scorned by Dickens, the carnal Jews of typology, and the "Judaized" Roman Catholic "junta" of *Villette*; and Macaulay's gossiping servants, the undeserving poor, thieves, vagrants, and begging-letter writers of Dickens, those who "won't work" in Mayhew – all are less than fully historical, less than fully human. Lesser than Man, they confirm the teleological impetus of history, the progress by which the barbarous practices of ages past have been surpassed, the inevitable development which ensures the advances of the future.

For Victorians of the middle class, "those intelligent, warm-hearted households, which are the strength of our country" (to recall Mrs Oliphant's words), history has led to the civilization of Europe in general, more particularly to an England of unprecedented humanity. Even those who predict dire things for an overly materialistic society, and who meditate on the fallen nations of the past, see history issuing in the present. England, then, becomes a nation in which reform is a "sacred business" and empire the civilizing advance of history itself, concepts produced in what may be called the "space of formation" of a certain discourse of history. As Stuart Hall has observed,

> Discursive formations (or ideological formations that operate through discursive regularities) "formulate" their own objects of knowledge and their own subjects; they have their own repertoire of concepts, and are driven by their own logics ... constitute their own way of acknowledging what is true and excluding what is false within their own regime of truth.[2]

The discourse which formulates "history" as teleology, as totality, clearly formulates much more besides, most importantly the subjects who recognize this history (this narrative of development, this concept of the historical) and say, " 'That's obvious! That's right! That's true!' "[3] Thus the respect accorded to George Eliot, and the closeness of Dickens's relationship with his audience, "personally affectionate, and like no other man's" – both writers work with extraordinary energy and creativity to elaborate the logic of "history." Thus the bewilderment and outrage generated by the "reso-lution" of Thackeray's *Henry Esmond*, and the uncertainty and hostility which greeted *Villette* – while both texts are driven by the logic of history, each also undermines that regime of truth.

Ideology, as Althusser and others have suggested, is a process of recognition, the internalization of a certain order, and a crucial aspect of the formation of subjectivity itself. Further, ideology is inseparable from the production of knowledge; the apparent inno-cence of ideology, its invisibility, is the effect of a powerful conception of knowledge, which is knowledge as reflection. That is, the real object which is known is *there*, waiting to be comprehended, and knowledge belatedly recognizes it, makes sense of it.[4] In the discursive formation which produces "history," this logic is at work, making history "itself" the object of knowledge, identifying history and knowledge. "We do nothing but enact history, we say little but recite it," Carlyle declares in an exemplary ideological statement of the obviousness of history. History is there to be known, to be read like a book.

Read differently, read so as to question its immanence, its inno-cence, this history appears as a vicious circle which can only lead to repetitions, to the same story, time after time, to the Same. For Victorians, however, the obviousness and omnipresence of history endows it with the imperturbable guise of Necessity. Thus history becomes the "Invisible Power" of *Daniel Deronda*, which rides on the wind "till the mountains smoke and the plains shudder under the rolling, fiery visitation." We have seen what happens to Gwendolen, while Deronda is wrapped up in the whirlwind and lifted to new historical heights. It is in the nature of man to be subject to history, that reality which presses down upon him, and to achieve his transcendence – his knowledge of himself and his history – through that subjection. Mind, spirit, consciousness, and knowledge are all given by history, come to man through history, and make him what he is. In the process, "women" become material and contingent, unhistorical, uncomprehending, for they are necessarily outside of history as Necessity, the limit at which the circle History <———> Knowledge is inscribed.

To read history not as a Necessity (necessarily real) comprehended after the fact by the subject, but as a concept produced by a particular discourse, is to break the guarantee that history will give one truth and to deny the innocence of any knowledge.[5] Furthermore, it is to reformulate the question of necessity, for "history" is no longer foundational, and reading is no longer an innocent process of discovery. Indeed, all readings are guilty of producing their object of knowledge, which is not to say that knowledge is false, or true. It is to insist on knowledge as active production rather than passive recognition, and to insist that any reading must, as Althusser writes, "[take] responsibility for its crime as a 'justified crime' and [defend] it by proving its necessity."[6]

Reading the Victorian discourse of history as a process which formulates certain objects (history "itself") and certain subjects (the "men" who find themselves confirmed in history; the "women" and other "others" who are positioned so as to confirm the truth of that operation) is necessary because of the material effects of that discourse. The extension of Britain's imperial power to Palestine in an alliance with Zionism is not *caused* by reading the Jews as history incarnate (a reading to which Eliot contributes), but it is quite literally unthinkable without it. Similarly, Macaulay's reading of history does not alone ensure "the authority of law [and] the security of property," but such glorifications of the Glorious Revolution and the constitution are integral to the hegemony of the bourgeoisie. My readings are also concerned with other specific effects – for instance, the development of the apparatus of the tutelary state, the "sacred business" of social reform. Crucial to all is the creation of the Victorian concept of "women" and the consolidation of middle-class domesticity; this is the most general effect, the one to which each text contributes in some way. The closed patriarchal family becomes a site of extraordinary social and symbolic productivity.

Refusing the guarantees of universal "history" means that one can begin to see these social and political effects. Otherwise one sees everything only through the terms of the truth produced by the text – the truth of humanity (Eliot), the truth of political enlightenment and national progress (Macaulay, Thackeray), the truth of an over-arching ethical order (Collins, Dickens, and sometimes Mayhew), the truth of Eternity (Ruskin, Fairbairn), and of consciousness (Brontë). These diverse truths are all constructed within the "space of for-mation" of the historical problematic, are driven by the logic of "history" and conform to its rules. To discover and explicate these truths – the project of much Victorian criticism – is a great deal, but is not enough, for such work stays within the limits set by the discourse, reflects its logic, repeats its truths as truth.

Finally, breaking the mirror of history is a "justified crime" because history is already fractured, necessarily so, by the traces of all that is excluded from its field. The limit of history does not enclose a field homogeneous with itself, nor close out a homogeneous exterior, for, as my readings have been at pains to show, history is constituted precisely by what it excludes, most notably "women." The essence of history is predicated on the inessential and unhis-torical.[7]

Reading these processes of exclusion is not, however, to argue for a history that really would encompass everything and everyone. Such a history could only be Messianic, a model of history as salvation, the consummation of all difference in total unity. As Walter Benjamin comments aphoristically,

> Only the Messiah himself consummates all history, in the sense that he alone redeems, completes, creates its relation to the Mes-sianic. For this reason nothing historical can relate itself on its own account to anything Messianic. Therefore the Kingdom of God is not the *telos* of the historical dynamic; it cannot be set as a goal. From the standpoint of history it is not the goal, but the end.[8]

To counter the promises and consolations – and costs – of the sacred, Benjamin argues in his *Theses on the Philosophy of History* that one must "make the continuum of history explode" and "brush history against the grain."[9] These figures, like Althusser's declarations of crime and guilt, insist that history is a concept which is always produced and declare that production is always political. As Benjamin knows, the past can always be made to speak the truth of historical necessity: in *Daniel Deronda* the words of the ancient Hebrew poet give voice to Hegelian truths by denying the specificity of Judaism; in Mayhew the destitute old man dying in the "two-pair back," attended by his crippled wife, bears witness to the sublimity of pious resignation, the reality of virtue and the benevolence of the middle class. Such readings ensure that those who rule (here, the English and European bourgeoisie) are justified by "history." History has made them victorious, and history has an irresistible necessity.

Benjamin moves to explode history as justification and to produce a concept of history as an open field, not a linear progression or development. This is, then, a history without guarantees, but it is not a history without costs. One of the costs is the loss of all guarantees, and another is the necessity of breaks and divisions, the loss of universality. Unitary history is broken by the reality of political struggles; the task of the historian is to articulate the fault-lines in the field, to "remember" (by producing a concept adequate to think it) that history is the violent, often surreptitious engagement of conflicting forces.[10]

Intervening as an "historical materialist" in the philosophy of history, Benjamin contributes to a complex tradition of marxist thought, as does Althusser, whose theories of the production of knowledge and of history are situated specifically in relation to Marx's *Capital*. Indeed, marxism is a "space of formation" that produces very different truths from Eliot's humanism, Dickens's sentimental radicalism, Macaulay's narrative of the triumph of justice and the law, and so on. It would be impossible at this point to enter the specific debates about the philosophy of history which mark the long and various tradition of marxism (and equally the texts of post-structuralist theorists working tangentially to marxism), except, perhaps, to observe that the theoretical conjunction of politics and history has incalculably opened up the historical field.

This epistemological opening is related to (but not identical with) another reconfiguring of the field of history, the writing of histories "from below." These histories – of women, of the working class, of Africans and African-Americans, of South Asians, and of all colonized peoples – are efforts to calculate and redress the high costs of a history predicated on their silence and invisibility. Just as marginalization was (and is) fully political in its impetus and effects, these histories are driven by a logic which insists that all history is imbricated with the political – as event and representation, as the event which is representation. Further, the project of these histories is as daunting as it is necessary, for in the historical record these collectivities are represented largely "from above." India, for instance, has been subjected to what Gayatri Spivak calls an "epistemic violence" which eradicated Indian categories, concepts, knowledge, and culture in the course of British domination and rule. How, then, is one to "recover" that history; how is one to reconstruct the subjected colonial other, who is known historically through the records of the colonizing subject? Similarly, any history of the working class, whether of men or women, must work with archival materials which record their lives in categories that are far from innocent; even statistics – *especially* statistics – are concepts saturated with politics, classifying what is visible and what counts.[11] And even middle-class women, however secure in their class position, are "hidden from history," hidden in the closed patriarchal family, in their private and intimate sphere.

The histories of the collectivities which inhabit the prohibited margins of universal history have thus necessarily changed how history is conceived, changed its objects and its methods and its ends. The discourse of history which so pervades the nineteenth century and still marks the twentieth has as its celebrated end the truth of man (to recall Macaulay's words, "the noblest earthy object of the contemplation of man is man himself"), who, because he is mortal, is to be known through history. Another end is more surreptitious, the political aim of consolidating that "man" at the expense of all the other collectivities we have seen. If a certain historical discourse is now overtly political, it is to contest these ends and to calculate their costs. And this is the point at which explicitly theoretical challenges to the problematic of (universal) history intersect with histories "from below": history is seen as a production of knowledge which cannot – and must not – be separated from politics. One does not "find" history, one commits historical acts.[12] What is more, this discourse of history crosses disciplinary boundaries and its effects are by no means limited to the practice of history *per se*, nor even to the academy. To the contrary, the conjunction of history and politics has reconfigured knowledge and how it is produced.[13]

To pose the question of how "women" figure in these reconfigured fields is far beyond the scope of this book. But women's studies, of which this study is a part, has been deeply engaged with the problem of its object ("women") over the last decade or more, and this problem is inseparable from the problem of history. To ask, then, whether the late twentieth-century feminist production of knowledge participates in the nineteenth-century discourse of universal history and its questionable ends, or if the conjunction of history and politics has fully displaced that problematic, is the question which must bring this study to a close.

This question is, of course, still too large, but may be approached by narrowing the field, by considering how feminist literary critics have read nineteenth-century texts and what understanding of women emerges from those readings. While Helene Moglen's 1976 study, *Charlotte Brontë: The Self Conceived*, is not a fully representative text, it is exemplary in the way it formulates its problem, insisting that Brontë's texts can be adequately understood only when one understands her life and the historical forces which constructed that life. Further, Moglen studies the nineteenth century in order to know the twentieth: "[T]he world in which Charlotte Brontë lived is the world which we have ourselves inherited," she writes. Thus, "as we too strive for autonomous definition, we see ourselves reflected in different aspects of Brontë's struggle.... I have pursued my own shadow through the beckoning recesses of another's mind, hoping to discover its substance at the journey's end."[14] Knowledge of another leads to knowledge of the self; knowledge of the self leads to the recognition of a unitary identity shared with all women (thus Moglen's "we," her first-person plural). Indeed, an anecdote which she told at a conference to explain the genesis of the book best summarizes these issues.[15] She explained that she had been teaching *Villette*, Lucy Snowe's retrospective narration of emotional suffering and fleetingly realized satisfaction. At the end of the last class, one of her students – a woman – made her way to Moglen's side, burst into tears and declared, "I *am* Lucy Snowe!" This striking testimony of recognition and identification moved Moglen to study Brontë's life and works to discover how "the self" is "conceived" in her writings, to discover, in short, how a novel like *Villette* represents an identity in which women readers see themselves reflected. This moment of recognition – "that's true! that's me!" – points to an identity common to women, and the founding moment of feminist consciousness is identifying as a woman with all women. In this reading, history is continuous from Brontë's time to the present and her struggle is "ours."

Other important feminist works such as Elaine Showalter's literary history, *A Literature of Their Own: British Women Novelists from Brontë to Lessing*, and Sandra Gilbert and Susan Gubar's critical study, *The Madwoman in the Attic: The Woman Writer and the Nineteenth-Century Literary Imagination*, proceed along similar lines, returning to the nineteenth century to discover there the lives and the literature which have been invisible, to bring to light the experience of being a woman in a world in which women are systematically silenced, reading the palimpsest (to use Gilbert and Gubar's figure) in which women tell the truths of their double lives, one of conformity to men and their desires, and the other of imaginative anger, rebellion, and rage.[16] In these works, to historicize is first to discover women where there had only been men, to see women in history, and recognize a fundamental experience which unites all women, the experience of being "the other." Surely one of the reasons that so much feminist criticism has focused on the nineteenth century has to do with the ways in which Victorian culture works up gender, the ways in which "women" there are so sharply differentiated from "men" and from "history." For the exaggerated separateness of women, the ideology of domesticity, the elevation of the angel in the house, and the degradation of the fallen woman all are evidence that being a woman is to be a woman for men, to be woman-as-other. So feminist critics have argued that to read this in history, to show that women's historical experience has been the experience of "otherness," is to see more clearly the social and symbolic relations of the present and to know better what it means to be a woman.[17]

Such a reading obviously is no longer wholly within the discourse which produces history as man's truth, no longer accepts that history has only to do with men. Yet in a fundamental way this feminist reading is still within the "space of formation" of that discourse, for where once history revealed the truth of man's identity as a finite being, revealed man's fate, now history reveals the truth of women's lives, the fate of being a woman, of being "the Other." The closed circle of recognition is still inscribed, for all women are women in the same way, and this discovery of identity is predicated on a whole series of exclusions. Such is the burden of the sharp questions which Audre Lorde posed in 1979 at a major international conference devoted to feminist theory. Lorde asked why white feminists didn't address the differences between women:

If white american [*sic*] feminist theory need not deal with the differences between us, and the resulting difference in our oppressions, then how do you deal with the fact that the women who clean your houses and tend your children while you attend conferences on feminist theory are, for the most part, poor women and women of Color? What is the theory behind racist feminism?[18]

Lorde poses the question of "the differences between us" as a question of theory, and quite rightly so, since overlooking differences is precisely a theoretical problem, a problem of what can be seen in the field delimited by theory. "Racist feminism," as Lorde argues, is predicated on the invisibility of "poor women and women of Color" and is enabled by a theory which universalizes women.

A feminism that conceptualizes "women" as a unitary category which can be recognized in history works within the circle of ideological reflection, guaranteeing that women will be found everywhere and will be everywhere similar. The benefits for some women's versions of feminism are obvious – the consolidation of a unified "we," the authorization to speak for all women, including those silenced in the past. But, as many have observed in the last decade, the unity is achieved at the expense of the differences of race and class, not to mention ethnicity, sexual preference, age, and all the other differences which divide women.

Yet simply to acknowledge "the differences between us" is not enough, either. Certainly academic U.S. feminism has been importantly modified in the years since Lorde's questions – refigured as African-American feminism, lesbian feminism, white middle-class feminism, Chicana feminism, and so on. But these many feminisms still too often repeat the discourse of history and identity which they are trying to displace, find identity in history, look to history for answers, for standpoints, for a ground for their politics. This means that women remain a substantive entity, substantially unified *before* the achieved unity of women which is feminism, modified by differences but fundamentally the same. History becomes a matter of personal consciousness and experience; the discontinuities of "women," the place of this collectivity in a specific system of discursive relations and the politics by which it is produced, are overlooked in the process of self-reflection.

The questions about differences and theorizing difference which are so central to U.S. feminisms need to be explicitly discussed as questions about history and theories of history. Pluralizing differences within an encompassing unity of women or within a universal history of women is not enough. Rather, the concepts "history" and "historicize" must be transformed, appropriated to signify the production of differences ("history") and the reading of the effects of that process ("historicizing"). Tracing the repressive hierarchies and violent exclusions of a certain "history" is to historicize history, to see that the production of historical knowledge is necessarily political and to read "history" and its "others" as political effects. Reading historically is in fact a necessity, for there is no end to history, no "beyond" of the historical; to project such an end is inevitably idealist, an ideological erasure of politics which can never be in the interests of feminism.[19]

To historicize without repeating the logic of universal history is to see "history" as a *pharmakon*, both poison and remedy.[20] That is, the (never ending, ever repeated) "cure" for history is history, a homeopathic remedy which appropriates the terms of a certain problematic not to finish off history, but to effect a theoretical transformation of the historical field. If the feminist problematic is to shift from the recognition of women in history, "history" must be posed as a theoretical problem. To historicize without surreptitiously returning to history as usual is to see that "being" a woman provides no ontological or epistemological foundation, as Denise Riley has argued, and to understand that the collectivity "women" is "historically, discursively constructed, and always relatively to other categories which themselves change."[21]

Reading "women" as an effect rather than recognizing women as a substantive entity which waits to be discovered is radically historical, a radical remedy to history-as-truth. This recasting of "history," this displacement of the anthrocentric problematic of history is necessary to feminism, as is the transformation of other intensely over-determined concepts – "consciousness," "experience," "identity" – which have been central to U.S. feminist discourse. This is a crucial aspect of Teresa de Lauretis's writing, for example; she has taken up these concepts in order to remake their theoretical status and political effectivity. "Identity," she writes, "is not the goal but rather the point of departure of the process of self-consciousness." While this sounds familiar (much like Moglen's formulation, in fact), de Lauretis quickly changes the terms of the argument. "Self" and "consciousness" are the product of "experience," but her concept of "experience" is theoretically precise, designating "an ongoing process by which subjectivity is constructed semiotically and historically ... a complex of habits resulting from the semiotic interaction of 'outer world' and 'inner world,' the continuous engagement of a self or subject in social reality."[22] She argues that a "feminist frame of reference" must be built "from women's own experience of difference, of our differences from Woman and of the differences among women" (p. 14). "Identity" must be "interpreted and reconstructed" within this frame of reference (p. 8), which means that identity is fully historical and political. "The personal," long said by white feminists to *be* the political, is displaced so that the *relation* between "experience" and history, the personal and the political can in fact be seen.

Such a displacement is a theoretical necessity since, as Gayatri Spivak has observed, "knowledge is made possible and sustained by irreducible difference, not identity." To assume that simply being a woman gives one knowledge about women is to make "the person identical with her predicament." This, Spivak writes, "is actually the figure of the impossibility and non-necessity of knowledge."[23] Absolute identity forecloses knowledge in an imaginary relation of direct reflection, in the imagined unity of subject and object of knowledge – there knowledge is at an end, just as the Messianic finishes off history. All that is left are ideological reflections of a preconceived unity, the unity of women.

A feminist frame of reference, then, the condition for feminist knowledge, would necessarily be historical, built as de Lauretis says from the historically and semiotically constructed experience of difference. "Experience" itself is thus an effect, as is the subject which "has" experience, effects that can only be read by attending to processes of differentiation. These processes make up the "general text," as Spivak says, "an immense discontinuous network ... of strands that may be termed politics, ideology, economics, history, sexuality, language, and so on," all of which configure subjectivity.[24] What is more, tracing these configurations, one can see that the category of "women" itself is not just internally divided, as in Lorde's "the differences between us," or de Lauretis's "the differences among us": "women" is not just modified by differences, it is a category that has no over-arching historical continuity even as it has the air of a fundamentally transhistorical entity. Riley reads the seeming immutability of gender itself, the apparent universality of the pair "men" and "women" as one of the grander constructs of modern thought. In a defiantly historical gesture, she announces that "there *aren't any* 'women,'" not to dissolve the reality of sexual categorization and its material effects, but to insist that "women" is historically variable, constituted differently in different social formations. Feminists must see, as she puts it, "the alterations in what 'women' are posed against, as well as established by – Nature, Class, Reason, Humanity and other concepts...."[25] In Victorian Britain, History is such an oppositional and establishing concept which formulates "women" in a certain way, ensuring that "the woman question" will be incessantly asked and never answered.

To see the experience of "being a woman" in Victorian Britain is thus to read the exile of women from History and their intimate relation with the new category of "the social." These are ideological processes, to be sure, but they are not thereby immaterial. Indeed, such a reading suggests that the long-standing opposition of the ideological and the real, words and things, divides what is inseparable, for women live "as women," live the consequences of the discursive production of "women."[26] So to declare that "there *aren't any* 'women'" is not to proclaim the end of women, the apocalypse of a beyond of sexual categorization, but to establish the conditions of possibility for an historically specific understanding of women. Finally, it is to see that women are only sometimes "women," that gender can at times recede in the face of other attributes – ethnicity, race, class, religion, and so on – and at other times be so dominant as to obscure anything else.

*

As for history, "there's no there there," no more than there "are" women. "'History' is a catachresis," Spivak says, "a metaphor without an adequate literal referent, in the last instance a model for all metaphors, all names."[27] Moreover, catachresis is a figure in which words are misused, used improperly, abused, and perverted.[28] To say that "history" is a catachresis is to deny that history has something proper to it, and, given the history of "history," this is decidedly perverse.

Since the nineteenth century, history has been endowed with foundational properties, has been taken to be proper to man himself, both the condition and guarantee of his knowledge.[29] While the conjunction of history and politics has displaced universal man from his privileged position, "history" has retained its explanatory power – indeed, "always historicize" is said to be the imperative of politically engaged reading. How can there be politics if history has no adequate literal referent? If history has nothing proper to it, no Necessity? Doesn't that mean the end of history altogether, the dream of a metaphysics or a theoreticism run wild?

These questions are all driven by the logic of history proper, and imply the answers which would confirm the questions. Only when one reads history and politics together, rather than seeing history as the cause of politics, can one see the truth of Spivak's formulation. That is, history is the reading of historical effects; history is no thing-in-itself, but a process that is always political. Not only is knowledge of history produced through readings, but the "events" of history, from the "world-historical" engagements of imperial Britain to the intimate exchanges of "private" life, are inseparable from discursive formations which work up certain subjects, certain objects. That there is no adequate referent is the possibility of history itself, the possibility of historical process, for adequation would be the end of history in totality: the totally adequate re-presentation of presence.

Totality *is* the end, the goal, of universal history, its *telos* which lifts up finite man, sublating his mortality in the knowledge of a total unity. Therefore, no reading of history which breaks with this problematic and refuses its costs can aim for adequation, for the literal truth of the empirical or the essential truth of the transcendental. However, the end of epistemological guarantees is not the end of history – only the displacement of a certain theory of history. In the opening of this gap is politics. History remains.

Notes

Introduction

1 Michel Foucault advances this argument in great detail in *The Order of Things: An Archaeology of the Human Sciences* (New York: Random House, 1973).

2 See Jacques Derrida, "The Ends of Man," for a reading of the teleological goals and eschatological limits of "man" (in *Margins of Philosophy*, trans. Alan Bass (Chicago: The University of Chicago Press, 1982), pp. 109–36).

3 I realize that this process can be read in the texts of the West from the ancients to the moderns (as Luce Irigaray does in *Speculum of the Other Woman*, trans. Gillian G. Gill (Ithaca: Cornell University Press, 1985) and *This Sex Which Is Not One*, trans. Catherine Porter (Ithaca: Cornell University Press, 1985)). In the nineteenth century it is specifically enacted through "history," and it is that specificity with which I am here concerned.

4 Carlyle, "On History," in Alan Sheridan (ed.), *Thomas Carlyle: Selected Writings* (Harmondsworth: Penguin Books, 1971), p. 51.

5 The Society of Antiquaries, The British Archaeological Association (1843), the Royal Historical Society (1868), the Society of Biblical Archaeology (1870), the Society for the Protection of Ancient Buildings (1877), the Egypt Exploration Fund (1882). These societies, whose members were overwhelmingly professional men of the middle class, raised money for historical preservation and exploration, printed manuscript collections, and studied the remains of Britain's Anglo-Saxon, Roman, and medieval past. For a detailed history of the development of historical disciplines in nineteenth-century England, see Philippa Levine, *The Amateur and the Professional: Antiquarians, Historians, and Archaeologists in Victorian Britain, 1838–1886* (Cambridge: Cambridge University Press, 1986).

6 John Stuart Mill, *The Spirit of the Age* (Chicago: University of Chicago Press, 1942), p. 1, quoted by Louis Menand, "The Victorian Historical Sense and Modernism," *Victorian Newsletter*, 61 (spring 1982), p. 5.

7 (London/Newcastle, 1851), pp. 40, 49, quoted by Levine, op. cit., p. 82.

8 *English Historical Review*, 1 (1886), p. 5.

9 Frederic Harrison, *The Meaning of History and Other Historical Pieces* (New York: Macmillan and Co., 1896), pp. 11, 12, 14.

10 Matthew Arnold, *On the Classical Tradition*, ed. R. H. Super (Ann Arbor: University of Michigan Press, 1960), p. 20, quoted by Frank Miller Turner, *The Greek Heritage in Victorian Britain* (New Haven: Yale University Press, 1981), p. 28.

11 *Antiquary: A Magazine Devoted to the Study of the Past*, 1 (January–June, 1880), p. iii. This magazine is one of a number devoted to historical subjects which were directed to a popular rather than scholarly audience. In the 1850s, *Historian* and *Historical Educator* published; from 1860 to 86, *Reliquary*; in the 1870s, *Antiquary* (a different magazine) and *Long Ago*. See Levine for a detailed discussion.

12 A. Dwight Culler, *The Victorian Mirror of History* (New Haven: Yale University Press, 1985), p. 4.

13 To note only two other instances of this reasoning: Adena Rosmarin, in "The Historical Imagination: Browning to Pound," writes, "To imagine ourselves thinking, writing, living, and dying in another time is to imagine ourselves as other selves. It is also to define ourselves as such" (*Victorian Newsletter*, 61 (spring 1982), p. 11). And in "The Victorian Historical Sense and Modernism," Louis Menand's logic is the same: "The imagination of history implies the imagination of oneself in relation to that history; imagining the past is a way of imagining oneself" (ibid., p. 5).

14 The Hegelianism of Eliot's thought, derived from her work with the Young Hegelians (particularly Feuerbach), ensures that history always aspires to totality. In general, Victorians sought to subsume differences and conflicts into a continuous History driven by necessity; the first chapter of this study is thus devoted to Eliot and Hegel since their texts clearly demonstrate the drive to conceptualize history in totalizing and universal terms. However, I am not claiming that all conceptions of history in nineteenth-century England are explicitly Hegelian or directly indebted to Hegelian philosophy, as subsequent chapters will show.

Chapter 1 George Eliot's apocalypse of history

1 "Prophetess of Humanity," "more like Bibles": W. H. Mallock, unsigned review of *Impressions of Theophrastus Such*, *Edinburgh Review*, cl (October 1879), pp. 557–86, in David Carroll (ed.), *George Eliot: The Critical Heritage* (London: Routledge & Kegan Paul, 1971), pp. 452, 453. "National blessing": John Blackwood, letter to George Eliot, 19 November 1874, in Gordon S. Haight (ed.), *The George Eliot Letters*, VI (New Haven: Yale University Press, 1955), p. 91.

2 Michel Foucault's important book, *Discipline and Punish: The Birth of the Prison*, trans. Alan Sheridan (New York: Random House, 1979), is a detailed study of the ways in which knowledge is implicated with power, and a reading of the formulation of social subjects.

3 For a powerful reading of Eliot's humanism as bourgeois ideology, see Daniel Cottom, *Social Figures: George Eliot, Social History, and Literary Representation* (Minneapolis: University of Minnesota Press, 1987).

4 Eliot, letter to Dr Joseph Frank Payne, 25 January 1876, in Haight (ed.), op. cit., VI, p. 216.

5 George Henry Lewes to John Blackwood, 1 December 1875, in Haight (ed.), op. cit., VI, p. 196.

6 Lord Acton, *Letters of Lord Acton to Mary, Daughter of the Right Hon. W. E. Gladstone*, ed. Herbert Paul (1904), in Carroll (ed.), op. cit., p. 462.

7 In this, Eliot's experiments confirm Michel Foucault's observation that "a discourse attempting to be both empirical and critical cannot but be both positivist and eschatological; man appears within it as a truth both reduced and promised" (*The Order of Things: An Archaeology of the Human Sciences* (New York: Random House, 1973), p. 320.)

8 Eliot, letter to Mrs William Smith, 1 July 1887, Haight (ed.), op. cit., VI, p. 64.

9 *Impressions of Theophrastus Such*, in *Works of George Eliot*, VIII (New York: The Nottingham Society, n. d.), p. 112.

10 "Leaves from a Note-Book," in ibid., VIII, p. 218.

11 Besides her novels, Eliot's particular contributions to the death of God are her translations and reviews of the German "Higher Criticism." Carlyle preceded her in his interest in German philosophy, but she is more rigorously philosophical than he, and her fiction was more widely read. All of her novels, from *Scenes of Clerical Life* to *Daniel Deronda*, bear witness to the truths not of God but of man.

12 Eliot, letter to Mme Eugène Bodichon, 2 October 1876, in Haight (ed.), op. cit., VI, p. 290.

13 F. R. Leavis, *The Great Tradition: George Eliot, Henry James, Joseph Conrad* (New York: New York University Press, 1964), p. 109.

14 Henry James, "Daniel Deronda: a Conversation," *Atlantic Monthly* xxxviii (Dec. 1876), 684–94, in Carroll (ed.), op. cit., p. 431.

15 Carroll (ed.), op. cit., p. 431.

16 George Eliot, *Daniel Deronda*, ed. Barbara Hardy (New York: Penguin Books, 1967), p. 875. Further references will be to this edition and will be given parenthetically in the text.

17 *Theophrastus Such*, *Works*, op. cit., VIII, p. 158.

18 Mordecai goes on to find in Israel an organic unity composed of law, religion, and morality: this is the unity of the nation. " 'Where else is there a nation of whom it may be truly said that their religion and law and moral life mingled as the stream of blood in the heart and made one growth . . . ?' " (p. 590).

19 Cynthia Chase, " 'The Decomposition of Elephants': Double-reading *Daniel Deronda*," *Publications of the Modern Language Association* (*PMLA*), 93:2 (March 1978).

20 While I am arguing that the explicitly feminist elements of *Daniel Deronda* are developed by Eliot only to be subsumed into a "world-historical" system which actually is antithetical to feminism, the fact that she is so eloquent about the specific sufferings of women works against the totalizing design of the book, no matter how strongly she asserts that totality and its necessity. This tension is not unique to *Daniel Deronda*; it appears throughout her work and has made her writing an

especially rich subject for feminist criticism. Indeed, the problem of Eliot's construction of her heroines and especially of her resolution of their stories has long been under discussion by feminist critics. Some have faulted Eliot for making her women characters subject to conventions she herself broke, citing Dinah's retirement from preaching when she marries Adam in *Adam Bede*, the death of Maggie in *The Mill on the Floss*, the ways in which both Romola and Dorothea (in *Romola* and *Middlemarch*) subside into domesticity, the truncated future left to Gwendolen in *Daniel Deronda*. See, for example, Jenni Calder, *Women and Marriage in Victorian Fiction* (New York: Oxford University Press, 1978); and Ellen Ringler, "*Middlemarch*: A Feminist Perspective," *Studies in the Novel*, 15 (spring 1983), pp. 55–61. Others have argued that Eliot is simply demonstrating the degree to which women are disadvantaged (see Lisa Gerrard, "Romantic Heroines in the Nineteenth-Century Novel: A Feminist View," *International Journal of Women's Studies*, 7 (January–February 1984), pp. 10–16), or say that Eliot is advocating the discredited womanly virtues of sympathy and renunciation (see Kathleen Blake, "Armgart: George Eliot on the Woman Artist," *Victorian Poetry*, 18 (1981), pp. 75–80).

Other critics have approached these problems by considering Eliot's relation to the dominant masculine literary tradition, reading in her novels a covert subversion of the received wisdom about women. Sandra M. Gilbert and Susan Gubar show in her works a violent, angry attack on the status quo that is in conflict with her ostensible celebration of traditionally feminine virtues (*The Madwoman in the Attic: The Woman Writer and the Nineteenth-Century Literary Imagination* (New Haven: Yale University Press, 1979)). Similarly, Margaret Homans, in "Eliot, Wordsworth and the Scenes of the Sisters Instruction" (chapter 6 of *Bearing the Word: Language and Female Experience in Nineteenth Century Women's Writing* (Chicago: University of Chicago Press, 1986)), argues that what seems to be Eliot's docile repetition of Wordsworthian ideas and themes is actually a charged and ambivalent reworking, not a simple case of influence at all; and in "Figuring the Mother: Madonna Romola's Incarnation" (chapter 8, ibid.) considers the contradictions of a text which celebrates literal, faithful representation, and transmission while recreating the literal historical world of Savonarola's Florence around the fully fictional figure of Romola. So, too, Nancy K. Miller, reading *The Mill on the Floss*, considers Eliot's relation to a masculine tradition, showing that this novel, like many other texts by women, is "about the plots of literature itself, about the constraints the maxim places on rendering a female life in fiction," and by its "improbable" end emphasizes the power of conventions not only in literature but in life, and protests against them ("Emphasis Added: Plots and Plausibilities in Women's Fiction," *PMLA*, 96 (1981)).

Judith Lowder Newton, in *Women, Power, and Subversion: Social Strategies in British Fiction, 1778–1860* (Athens, Georgia: University of Georgia Press, 1981), argues that in *The Mill on the Floss* Eliot's "potentially radical analysis of Maggie's oppression by the community" is compromised by "her attenuation of protest and valorization of corporate loyalty"; Newton stresses Eliot's "brilliant resistance to ideology" while acknowledging the ambivalence of the novel. Mary Jacobus reads the text as more fully subversive by analyzing Eliot's challenges to a masculine demand for social, linguistic, and philosophical mastery ("The Question of Language: Man of Maxims and *The Mill on the Floss,*" *Critical Inquiry,* 8 (winter 1981), pp. 207–22). Elizabeth Weed, in "*The Mill on the Floss,* or the Liquidation of Maggie Tulliver," is equally concerned with the problem of signification, arguing that Maggie, as a woman, cannot be "representative," an impossibility suggested by various logical impossibilities in the text (*Genre* 11:2 (fall 1978), pp. 427–44).

Because of Eliot's intense focus on Maggie in *The Mill on the Floss,* and because hers is a gender-specific tragedy, many feminist critics have written on that novel. *Daniel Deronda* has more recently been the subject of attention, particularly for critics interested in the political ideological implications of Eliot's writing. Thus both Catharine Bealsey ("Rereading the Great Tradition," in Peter Widdowson, (ed.), *Rereading English* (London: Methuen, 1982)) and John Good ("'The Affections Clad with Knowledge': Woman's Duty and the Public Life," *Literature and History,* 9 (spring 1983), pp. 38–51) argue that Eliot makes sexual politics an irreducible problem in *Daniel Deronda* which subverts the liberal humanism of the novel (conclusions with which I disagree). Mary Wilson Carpenter, in "'A Bit of Her Flesh': Circumcision and 'The Signification of the Phallus' in *Daniel Deronda,*" *Genders* 1:1 (1988), pp. 1–23, also argues that the text is subversive; her reading focuses not so much on sexual politics *per se* as on the textual figure of circumcision, the "identifying" inscription of Jewishness and masculinity which she sees linked to Gwendolen in an undoing of religious and gendered identity. In "George Eliot and *Daniel Deronda*: The Prostitute and the Jewish Question," Catherine Gallagher considers Eliot's complicated relation to literary, economic, and sexual systems of production and exchange (in Ruth Bernard Yeazell (ed.), *Sex, Politics, and Science in the Nineteenth-Century Novel* (Baltimore: Johns Hopkins University Press, 1984), pp. 39–62). Gallagher has also written on *Felix Holt* in *The Industrial Reformation of the English Novel: Social Discourse and Narrative Form: 1832–1867* (Chicago: University of Chicago Press, 1985), analysing Eliot's contributions to the debates on artistic and political representation, contributions which reveal Eliot's deeply conservative positions. So, too, Ruth Bernard Yeazell has discussed the politics of *Felix Holt,* showing how Eliot displaces political conflict on to a story of courtship ("Why Political Novels Have Heroines: *Sybil, Mary Barton,* and *Felix Holt,*" *Novel,* 18 (winter 1985), pp. 126–44).

Jacqueline Rose in "George Eliot and the Spectacle of the Woman" (in *Sexuality in the Field of Vision* (London: Verso, 1986)) develops a psychoanalytic reading of the sexual politics of the text, interpreting Gwendolen as an hysteric, a spectacle for the other characters, for the narrator, and for the readers. Rose sees in this a contradiction, both a critique and an affirmation of the whole system which produces "woman" as the object of the gaze: "the hysteria of the woman is given as a fantasy of the man at the same time as George Eliot qua narrator implicates herself so directly in the perversity, and even pleasure, of the process" (p. 120). I think that some of the recent work on Eliot indicates a new direction in feminist criticism of her writings, one which stresses the ways in which Eliot is implicated in the political, ideological, and discursive scene of Victorian Britain.

I would like to acknowledge my indebtedness to the feminist critics of Eliot whose work has helped me understand the inescapable importance of gender both in Eliot's texts and in the work of criticism.

21 Eliot, letter to Emily Davies, 8 August 1868, in Haight (ed.) op. cit., IV, p. 468.

22 Michel Foucault, *The Archaeology of Knowledge*, trans. A. M. Sheridan Smith (New York: Harper & Row, 1972), p. 12.

23 John Kucich develops a significant revisionary reading of Eliot's work, including *Daniel Deronda*, in *Repression in Victorian Fiction: Charlotte Brontë, George Eliot, and Charles Dickens* (Berkeley: University of California Press, 1987). He argues that repression is a productive force, one which produces the modern subject as a deeply privitized entity; he sees Gwendolen's "experience" in *Daniel Deronda* as illustrative of this and a demonstration that "what is missing in Eliot is not fulfilled desire or passion, but the truly social, interdependent vision she tried so hard to achieve" (p. 200). I agree with Kucich that Eliot fails on this count – necessarily, given the terms of her project. But I find that gender makes a difference in the way repression works in *Daniel Deronda*, and think that Gwendolen is repressed in a far more punitive way than Deronda.

24 Edward Said, *Orientalism* (New York: Random House, 1979). Matthew Arnold, *Culture and Anarchy*, in A. Dwight Culler (ed.), *Poetry and Criticism of Matthew Arnold* (New York: Houghton Mifflin Co., 1961), pp. 407–75. Further references to *Culture and Anarchy* will be given parenthetically in the text.

25 *Theophrastus Such*, *Works*, op. cit., VIII, p. 87.

26 The entry for "Hebraism-Hellenism" in Alex Preminger (ed.), *Princeton Encyclopedia of Poetry and Poetics* (Princeton: Princeton University Press, 1974), p. 336, notes that "Ernest Renan foreshadowed Arnold's historical development of Hebraic-Hellenic strains in *Les Origines du Christianisme* (1863) and later expanded this idea in a preface to his *Histoire des peuples d'Israel* (1887–93)." See Said, op. cit., pp. 123–48, for an extensive discussion of the anti-Semitism of Renan's Orientalist work.

27 Eliot, letter to Mrs Harriet Beecher Stowe, 29 October 1876, in Haight (ed.), op. cit., VI, p. 302.

28 *Theophrastus Such*, *Works*, op.cit., VIII, p. 156.

29 "Leaves from a Notebook," ibid., VIII, p. 218.

30 Eliot, letter to Mrs Harriet Beecher Stowe, 29 October 1876, in Haight (ed.), op. cit., VI, p. 301.

31 *Theophrastus Such*, *Works*, op. cit., VIII, p. 161.

32 ibid., p. 150.

33 Jacques Derrida, *Glas*, trans. John P. Leavey Jr and Richard Rand (Lincoln: University of Nebraska Press, 1986), p. 56a. In *Glas*, Derrida

considers the inseparability of idealist philosophy and Christianity – and the difference of Judaism – in a lengthy reading of Hegel's works, especially Hegel's analysis of the Holy Family. He writes, "Philosophy is descended, as its own proper object, from Christianity of which it is the truth, from the Holy Family which it falls under (whose relief it is) [dont elle (est la) relève]" (p. 95a). As for the Jews,

> they consider the family nomination of the relation of God to men or to Jesus as images [Bilde], in the most external sense, as ways of speaking or imagining. Thus do they disqualify what essential the advent of Christianity can include in the history of the spirit.
>
> (p. 84a)

In thinking about the relation of Judaism and the Greco-Christian philosophical tradition, I found very useful Susan Handelman's essay, "Jacques Derrida and the Heretic Hermeneutic," in Mark Krupnick (ed.), *Displacement: Derrida and After* (Bloomington: Indiana University Press, 1983), pp. 98–129).

34 Burleigh Taylor Wilkins, *Hegel's Philosophy of History* (Ithaca: Cornell University Press, 1974), p. 57.

35 *The Philosophy of History*, quoted by Wilkins, p. 57.

36 Hegel grants the Jews a certain importance in that they were the first to conceive of the Fall:

> from it has sprung the higher development by which the spirit arrived at absolute self-consciousness.... Man, created in the image of God, so the tale goes, had lost his absolute contentment, because he had eaten of the tree of knowledge of good and evil.... This is a deep truth that evil results from consciousness.... Only consciousness produces the splitting of the ego.
>
> (quoted by Wilkins, p. 86)

But this concept of the splitting necessary to consciousness is still a primitive idea; according to Hegel, the ancient Greeks, whose gods are anthropomorphic, actually come closer to the Christian idea of the incarnation.

> The Greek gods, while they are represented as human, each have an individual character; this anthropomorphism has been described as a defect. Quite on the contrary, man as a spiritual being constitutes the element of truth in the Greek gods which render them superior to all other natural deities, and superior also to all mere abstractions of the one and highest essence. It may be posited as an advantage of the Greek gods that they are represented as men....

(*The Philosophy of History*, trans. Carl F. Friedrich and Paul W. Friedrich, in Carl F. Friedrich (ed.), *The Philosophy of Hegel* (New York: Random House, 1953), p. 59)

37 Hegel, *The Philosophy of History*, in ibid., p. 23.

38 ibid., p. 14.

39 Hegel, *Reason in History*, quoted by Wilkins, op. cit., p. 53.

40 Hegel, *The Philosophy of History*, in Friedrich (ed.), op. cit., pp. 36, 42.

41 See Hani al-Raheb, *The Zionist Character in the English Novel* (London: Zed Books, 1965), for a discussion of Mordecai's Zionism. He writes, "It is perhaps through this conservative concept of restoring the past, in which agnosticism leaves its place to mysticism in the case of the Deronda group, that George Eliot's much-regretted failure in artistry and sensibility can be explained" (p. 91). I think that the "mysticism" is simply nationalism, quite secular in fact.

42 Nahman Krochmal, "A Philosophy of Jewish History," in Michael A. Meyer (ed.), *Ideas of Jewish History* (New York: Behrman House, Inc., 1974), p. 199. Henrich Graetz (the great nineteenth-century historian of Jewish life) notes that for some of his contemporaries, "Judaism [is] an elaboration of speculative theology, an early anticipation of Hegelianism ..." (ibid., p. 219). He may have had in mind Krochmal or perhaps Immanuel Wolf, one of the founders in Berlin in 1819 of the "Society for Culture and Science of the Jews." Wolf was deeply influenced by German idealism, and argues that Jewish history is the history of a concept, the concept of God. See ibid., pp. 141–55.

43 ibid., pp. 201, 203.

44 For a discussion of Krochmal's work, see Shlomo Avineri, "The Fossil and the Phoenix: Hegel and Krochmal on the Jewish Volkgeist" and Leo Rauch's "Comments" on Avineri's essay, in Robert Perkins (ed.), *History and System: Hegel's Philosophy of History* (Albany: State University of New York Press, 1984), pp. 47–71.

45 Eliot stresses repeatedly the Kabbalistic elements of Mordecai's thinking, as in the scene when he hails Deronda from the bridge at sunset. He says to Deronda,

> "I have always loved this bridge: I stood on it when I was a little boy. It is a meeting place for the spiritual messengers. It is true – what the Masters said – that each order of things has its angel: that means the full message of each from what is afar."
>
> (p. 551)

And again, when Deronda has revealed to him the fact of his Jewish identity, Mordecai replies in Kabbalistic terms:

> "Daniel, from the first, I have said to you, we know not all the pathways. Has there not been a meeting among them, as of the operations in one soul, where an idea being born and breathing draws the elements towards it, and is fed and grows? For all things are bound together in that Omnipresence which is the place and habitation of the world, and events are as a glass where-through our eyes see some of the pathways."
>
> (p. 818)

46 Harold Bloom, *Kabbalah and Criticism* (New York: Seabury Press, 1975), pp. 24–5 and *passim*.

47 Michael Fishbane has declared that "the most characteristic feature of the Jewish imagination [is] the interpretation and rewriting of sacred texts" ("Inner Biblical Exegesis," in Geoffrey Hartman and Sanford Budick (eds) *Midrash and Literature* (New Haven: Yale University Press, 1986), p. 36).

48 Joseph Dan, "Midrash and the Dawn of Kabbalah," in ibid., p. 128.

49 "The Death of Moses," *Works*, op. cit., VIII, p. 395.

50 Richard Jacobson, "Absence, Authority, and Text," *Glyph*, 3 (1979), p. 146.

51 James L. Kugel, "Two Introductions to Midrash," in Hartman and Budick (eds), op. cit., p. 80.

52 John Blackwood, letter to Eliot, 1 April 1874, in Haight (ed.), op. cit., VI, p. 37.

53 Jacques Derrida, "Edmund Jabés and the Question of the Book," in *Writing and Difference*, trans. Alan Bass (Chicago: University of Chicago Press, 1978), p. 71.

54 John Freccero, "The Fig Tree and the Laurel: Petrarch's Poetics," *Diacritics*, 5 (1975), p. 37, quoted by Handelman, op. cit., p. 107.

55 For the classic psychoanalytic discussion of fetishism, see Freud's essay, "Fetishism," in James Strachey (ed.) *The Standard Edition of the Complete Psychological Works of Sigmund Freud*, XXI (London: The Hogarth Press, 1961), pp. 152–58.

56 *Simcox Autobiography*, 9 March 1880, quoted by Gordon Haight, *George Eliot: A Biography* (New York, Penguin Books, 1985), p. 535. Simcox has been criticized as an unreliable source; let me say that I am not citing this passage to "condemn" Eliot with true words out of her own mouth, but as an indication of her contradictory position: a woman who is the pre-eminent Victorian spokesman for a humanism that universalizes Man.

57 Haight (ed.), *Letters*, op. cit., V, p. 333, quoted by Haight, *George Eliot*, op. cit., p. 445.

Chapter 2 *Henry Esmond* and the subject of history

1 In a letter to the Rev. Whitwell Elwin, 24–31 May 1861, Thackeray writes,

> I wonder shall I have life and health to write Queen Anne? I long to get at it in my old age, feeling that the days of novels & romances and love making are over ... what about Books? You know we don't read 'em in London. I admire but can't read Adam Bede and the books of that Author.

(Gordon N. Ray (ed.), *The Letters and Private Papers of William Makepeace Thackeray*, IV (New York: Farrer, Straus & Giroux, 1980), p. 238)

2 Thomas Carlyle, "The Waverley Novels," *Edinburgh Review*, lv (April 1832), pp. 77–8, quoted by James C. Simmons, *The Novelist as Historian: Essays on the Victorian Historical Novel* (The Hague: Mouton, 1973), p. 28.

3 Macaulay, from a letter quoted by Sir Charles Firth, *A Commentary on Macaulay's History of England* (London: Macmillan & Co., 1938), p. 7.

4 Goldwin Smith, review in the *Edinburgh Review*, cx (October 1859), pp. 438–53, in Geoffrey Tillotson and Donald Hawes (eds), in *Thackeray:*

the Critical Heritage (London: Routledge & Kegan Paul, 1968), pp. 292–3.

5 Michel de Certeau, *Heterologies: Discourse on the Other*, trans. Brian Massumi (Minneapolis: University of Minnesota Press, 1986), p. 201.

6 ibid, p. 219.

7 Thomas Babington Lord Macaulay, from his Journal, quoted by T. F. Henderson in the "Editor's Introduction" to *History of England from the Accession of James II*, I (1849, reprinted London: Oxford University Press, 1931), pp. xiii, xiv.

8 Macaulay, "History," in *Critical, Historical and Miscellaneous Essays*, I (New York: Sheldon & Co., 1860), p. 340.

9 Macaulay, from his Journal, 28 June 1849, quoted by Sir Charles Firth, op. cit., p. 9.

10 Thackeray, letter to Mrs Carmichael-Smyth, 26 March 1851, Ray (ed.), *Letters*, op. cit., II, p. 761.

11 Certeau, op. cit., p. 218.

12 George Eliot, letter to Mr and Mrs Charles Bray, 13 November 1852, Gordon S. Haight (ed.), *The George Eliot Letters*, II (New Haven: Yale University Press) in Tillotson and Hawes (eds), op. cit., p. 151.

13 Mrs Oliphant, "Mr Thackeray and His Novels," *Blackwood's Magazine*, lxxvii (January 1855), pp. 86–96, in Tillotson and Hawes (eds), op. cit., p. 209.

14 John Forster, review in the *Examiner* (13 November 1852), pp. 723–6, in Tillotson and Hawes (eds), ibid., p. 150.

15 N. S. V. (January 1853), pp. 37–49, quoted by Gordon Ray, *Thackeray: The Age of Wisdom: 1847–1863* (New York: McGraw Hill, 1958), p. 192.

16 Mrs Oliphant, op. cit., p. 208.

17 G. H. Lewes, "Thackeray's New Novel," *Leader*, iii (6 November 1852), pp. 1071–3, in Tillotson and Hawes (eds), op. cit., p. 137; Anthony Trollope, "W. M. Thackeray," *Cornhill Magazine*, ix (February 1864), pp. 134–7, in Tillotson and Hawes (eds), op. cit., p. 327.

18 *The History of Henry Esmond, Esq. A Colonel in the Service of Her Majesty Queen Anne, Written by Himself* [and] *The English Humourists of the Eighteenth Century* [and] *The Four Georges* [and] *"Charity and Humour,"* ed. Mrs Anne Thackeray Ritchie (New York: Harper and Brothers, 1900), p. 11. All subsequent references to *Henry Esmond* and *The Four Georges* will be to this edition.

19 *The Four Georges*, pp. 621, 671.

20 ibid., p. 638.

21 Stephan Bann, in his essay "L'anti-histoire de *Henry Esmond*," *Poetique*, 9 (1972), 61–79, and J. Hillis Miller, in *Fiction and Repetition: Seven English Novels* (Cambridge, Mass.: Harvard University Press, 1982), pp. 73–115, both analyze the repetitions of astronomical imagery.

22 Thackeray's ironic distance from Esmond, which I discuss below, does not extend to Esmond's status as a slave-owning southern planter. On the whole, Thackeray thought that the critics of the slave system were misled by sentimental appeals, and that with a few natural exceptions, the owners treated the slaves quite well. While he protested that it is

wrong to hold a "fellow creature in bondage and make goods and chattle out of him and his issue," he was hardly persuaded that black people were his fellows, writing in the same letter that "they are not my men and brethren, these strange people with retreating foreheads, with great obtruding lips and jaws: with capacities for thought, pleasure, endurance quite different from mine ..." (Ray (ed.), op. cit., *Letters*, III, p. 187, quoted by Ray, *Thackeray*, op. cit., p. 216). See Ray on Thackeray's first trip to America, ibid., pp. 216–17.

23 Juliet McMaster, "Thackeray's Things: Time's Local Habitation," in Richard Levine (ed.), *The Victorian Experience: The Novels* (Athens Ohio: Ohio University Press, 1976), p. 67.

24 See especially Stephan Bann's discussion of the ironic complications of the text in "L'anti-histoire de *Henry Esmond*," op. cit., and in *The Clothing of Clio: A Study of the Representation of History in Nineteenth-Century Britain and France* (Cambridge: Cambridge University Press, 1984), pp. 140–51. Also, J. Hillis Miller demonstrates in *Fiction and Repetition* how Thackeray undoes any possibility of omniscience (op. cit., pp. 94–5).

25 For the homage of these three, see pp. 302, 372, 415. Thackeray, who while writing the novel called Esmond "a handsome likeness of your ugly son" in a letter to his mother, later had something else to say about this character, as his daughter reports: "I said to Papa that I thought he was very like Esmond and Papa said he thought he was perhaps only Esmond was a little bilious fellow" (Anny Thackeray, "Reminiscences," quoted by Ray, *Thackeray*, op. cit., n. 5, p. 462). Interestingly, Ray gives this quotation only in a footnote, for this evidence of Thackeray's ironic distance from his narrator is a problem for Ray's thesis that *Esmond* reads most convincingly as a biographical text. Calling him likewise a "bore" (Ray (ed.), *Letters*, op. cit., III, p. 72) and a "prig" (Trollope, quoting Thackeray, in Tillotson and Hawes (eds), op. cit., p. 166), Thackeray makes explicit the distance he implicitly takes from Esmond in *Henry Esmond*.

26 Miller, op. cit., p. 83.

27 C. C. Harris, *The Family in Industrial Society* (London: George Allen and Unwin, 1983), p. 164. See also Richard Sennett, *The Fall of Public Man* (Cambridge: Cambridge University Press, 1974), and Michel Foucault, *The History of Sexuality, Volume I, An Introduction*, trans. Robert Hurley (New York: Random House, 1980).

28 Macaulay, *The History of England*, op. cit., II, p. 576.

29 Macaulay, *Essays*, op. cit., p. 423.

30 One can open Macaulay's *History* virtually anywhere and find a scene set and men described in these terms. An example is his account of James's response to Monmouth's rebellion. Here is his final judgment on James II:

> No English sovereign has ever given stronger proofs of a cruel nature than James the Second. Yet his cruelty was not more odious than his mercy. Or perhaps it may be more correct to say that his mercy and his cruelty were such that each reflects infamy on the other.... The

rule by which a prince ought, after a rebellion, to be guided in selecting rebels for punishment is perfectly obvious. The ringleaders, the men of rank, fortune, and education, whose power and whose artifacts have led the multitude into error, are the proper objects of severity. The deluded populace, when once the slaughter on the field of battle is over, can scarcely be treated too leniently. This rule, so evidently agreeable to justice and humanity, was not only not observed: it was inverted. While those who ought to have been spared were slaughtered by hundreds, the few who might with propriety have been left to the utmost rigour of the law were spared. This eccentric clemency has perplexed some writers, and has drawn forth ludicrous eulogies from others. It was neither at all mysterious nor at all praiseworthy. It may be distinctly traced in every case either to a sordid or to a malignant motive, either to thirst for money or to thirst for blood.

(Macaulay, *History*, op. cit., I, pp. 569–71)

31 Macaulay, *Essays*, op. cit., p. 427.
32 P. B. M. Blass argues in *Continuity and Anachronism: Parliamentary and Constitutional Development in Whig Historiography and in the Anti-Whig Reaction Between 1890 and 1930* (The Hague: Martinus Nijhoff, 1978), that Macaulay "hypostatizes" the constitution: "It came to be almost regarded as an autonomous historical force: the object to be interpreted had developed into a means for interpretation" (p. 34).
33 Hayden White, "The Value of Narrativity in the Representation of Reality," *Critical Inquiry*, 7 (autumn 1980), p. 17.
34 Macaulay, *Essays*, op. cit., p. 423.
35 ibid., pp. 425, 432.
36 ibid., pp. 385, 379.
37 For Macaulay, historical representation is necessarily a matter of perspective, a representation adjusted to emphasize what is significant and to de-emphasize the trivial:

History has its foreground and its background.... Some events must be represented on a large scale, others diminished; the great majority will be lost in the dimness of the horizon; and a general idea of the joint effect will be given by a few slight touches.

(ibid., p. 388)

38 ibid., p. 391.
39 Lawyers are a slightly different case, but the logic is the same: they simply manipulate the law for specific ends without comprehending its significance.
40 Thackeray, *The Four Georges*, op. cit., p. 642.
41 Thackeray, letter to Mrs Carmichael-Smyth, 17–18 April 1852, Ray (ed.), *Letters*, op. cit., III, p. 38.
42 Walter Bagehot, "Sterne and Thackeray," *National Review*, xviii (April 1864), pp. 523–53, in Tillotson and Hawes (eds), op. cit., p. 350.
43 George Brimley, "Thackeray's Esmond," the *Spectator*, xxv (6 November 1852), in Tillotson and Hawes (eds), op. cit., p. 144; Anthony Trollope, *Thackeray*, in Tillotson and Hawes (eds), op. cit.,

p. 167; Trollope, "W. M. Thackeray," in Tillotson and Hawes (eds), op. cit., p. 325.

44 Thackeray, manuscript letter, 14–16 February 1856, in Ray, *Thackeray*, op. cit., p. 209.

45 Brimley, in Tillotson and Hawes (eds.), op. cit., p. 144.

46 Certeau, op. cit., p. 5.

47 Jacques Lacan, *Ecrits*, trans. Alan Sheridan (New York: Norton, 1977), pp. 52, 49.

48 Friedrich von Schiller, letter to Goethe, 2 October 1797, in *The Correspondence Between Schiller and Goethe*, I (London: George Bell, 1877), reprinted in Albert Cook (ed.), *Oedipus Rex: A Mirror for Greek Drama* (Prospect Heights, Illinois: Waneland Press, 1982), p. 86.

49 I am emphasizing the way psychoanalysis confirms sexual difference as an answer to man's identity, but psychoanalysis can do much more than shore up sexed subjectivity – after all, Freud insists repeatedly on the instability and uncertainty of all identity. See Jacqueline Rose, "Introduction II" to Juliet Mitchell and Jacqueline Rose (eds), *Feminine Sexuality: Jacques Lacan and the école freudienne* (New York: Norton, 1982); and Stephen Heath, *The Sexual Fix* (New York: Schoken Books, 1984), especially chapter IV.

50 Foucault, *The History of Sexuality*, op. cit. p. 109. Here Foucault argues that the importance accorded to the prohibition of incest is part of a specific historical moment in which sexuality is produced as a problem of truth. The fascination with incest is a part of the whole modern incitement of sexuality, in conjunction with the requirements of an older system of family alliances:

> [Incest] is manifested as a thing that is strictly forbidden in the family insofar as the latter functions as a deployment of alliance; but it is also a thing that is constantly demanded in order for the family to be a hotbed of constant sexual incitement.

51 Roland Barthes, *S/Z*, trans. Richard Miller (New York: Hill and Wang, 1974), p. 162.

52 Certeau, op. cit., p. 218.

53 Just after finishing the novel Thackeray wrote, "It's only acting, our business. We are but quacks and mountebanks more or less painted and gay and solemn," a recognition of performance that is antithetical to objective history (Ray (ed.), *Letters*, op. cit., III, pp. 52–3).

54 See Gilles Deleuze and Félix Guattari, *Anti-Oedipus: Capitalism and Schizophrenia*, trans. Robert Hurley, Mark Seem, and Helen R. Lane (Minneapolis: University of Minnesota Press, 1983) for an analysis of the conjunction of capitalism and Oedipal family structures, and a remarkable attempt to think about the production of desire without privileging the law of the father.

Chapter 3 History and the melodramatic fix

1 The *Leader*, 18 July 1857, p. 692, in Robert Louis Brannan, "*The Frozen Deep*": Under the Management of Mr Charles Dickens," diss., Cornell University (Ann Arbor: University Microfilms, 1966), p. 69.

2 Quoted by Raymund Fitzsimons, *The Charles Dickens Show: An Account of His Public Readings 1858–1870*, (London: Geoffrey Bles, 1970), p. 21.
3 I am referring to the Penguin edition of *Little Dorrit* (Harmondsworth, 1967). Further references will appear parenthetically.
4 Dickens, letter to John Forster, 30 January 1856, in Forster, *The Life of Charles Dickens*, 2 (1872–3; London: J. M. Dent and Sons, 1966), p. 183.
5 Laura Mulvey, "Notes on Sirk and Melodrama, *Movie*, 25 (winter 1977–8), p. 53.
6 The edition to which I refer is Wilkie Collins's 1857 script, edited by Robert Louis Brannan. In the reading which follows I am indebted to Brannan's research and his interpretation of the play. He argues that the real drama of *The Frozen Deep* is the tension between savagery and civilization embodied in Wardour himself.
7 John Cordy Jeaffreson, *Novels and Novelists from Elizabeth to Victoria* (1858), in Philip Collins (ed.), *Dickens: The Critical Heritage* (New York: Barnes & Noble, 1971), p. 381.
8 Hippolyte Taine, "Charles Dickens: son talent et ses oeuvres," *Revue des deux Mondes*, 1 February 1856, 2nde pèriode, i, 618–47, in Collins (ed.), op. cit., p. 339.
9 *The Times* (23 October 1854), p. 7, in Brannan, op. cit., p. 13.
10 *Household Words* (9 December 1854), in Brannan, op. cit., p. 19.
11 Dickens, letter to Forster, April 1856, *The Letters of Charles Dickens*, ed. Walter Dexter (Bloomsbury, 1938), vol. III, p. 768, in Brannan, op. cit., p. 20.
12 For a lucid and comprehensive analysis of this fundamental aspect of English middle-class consciousness, and the crucial role of the novel in the formation of that consciousness, see Nancy Armstrong, *Desire and Domestic Fiction: A Political History of the Novel* (New York: Oxford University Press, 1987).
13 *The American Heritage Dictionary of the English Language* (New York: Houghton Mifflin Co., 1975), p. 896.
14 Michel Foucault, *The Archaeology of Knowledge*, trans. A. M. Sheridan Smith (New York: Harper and Row, 1972), p. 12.
15 The "melodramatic fix" is a variation of Stephen Heath's phrase, "the sexual fix." See *The Sexual Fix* (New York: Schocken, 1984).
16 Peter Brooks, *The Melodramatic Imagination: Balzac, Henry James, Melodrama, and the Mode of Excess* (New Haven: Yale University Press, 1976), p. 11.
17 ibid., p. 15.
18 Dickens, letter to Macready, 4 October 1855, in David Paroissien (ed.), *Selected Letters of Charles Dickens* (Boston: Twayne, 1985), p. 268.
19 Dickens, letter to Forster, 30 September 1855, in Forster, op. cit., 2, p. 387.
20 See Norris Pope, *Dickens and Charity* (New York: Columbia University Press, 1978), for an account of his charitable work.
21 Chesterton, quoted by Sir Arthur Quiller Couch, *Charles Dickens and Other Victorians* (New York: G. P. Putnam's Sons, 1925), p. 10.
22 Mrs Oliphant, "Charles Dickens," *Blackwood's Magazine* (April 1855),

lxxvii, 451–66, in Collins (ed.), op. cit., pp. 327, 328. Humphry House also makes this point in *The Dickens World* (1942; London: Oxford University Press, 1960):

> Detached now from his time he may seem more original and adventurous than he was; for then he was only giving wider publicity in "inimitable" form to a number of social facts and social abuses which had already been recognized if not explored before him ... [H]e so exploited his knowledge that the public recognized its master in knowing; but he also shared with it an attitude to what they both knew, and caught exactly the tone which clarified and reinforced the public's sense of right and wrong, and flattered its moral feelings.
>
> (p. 41)

23 House, ibid. p. 88.
24 John Holloway, "Introduction" to *Little Dorrit* (Harmondsworth: Penguin Books, 1967), p. 16; Carlyle, *Sartor Resartus*, quoted by Holloway, ibid., p. 16.
25 Claude Lévi-Strauss, *Structural Anthropology*, trans. Claire Jakobson and Brooke Grundfest Schoepf (New York: Basic Books, 1963), p. 221.
26 ibid., p. 229.
27 Christine Gledhill, "Melodrama," in Pam Cook (ed.), *The Cinema Book* (New York: Pantheon Books, 1986), p. 89.
28 Humphry House discusses this point; see op. cit., p. 221.
29 Franco Moretti, *Signs Taken for Wonders: Essays in the Sociology of Literary Forms*, trans. Susan Fischer, David Forgacs, and David Miller (London: Verso and NLB, 1983), p. 162.
30 Steve Neale, "Melodrama and Tears," *Screen*, 27 (November–December 1986), p. 11.
31 Martin Meisel, *Realizations: Narrative, Pictorial, and Theatrical Arts in Nineteenth-Century England* (Princeton: Princeton University Press, 1983), p. 303.
32 Lévi-Strauss, op. cit., p. 229.
33 See Roland Barthes, *Mythologies*, trans. Annette Lavers (New York: Hill and Wang, 1972), p. 9 and *passim*.
34 *Household Words*, 1 (18 May 1850), pp. 171–2.
35 *Household Words*, 3 (14 June 1851), pp. 268, 269.
36 *Household Words*, 3 (26 April 1851) p. 104.
37 *Household Words*, 1 (30 August 1850), p. 549.
38 D. A. Miller makes this logic clear in his book, *The Novel and the Police* (Berkeley: University of California Press, 1988):

> [O]ne can correlate the two causes that Dickens's novels regularly ascribe to the faultiness of the family: on one hand, the external interference of institutions that ... dislocate and disjoin the family; and on the other, the internal dynamic that ... determines its own divisions and displacements.... In the first instance, Dickens advises society to police for the family, which would thereby be safeguarded as the home of freedom; in the second, he counsels the family to police itself, that it might remain free by becoming its own house of correction.
>
> (p. 103)

39 *Household Words*, 3 (30 August 1851), p. 549.
40 Unsigned review, *Bentley's Miscellany*, xxxiv (October 1853), pp. 372–4, in Collins (ed.) op. cit., p. 289.
41 Dickens, letter to Wilkie Collins, 6 June 1856, in Paroissien (ed.), op. cit., p. 46.
42 Dickens, in Fitzsimons, op. cit., p. 64.
43 Dickens, in ibid., pp. 66, 156.
44 Dickens, in ibid., p. 66.
45 Dickens' letter to Forster, 1856, in Forster, op. cit., p. 197–8.
46 The phrase is Eileen Yeo's in "Mayhew as a Social Investigator," an introduction to E. P. Thompson and Eileen Yeo (eds), *The Unknown Mayhew: Selections from the Morning Chronicle, 1849–1850* (London: Merlin Press, 1971), p. 51.
47 William Thackeray, *Punch*, 9 March 1950, quoted by Anne Humpherys, *Travels into the Poor Man's Country: The Work of Henry Mayhew* (Athens, Georgia: The University of Georgia Press, 1977), p. ix.
48 Henry Mayhew, *The Morning Chronicle Survey of Labour and the Poor: The Metropolitan Districts*, 6 vols. (Sussex: Caliban Books, 1980), 2, p. 45. Further references will appear parenthetically.
49 Peter Razzell, "Introduction," ibid., 1, p. 4.
50 James Bennett, "Human Values in Oral History," *Oral History Review*, 11 (1983), pp. 3, 5.
51 *Voices of the Poor* is the title Anne Humpherys gives to a selection of Mayhew's *Morning Chronicle* work (London: Frank Cass and Co., 1971).
52 Mayhew, quoted in *Report of the Speech of Henry Mayhew ... at a Public Meeting ... on Oct. 28, 1850 ...* (London: Bateman, Hardwicke, 1850), p. 6, in Anne Humpherys, *Henry Mayhew* (Boston: Twayne, 1984), p. 89.
53 See Raymond Williams's entries in *Keywords: A Vocabulary of Culture and Society* (New York: Oxford University Press, 1976) for "Science" (pp. 232–4), "Society" (pp. 243–6), and "Sociology" (pp. 247–8). See also Yeo, op. cit., pp. 88–95.
54 Yeo, ibid., p. 72.
55 See Joan Wallach Scott, *Gender and the Politics of History* (New York: Columbia University Press, 1988) for an analysis of the discourse of political economy (both right and left), concerning women workers in Paris:

> Workers but not workers, these women were marginal to, yet part of, the world of Parisian industry. In their behavior lay the threat to moral order, the destruction not only of work discipline but of all social relationships. Lacking proper appreciation of their subordination to a parent or husband, these women lived as outlaws. The very ambiguity of their situation, the fact that they defied categorization, was the measure of their dangerousness.
> ("A Statistical Representation of Work: *La Statistique de l'industrie à Paris, 1847–1848*," p. 136)

(Equally relevant is "'L'ouvrière! Mot impie, sordide ...' Women Workers in the discourse of French Political Economy, 1840–1860," pp. 139–67).

56 She should have made the wage Dickens allots to Little Dorrit: 1/2 crown (5 shillings) a day (p. 680).

57 Yeo, op. cit., p. 81. Yeo is quick to recognize that, as she says, "Mayhew was no socialist," pointing out that he was for worker cooperation and profit sharing, but had no critical analysis of private ownership.

58 ibid., p. 88.

59 Fredric Jameson, *The Political Unconscious: Narrative as a Socially Symbolic Act* (Ithaca: Cornell University Press, 1981), p. 102.

60 ibid., p. 35.

61 ibid., p. 19.

62 Michel Foucault, *Power/Knowledge: Selected Interviews and Other Writings, 1972–1977*, trans. Colin Gordon, Leo Marshall, John Mepham, and Kate Soper; Colin Gordon (ed.) (New York: Pantheon Books, 1980), p. 115. Foucault argues that history should be conceived along the model of "war and battle":

> History has no "meaning," though this is not to say that it is absurd or incoherent. On the contrary, it is intelligible and susceptible of analysis down to the smallest detail – but this in accordance with the intelligibility of struggles, of strategies and tactics. Neither the dialectic, as a logic of contradictions, nor semiotics, as the structure of communication, can account for the intrinsic intelligibility of conflicts. "Dialectic" is a way of evading the always open and hazardous reality of conflict by reducing it to a Hegelian skeleton, and "semiology" is a way of avoiding its violent, bloody and lethal character by reducing it to the calm Platonic form of language and dialogue.

This is polemical and therefore exaggerated and contentious, but the point Foucault is making here suggests why I think Mayhew's work is important.

63 E. P. Thompson, "Mayhew and the "Morning Chronicle,'" an introduction to Thompson and Yeo (eds), op. cit., pp. 44, 49.

64 Anatole Broyard, "All the Comforts of Dickens," *The New York Times Book Review* (15 May 1988), p. 13.

Chapter 4 *Villette* and the end of history

1 *Villette* (1853; New York, Harper & Row, 1972), p. 41. All further references will be to this edition and will be given parenthetically.

2 John Bunyan, *The Pilgrim's Progress* (Harmondsworth: Penguin, 1987), pp. 51, 52.

3 Barbara Keifer Lewalski, "Typological Symbolism and the 'Progress of the Soul' in Seventeenth-Century Literature," in Earl Miner (ed.), *Literary Uses of Typology From the Late Middle Ages to the Present* (Princeton: Princeton University Press, 1977), p. 107 and *passim*.

4 Brontë, letter to W. S. Williams, 6 November 1852, in Muriel Spark (ed.), *The Letters of the Brontës* (Norman: University of Oklahoma Press, 1954), p. 190.

5 Harriet Martineau, unsigned review, *Daily News* (3 February 1853), in Miriam Allott (ed.), *The Brontës: The Critical Heritage* (London: Routledge & Kegan Paul, 1974), p. 172.

6 Unsigned notice, *Guardian* (23 February 1853), in Allott (ed.), ibid., p. 193.

7 Thackeray, letter to Mrs Carmichael-Smyth, 25–8 March 1853, in Allott (ed.), ibid., p. 198.

8 H. F. Lowry (ed.), *The Letters of Arnold to Arnold Hugh Clough* (London and New York: Oxford University Press and H. M. Milford, 1932), p. 146, quoted by Walter E. Houghton, *The Victorian Frame of Mind: 1820–1870* (New Haven: Yale University Press, 1957), p. 321.

9 Arnold, letter to Mrs Forster, 14 April 1853, in Allott (ed.), op. cit., p. 201.

10 Unsigned review, *Athenaeum* (12 February 1853), in ibid., p. 188.

11 Elizabeth Gaskell, *The Life of Charlotte Brontë*, Thornfield Edition (New York: Harper & Brothers, 1900), p. 358.

12 Caroline Fox, from her Journal, 9 July 1857, in Allott (ed.), op. cit., p. 371.

13 Leslie Stephen, *Cornhill Magazine* (December 1877), in ibid., p. 415.

14 Brontë, letter to George Smith, 30 October 1852, in Spark (ed.), op. cit., p. 188.

15 George Eliot, letter to Mrs Bray, 15 February 1853, in Allott (ed.), op. cit., p. 192.

16 Patrick Fairbairn, *The Typology of Scripture, Viewed in Connection with the Whole Series of The Divine Dispensations*, vol. 1, 5th edn (Edinburgh: T. & T. Clark, 1870), p. 99. Here Fairbairn notes that he is quoting "Jacobi, as quoted by Sack, Apologetik, p. 356."

17 ibid., 1, p. 19.

18 Gaskell, op. cit., p. 361.

19 Unsigned review, *Spectator*, (12 February 1853), in Allott (ed.), op. cit., p. 183.

20 Unsigned review, *Examiner* (5 February 1853), in ibid., p. 177.

21 Kate Millett, *Sexual Politics* (New York: Avon Books, 1971), p. 147.

22 Sandra M. Gilbert and Susan Gubar, *The Madwoman in the Attic: The Woman Writer and the Nineteenth-Century Literary Imagination* (New Haven: Yale University Press, 1979), pp. 439, 440. See also Carol Ohmann, "Historical Reality and 'Divine Appointment' in Charlotte Brontë's Fiction," *Signs*, 2, (1977) 757–78. She argues that *Villette* is radical in its "rendering of deprivation," but that its ideology of divinely ordained suffering is "profoundly conservative."

23 Fredric Jameson, *The Political Unconscious: Narrative as a Socially Symbolic Act* (Ithaca: Cornell University Press, 1981), p. 18.

24 Annette Hopkins, *The Father of the Brontës* (Baltimore: Johns Hopkins University Press, 1958), pp. 51–8.

25 Fairbairn, quoting *Life and Remains of Bengel*, p. 245, in his *Hermeneutical Manual, Or, Introduction to the Exegetical Study of the Scriptures of the New Testament* (Edinburgh: T. & T. Clark, 1858), pp. 106–7.

26 ibid., p. 125.

27 ibid., p. v.

28 Ellen Nussey, "Reminiscences of Charlotte Brontë," quoted by Winifred Gerin, *Charlotte Brontë: The Evolution of Genius* (London: Oxford University Press, 1967), p. 75. As the Old Testament book in which Immanuel is prophesied, Isaiah is a text of particular significance in the typological scheme, truly sublime in its prophetic vision, its vivid anticipation of Christ.

29 Brontë, letter to W. S. Williams, 4 June 1849, in Spark (ed.), op. cit., p. 164.

30 Brontë, letter to Laetitia Wheelwright, 12 April 1852, in Clement K. Shorter, *Charlotte Brontë and Her Circle* (New York: Dodd, Mead and Co. 1896), p. 470.

31 Fairbairn, *Hermeneutical Manual*, op. cit., p. 107.

32 See George Landow, *Victorian Types, Victorian Shadows: Biblical Typology in Victorian Literature, Art, and Thought* (Boston: Routledge & Kegan Paul, 1980); Herbert L. Sussman, *Fact into Figure: Typology in Carlyle, Ruskin, and the Pre-Raphaelite Brotherhood* (Columbus: Ohio State University Press, 1979); Chris Brooks, *Signs for the Times: Symbolic Realism in the Mid-Victorian World* (London: George Allen & Unwin, 1984); Miner (ed.), op. cit.; Barry Qualls, *The Secular Pilgrims of Victorian Fiction: The Novel as Book of Life* (Cambridge: Cambridge University Press, 1982); Thomas Vargish, *The Providential Aesthetic in Victorian Fiction* (Charlottesville: University Press of Virginia, 1985).

33 Thomas Carlyle, "On History," in Alan Shelton (ed.), *Thomas Carlyle: Selected Writings* (Harmondsworth: Penguin Books, 1971), p. 56.

34 Carlyle, *Sartor Resartus*, in ibid., p. 106. The Reverend Patrick Brontë, who had his own literary aspirations, published several pieces, among them a pamphlet, *The Signs of the Times; or a Familiar Treatise on some Political Indications in the Year 1835*. Mr Brontë's title repeats that of Carlyle's essay, "Signs of the Times," published six years earlier in the *Edinburgh Review*, and is another indication of a generalized use of typology.

35 John Ruskin, *Modern Painters* (Boston: Dana Estes and Co., n.d.), 2, p. 376.

36 Ruskin, ibid., 1, pp. 357, 154.

37 Brontë, letter to W. S. Williams, 5 April 1849, in Shorter, op. cit., p. 440; letter to W. S. Williams, 1851, in Gaskell, op. cit., p. 518.

38 Brontë, letter to W. S. Williams, 14 August 1848, in Shorter, op. cit., p. 413.

39 Paul de Man, "The Rhetoric of Temporality," in *Blindness and Insight: Essays in the Rhetoric of Contemporary Criticism*, 2nd edn, revised (Minneapolis: University of Minnesota Press, 1983), p. 189.

40 See Paul de Man, *Blindness and Insight*, ibid.; also, *Allegories of Reading: Figural Language in Rousseau, Nietzsche, Rilke, and Proust* (New Haven: Yale University Press, 1979), and *The Rhetoric of Romanticism* (New York: Columbia University Press, 1984). For an historical summary of the issues in Victorian England, see George Landow, *The Aesthetic and Critical Theories of John Ruskin* (Princeton: Princeton University Press, 1971), especially chapter 5, "Ruskin and Allegory."

41 Paul Ricoeur, *The Rule of Metaphor*, trans. Robert Czervy, with

Kathleen McLaughlin and John Costello, SJ (Toronto: University of Toronto Press, 1977), pp. 27, 61.

42 ibid., p. 57.

43 Jacques Derrida, "White Mythology," in *Margins of Philosophy*, trans. Alan Bass (Chicago: University of Chicago Press, 1982), p. 215.

44 Thomas Hartwell Horne, *A Compendious Introduction to the Study of the Bible* (London: Longman, Brown, Breen & Longmans, 1852), 9th edn, p. 173.

45 de Man, "The Rhetoric of Temporality," op. cit., p. 189. For instance, Ruskin, with his extensive Evangelical training could anticipate with assurance the sermon which would be delivered on the biblical text, "Unto Adam also, and to his wife, did the Lord God make coats of skins": as he wrote to a friend, " 'Now,' thought I, when [the preacher] began, 'I know what you're going to say about that; you'll say that the beasts were sacrificed, and that the skins were typical of the robe of Christ's righteousness' " (in Landow, *John Ruskin*, op. cit., p. 336).

46 Wordsworth, *The Prelude*, VI, 636–40, quoted in de Man, *The Rhetoric of Romanticism*, op. cit., p. 12.

47 Ruskin, *Modern Painters*, op. cit., 2, p. 385.

48 Gilbert and Gubar, op. cit., p. 400.

49 Fairbairn, *Typology*, op. cit., 1, p. 79.

50 Of thirty-three references to the Bible in *Villette*, only eight are to the New Testament, and are all clustered around Lucy and Paul Emmanuel. Landow devotes the entire last chapter of *Victorian Types, Victorian Shadows* to an extensive discussion of Moses's death on Nebo as one of the best-known types of the Victorian period (op. cit., pp. 204–31). The biblical text is Deuteronomy 35: 1–6.

51 Henry Melvill, "The Death of Moses," in *Sermons* (London, 1936), 2, p. 185, in Landow, *Victorian Types, Victorian Shadows*, op. cit., p. 206.

52 G. H. Lewes, *Leader* (12 February 1853), in Allott (ed.), op. cit., p. 184.

53 For the story of Esau, see Genesis 27.

54 Margot Peters, *Charlotte Brontë: Style in the Novel* (Madison: University of Wisconsin Press, 1973), p. 123; Gilbert and Gubar, op. cit., p. 408, Barbara Hardy, *Forms of Victorian Fiction* (Athens, Ohio: Ohio University Press, 1985), pp. 118–30; Robert Martin, *Accents of Persuasion: Charlotte Brontë's Novels* (London: Faber & Faber, 1966); Helene Moglen, *Charlotte Brontë: The Self Conceived* (New York: Norton, 1976), pp. 207–8.

55 S. T. Coleridge, *Essays and Lectures on Shakespeare and Some Other Old Poets and Dramatists* (London: Everyman, 1907), p. 46, in de Man, *Blindness and Insight*, op. cit., p. 191.

56 Judges 4:15–21; 5:24.

57 Fairbairn, *Hermeneutical Manual*, op. cit., p. 121.

58 Peter Brooks, *Reading for the Plot: Design and Intention in Narrative* (New York: Alfred A. Knopf, 1984), p. 141.

59 Gaskell, op. cit., p. 120.

60 Anne Mozley, *Christian Rembrancer* (April 1853), in Allott (ed.), op. cit., p. 206.

61 Derrida, op. cit., p. 237.

62 Peter Brooks, op. cit., p. 108.
63 ibid., p. 93.
64 Naomi Schor, *Reading in Detail: Aesthetics and the Feminine* (New York: Methuen, 1987), p. 157.
65 The passage is quoted in full on p. 129 above.
66 Fairbairn, *Typology*, op. cit., 1, pp. 18–19.
67 Derrida, op. cit., pp. 247–8.
68 Brontë, letter to G. H. Lewes, 12 January 1848, in Gaskell, op. cit., p. 360.
69 As de Man has observed, "the inference of identity and totality that is constitutive of metaphor is lacking in the metonymic contact: an element of truth is involved in taking Achilles for a lion but none in taking Mr Ford for a motor car" (*Allegories of Reading*, op. cit., p. 14).
70 See Schor's argument about the "detotalized" and "desublimated" detail of modernity. As she says, "The modern allegorical detail is a parody of the traditional theological detail. It is the detail deserted by God" – this in a discussion of Lukacs's theory of "concrete typicality" (op. cit., p. 61). *Villette*'s details are not "desublimated" in the same way as details are in modern texts, but are none the less similarly fatal to theological totality, which may be one reason the novel is so often thought to be "ahead of its time."
71 Important exceptions are Mary Jacobus, "The Buried Letter: Feminism and Romanticism in *Villette*," in Mary Jacobus (ed.), *Women Writing and Writing about Women* (London: Croom Helm, 1979); the chapter on Brontë in John Kucich, *Repression in Victorian Fiction: Charlotte Brontë, George Eliot, and Charles Dickens* (Berkeley: University of California Press, 1987); and the chapter on the Brontës in Nancy Armstrong, *Desire and Domestic Fiction: A Political History of the Novel* (New York: Oxford University Press, 1987).
72 Derrida, op. cit., p. 248.

Conclusion

1 Ellen Rooney, *Seductive Reasoning: Pluralism as the Problematic of Contemporary Theory* (Ithaca: Cornell University Press, 1989), p. 13.
2 Stuart Hall, "The Toad in the Garden: Thatcherism among the Theorists," in Cary Nelson and Lawrence Grossberg (eds), *Marxism and the Interpretation of Culture* (Urbana: University of Illinois Press, 1988), p. 51.
3 Louis Althusser, *Lenin and Philosophy and Other Essays*, trans. Ben Brewster (New York: Monthly Review Press, 1971), p. 172.
4 The structure of identity between knowledge and the real holds in both speculative and empiricist thought: in speculative philosophy, "reality" is the realization, the embodiment, of a concept, and in empiricism the real object defines the concept. See Althusser, *Reading Capital*, trans. Ben Brewster (London: Verso, 1970), especially pp. 15–17 and 34–40; and Michel Foucault, *The Order of Things: An Archaeology of the Human Sciences* (New York: Vintage Books, 1973), p. 244 and *passim*.
5 For an excellent discussion of the concept of Necessity, see Rooney's

chapter on Jameson's *The Political Unconscious*, op. cit., pp. 198–240. Indeed, Rooney's book as a whole has helped me develop my argument not only about this matter, but more generally to understand the problem of the production of knowledge, the relation of politics and knowledge.

6 Althusser, *Reading Capital*, op. cit., p. 15.

7 My language paraphrases Derrida:

> The closure of metaphysics, above all, is not a circle surrounding a homogeneous field, a field homogeneous with itself on its inside, whose outside then would be homogeneous also. The limit has the form of always different faults, of fissures whose mark or scar is borne by all the texts of philosophy.

He makes these remarks in the course of a discussion of history in *Positions*, trans. Alan Bass (Chicago: The University of Chicago Press, 1981), p. 57.

8 Walter Benjamin, "Theological-Political Fragment," in *Reflections: Essays, Aphorisms, Autobiographical Writings*, trans. Edmund Jophcott (New York: Harcourt Brace Jovanovich, 1978), p. 312. In an essay on Benjamin's "The Task of the Translator" which considers the relation between translation and history, Paul de Man notes the difficulty of translating this passage "because the English word for 'aim' can also be 'end.'" His translation reads:

> Only the messiah himself puts an end to history, in the sense that it frees, completely fulfills the relationship of history to the messianic. Therefore, nothing that is truly historical can want to relate by its own volition to the messianic. Therefore the kingdom of God is not the telos of the dynamics of history, it cannot be posited as its aim; seen historically it is not its aim but its end.

> (*The Resistance to Theory* (Minneapolis: University of Minnesota Press, 1986), p. 93)

9 Walter Benjamin, "Theses on the Philosophy of History," in *Illuminations*, trans. Harry Zohn (New York: Schocken, 1977), pp. 261, 257.

10 Cf. Foucault:

> If interpretation were the slow exposure of the meaning hidden in an origin, then only metaphysics could interpret the development of humanity. But if interpretation is the violent or surreptitious appropriation of a system of rules, which in itself has no essential meaning, in order to impose a direction, to bend it to a new will, to force its participation in a different genre, to subject it to secondary rules, then the development of humanity is a series of interpretations.

> (*Language, Counter-Memory, Practice*, trans. Donald F. Bouchard and Sherry Simon (Ithaca: Cornell University Press, 1977) p. 151)

11 See Joan Wallach Scott, "A Statistical Representation of Work: *La Statistique de l'industrie à Paris, 1847–1848*," in Scott, *Gender and the Politics of History* (New York: Columbia University Press, 1988), pp. 113–38.

12 This is how Donald Scott describes what he asks his students to do in his freshman seminar, "History as a Way of Knowing," taught at Lang College of the New School for Social Research.

13 Some would argue that history as we have known it is impossible to reconfigure in any way meaningful to radical politics and knowledge. Such is Sande Cohen's argument:

> *History* ... is a concept of last resort, a floating signifier, the alibi of an alignment with obligatory values. It pertains to no signified at all; depending on how the past is positioned, it can preclude confusion of temporal coordinates, preserve the imaginary idea of collective relations, substitute when for where, or dismiss present intensities.
>
> (*Historical Culture: On the Recoding of an Academic Discipline* (Berkeley: University of California Press, 1986), p. 329)

14 Helene Moglen, *Charlotte Brontë: The Self Conceived* (New York: Norton, 1976), p. 14.

15 Helene Moglen's remarks were made at a conference sponsored by *Novel: A Forum on Fiction* at Brown University in 1976.

16 Elaine Showalter, *A Literature of Their Own: British Women Novelists from Brontë to Lessing* (Princeton: Princeton University Press, 1977); Gilbert and Gubar, *The Madwoman in the Attic: The Woman Writer and the Nineteenth-Century Literary Imagination* (New Haven: Yale University Press, 1979).

17 See Elizabeth Weed on the power and seductiveness of reading woman-as-other. She points to

> the extraordinary explanatory power of [white feminism's] own critical reading of Western Man and his Other and of the semantic richness of the figure of the feminine. For white middle-class women this entailed a reading of one's identity from the other side as it were, and in that sense was compelling as negative identification, as identification with the negative.... Although "Woman" does not exist, of course, other than as man's support, the very unified nature of the concept has had its own seductive history and effects.
>
> ("Introduction: Terms of Reference," in Elizabeth Weed (ed.), *Coming to Terms: Feminism, Theory, Politics* (New York: Routledge, 1989), p. xx)

18 Audre Lorde, *Sister Outsider* (Trumansburg, New York: The Crossing Press, 1984), p. 112.

19 That conceptualizing the "end of history" involves the erasure of politics is evident in a recent essay by Francis Fukuyama, "The End of History?" (*The National Interest* (summer 1989)). This piece, which has attracted enough attention to be reported in the "The Week in Review" section of *The New York Times* (27 August 1989, section E, p. 5), is a Hegelian explanation of the late twentieth-century development of a global market and culture. Fukuyama writes,

> The triumph of the West, of the Western *idea*, is evident first of all in the total exhaustion of viable systematic alternatives to Western

liberalism.... What we may be witnessing is not just the end of the Cold War, or the passing of a particular period of postwar history, but the end of history as such: that is, the end point of mankind's ideological evolution and the universalization of Western liberal democracy as the final form of human government.

Fukuyama is already nostalgic for a history which allowed men to be men. He declares,

The end of history will be a very sad time. The struggle for recognition, the willingness to risk one's life for a purely abstract goal, the world-wide ideological struggle that called forth daring, courage, imagination, and idealism, will be replaced by economic calculation, the endless solving of technical problems, environmental concerns, and the satisfaction of sophisticated consumer demands.

Fukuyama explains the global expansion of capitalism in unabashedly idealist terms, and he imagines the end of history as a problematic descent from heroic (masculine) history into the mundane details of daily life, a feminized world of calculation, technique and consumption. That the essay has been excerpted in various newspapers, reprinted, and translated into French, Japanese, Italian, Dutch and Icelandic, indicates the continuing power of the discourse of universal history.

20 I am grateful to Ellen Rooney for suggesting this formulation of the issue. The classic deconstructive reading of the double logic of the *pharmakon* is Derrida's "Plato's Pharmacy," in *Dissemination*, trans. Barbara Johnson (Chicago: University of Chicago Press, 1981), pp. 61–171.

21 Denise Riley, *"Am I That Name?" Feminism and the Category of "Women" in History* (Minneapolis: University of Minnesota Press, 1988), pp. 1–2.

22 Teresa de Lauretis (ed.), *Feminist Studies/Critical Studies* (Bloomsburg: Indiana University Press, 1986), p. 9. Cited hereafter parenthetically.

23 Gayatri Chakravorty Spivak, *In Other Worlds: Essays in Cultural Politics* (New York: Routledge, 1988) p. 204. Derrida makes explicit the historicity of differences in "Différance:"

[T]he signified concept is never present in and of itself, in a sufficient presence that would refer only to itself. Essentially and lawfully, every concept is inscribed in a chain or in a system within which it refers to the other, to other concepts, by means of the systematic play of differences. Such a play, *différance*, is thus no longer simply a concept, but rather the possibility of conceptuality, of a conceptual process and system in general.... [D]ifferences are themselves *effects*. They have not fallen from the sky fully formed.... If the word "history" did not in and of itself convey the motif of a final repression of difference, one could say that only differences can be "historical" from the outset and in each of their aspects.

(*Margins of Philosophy*, trans. Alan Bass (Chicago: University of Chicago Press, 1982), p. 11)

24 Spivak, op. cit., p. 204.
25 Riley, op. cit., p. 7.
26 Weed, in considering the specificity of "women," argues that

> [a]lthough the term is in itself unstable and unreliable, there is little danger of lapsing into "sexual indifference," or indifference to gender, because "women" are indeed continually produced by social formations. The whole problem of establishing a positive identity for women is thus displaced since such a project makes sense only if the term "women" can be somehow isolated or essentialized. And the lack of a reliable positive identity does not mean an endless proliferation of differences. It means, rather, that the very categories of difference are displaced and denaturalized through the articulation of those categories with the structures of domination in which they were historically produced.
>
> (op. cit., p. xix)

27 Gayatri Spivak, "The New Historicism: Political Commitment and the Postmodern Critic," in H. Aram Veeser (ed.), *The New Historicism* (New
28 York: Routledge, 1989), p. 279.

> The misapplication of a word, especially in a strained or mixed metaphor or in an implied metaphor. It need not be a ridiculous misapplication as in bad poetry, but may be a deliberate wresting of a term from its normal and proper significance.
>
> (Alex Preminger (ed.), *Princeton Encyclopedia of Poetry and Poetics* (Princeton: Princeton University Press, 1974), p. 104)

"Improper use of words, application of a term to a thing which it does not properly denote, abuse or perversion of a trope or metaphor" (the *Oxford English Dictionary*, quoted by Spivak, "The New Historicism," op. cit., p. 279).
29 Joan Wallach Scott, in "History in Crisis? The Other's Side of the Story," shows how the discipline of history from its professionalization in the nineteenth century to the present can be read to demonstrate what is at stake in defining "history." Using the documents of the American Historical Association, she analyzes "the process by which a particular approach to historical inquiry claims to embody the entire discipline by defining itself as 'History' and declaring challenges to it to be non-history, unacceptable and irrelevant because outside the boundaries of the field" (*American Historical Review*, 94:3 (June 1989), p. 681). She shows that defining "History" and determining what is proper to it has been a way of keeping the profession the preserve of white, middle-class, Protestant men, and a way of ensuring certain truths – of historical development, historical necessity, and historical truth itself.

Index